About the author

Emma Mawdsley is a senior lecturer in the Geography Department, University of Cambridge, and a Fellow of Newnham College. Her recent work on development politics focuses on the 'rising powers', and includes a co-authored book (with Gerard McCann) on contemporary India–Africa relations, and publications on China and Africa. She recently led a project examining public perceptions of development cooperation in China, India, Poland, Russia and South Africa.

This book is dedicated to my mother, to whom I owe so much and whom I love dearly.

From recipients to donors

Emerging powers and the changing development landscape

EMMA MAWDSLEY

Zed Books
LONDON | NEW YORK

From Recipients to Donors: Emerging powers and the changing development landscape was first published in 2012 by Zed Books Ltd, 7 Cynthia Street, London N1 9JF, UK and Room 400, 175 Fifth Avenue, New York, NY 10010, USA

www.zedbooks.co.uk

Set in OurType Arnhem and Monotype Futura by Ewan Smith, London
Index: ed.emery@thefreeuniversity.net
Cover designed by Rogue Four Design
Printed and bound by CPI Group (UK) Ltd, Croydon, CR0 4YY

Distributed in the USA exclusively by Palgrave Macmillan, a division of St Martin's Press, LLC, 175 Fifth Avenue, New York, NY 10010, USA

A catalogue record for this book is available from the British Library
Library of Congress Cataloging in Publication Data available

ISBN 978 1 84813 947 3 hb
ISBN 978 1 84813 946 6 pb

Contents

Tables and boxes

Tables

Boxes

Acknowledgements

This book has been nearly three years in the making, and I have countless people to thank for their intellectual stimulation and collegial support over this time. Many of the ideas and arguments have been presented in departmental seminars, workshops and conferences, and I am grateful to organizers, other presenters and audiences for being such a rich source of feedback and advice. These include events at the Royal Geographical Society with the Institute of British Geographers; the Developing Areas Research Group; the Annual Association of American Geographers; the Institute of Development Studies; the departments of Geography and of International Relations and Politics at Otago University, New Zealand; the Paekakariki Institute of Social Science in New Zealand; Durham University Geography Department; Trinity College Dublin Geography Department; Sheffield University Geography Department; DANIDA, Denmark; the Polish Ministry of Foreign Affairs; and the NGO Polish Humanitarian Action. A number of research grants have contributed to the analysis in this book, and I am very grateful to the British Academy, the Department for International Development (Futures of Aid Programme) and Newnham College, Cambridge, for their support.

In the closing stages of writing this book I was awarded the Ron Lister Visiting Fellowship by the Department of Geography at Otago University in New Zealand. I had four very happy months getting to know the lovely city of Dunedin as well as New Zealand a little, and meeting students and staff in Unicol and in the Geography Department. I am grateful for the enormous personal and professional generosity and warmth I experienced, and the tremendous opportunity to learn from my colleagues in Otago, Auckland, Massey and Victoria universities, while getting a sense of seeing the world from the Pacific. Kia ora!

Many individuals have contributed to the ideas expressed in this book, all of whom have been generous with their time and their expertise. In particular, I would like to thank Glenn Banks, Richa Bansal, Tony Binns, Deborah Bräutigam, Laura Collins, Jennifer Constantine, Penny Davies, Ela Drazkiewicz, Thomas Fues, Patty Gray, Nilima Gulrajani, Doug Hill, Soyeun Kim, Sungmi Kim, Kenneth King, Colin Lawson, Simon Lightfoot, Gerard McCann, Cheryl McEwan, Giles Mohan, Warwick Murray, Etienne Nel, Philippe Nel, John Overton, Dinesh Paudel, Sarah Radcliffe, Venkat Ramanujam Ramani, Regina Scheyvens, Alex Shankland, Pranay Sinha, Katia Taela, Lena Tan, May Tan-Mullins and Helen Yanacopolos. I would also like to take this opportunity to thank Stuart Corbridge, who has been a generous supervisor, mentor and friend over many years, as well as a great intellectual inspiration. I appreciate being among supportive and stimulating students, colleagues and staff at the Department of Geography and Newnham College in Cambridge University.

Particular thanks to Jenny Constantine, Penny Davies, Cheryl McEwan, Thomas Fues, Sungmi Kim, Colin Lawson, Simon Lightfoot, Pranay Sinha and Katie Willis, who read all or parts of the manuscript at various stages. All deficiencies remain my own. Amy Carrithers, George Carrothers, Regina Hansda and Sungmi Kim were press-ganged into helping out with the bibliography, which they did with grace and efficiency.

I have lost count of the number of times I have read acknowledgments in other books that include thanks to publishers and apologies for being somewhat late in meeting deadlines. The full force of this has been brought home to me over the last year and more, so I would like to say a sincere thank you to Jakob Horstmann and Tamsine O'Riordan at Zed Books, who have been more than patient in the face of repeated delays.

Abbreviations

ACGI	Arab Coordination Group Institutions
ADB	Asian Development Bank
BPD	Busan Partnership Document
BRIC	Brazil, Russia, India, China
CEE	Central and Eastern Europe
CIDA	Canadian International Development Agency
COMECON	Soviet Council for Mutual Economic Assistance
CRS	Creditors Reporting System
CSO	civil society organization
DAC	Development Assistance Committee
DCF	Development Cooperation Forum
DE	development effectiveness
DfID	Department for International Development
ECOSOC	Social and Economic Council of the United Nations
FOCAC	Forum on China–Africa Cooperation
FTS	Financial Tracking Service
GNI	gross national income
HIPC	Heavily Indebted Poor Country
HLF	High Level Forum
IATI	International Aid Transparency Initiative
IBSA	India, Brazil, South Africa
ICT	information and communication technology
IDA	International Development Agency
IECDF	International Economic Cooperation Development Fund
IMF	International Monetary Fund
IR	international relations
ITEC	Indian Technical and Economic Cooperation
JICA	Japan International Cooperation Agency
KJAS	Kenya Joint Assistance Strategy
LoC	line of credit
MDG	Millennium Development Goal
NAM	Non-Aligned Movement
NDD	non-DAC donor
NEPAD	New Partnership for Africa's Development

NGO	non-governmental organization
NIEO	New International Economic Order
OCHA	UN Office for the Coordination of Humanitarian Affairs
ODA	official development assistance
OECD	Organisation for Economic Co-operation and Development
OOF	other official flows
OPEC	Organization of the Petroleum Exporting Countries
PCD	policy coherence for development
PKI	Partai Komunis Indonesia
PRC	People's Republic of China
PRSP	poverty reduction strategy plan
R2P	responsibility to protect
ROC	Republic of China (Taiwan)
SADPA	South African Development Partnership Agency
SSA	sub-Saharan Africa
SSC	South–South cooperation
SSDC	South–South development cooperation
TC	technical cooperation
TDC	trilateral development cooperation
TEAM-9	Techno-Economic Approach for Africa-India Movement
TT-SSC	Task Team on South–South Cooperation
UAE	United Arab Emirates
UNCTAD	United Nations Conference on Trade and Development
UNDAC	United Nations Disaster Assessment and Coordination
UNDP	United Nations Development Programme
UNHCR	United Nations High Commissioner for Refugees
WFP	World Food Programme
WP-EFF	Working Party on Aid Effectiveness
WTO	World Trade Organization

Introduction

This book is about the emergence, or in many cases the re-emergence, of a large number of states that are active as partners and donors in international development. They include growing global giants like China, India and Brazil; regional powers like South Africa and Saudi Arabia; rapidly industrializing countries like Thailand and Turkey; and former socialist states, such as Russia, Poland and the Czech Republic.[1] The visibility, presence and impact of these countries in international development have grown sharply over the last few years. As a result, they have gone from being almost entirely neglected within Western-dominated analyses of foreign aid and development (except in many cases as recipients) to being a subject of intense interest and analysis as *providers* of foreign aid and development assistance.

The tremendous diversity and growing numbers of the (re-)emerging donors and development partners present a range of opportunities and challenges for poorer countries and peoples around the world; and for foreign aid and development policies, ideologies and governance regimes in the new millennium. Many within the 'mainstream' aid community now welcome the specific expertise and additional resources that the (re-)emerging development partners provide, but also express concerns that the fragile gains made by the so-called traditional donor community towards good governance, aid effectiveness and poverty reduction will be undermined by the sheer proliferation of new actors and, in some cases, by their lower levels of transparency and their different approaches to development (Manning 2006; Davies 2008; Grimm et al. 2009; Zimmerman and Smith 2011). Some commentators take a more hostile view of what they consider to be the sinister agendas and impacts of 'rogue donors', such as China, Iran, Saudi Arabia and Venezuela. These are accused of using 'toxic aid' to promote their national self-interest at the expense of poor people and countries, while undermining liberal global governance (Collins 2007; Naím 2007). For others, however, the fracturing of the Western-dominated aid cartel is viewed in a more positive light – here the (re-)emerging donors and development partners are expected to be instrumental in rebalancing global power, offering recipient nations greater choices in their sources of financing and assistance, as well as demonstrating alternative models and approaches to economic growth that may well prove more effective in increasing productivity and wealth creation (Kondoh et al. 2010; Rhee 2010; Sato et al. 2010). How these might impact on poverty reduction, social justice, gender equality and environmental sustainability remains an open question. The reality is likely to be a complex one: (re-)emerging foreign aid donors and development partners have diverse histories, embody a range of ideologies and practices, and will have a wide variety of direct and indirect impacts, for better and worse, on the lives and livelihoods of poorer people and poorer countries around the world.

The context for this rapidly changing landscape of aid and development is the seismic shifts taking place in the geographies of power and wealth. The world is becoming increasingly multipolar in terms of the distribution of economic growth, and in the balance of political power within and across state, regional and global institutions (Hurrell 2006, 2007; Nye 2011; World Bank 2011a; Sidaway 2012). Foreign aid and development cooperation constitute a relatively small element within this turbulent sea of global change, but it is an arena that is revealing of wider patterns and trends in political, economic and cultural power. It is increasingly obvious that the (Western-dominated) 'international' development community, including bilateral agencies, multilateral organizations and even NGOs, foundations and other non-state actors, can no longer neglect the large number of (re-)emerging donors and development partners (Kragelund 2008, 2011; Woods 2008; Grimm et al. 2009; King 2010; Lightfoot 2008, 2010; Scott et al. 2010; Sorensen 2010; Mitchell 2011; Kharas et al. 2011; Kim and Lightfoot 2011; Park 2011; Amar 2012; Chaturvedi et al. 2012).

These shifts are being closely observed and experienced by poorer countries around the world – the recipients of both 'traditional' Western-led foreign aid and 'non-traditional' development assistance from Southern, Arab and post-socialist states. The evidence suggests that their governments, civil society organizations and peoples frequently welcome the emerging powers in terms of the wider impact they are having on the global economy, their supply of relatively cheaper consumer goods, and their growing assertiveness in international forums and institutions. More specifically, as development partners, they bring additional financing and resources; and some tend to conduct their partnerships differently and in ways that are appreciated by their recipients, while providing alternative development discourses, approaches and ideologies (Mohan and Power 2008; South Centre 2008; Kagame

2009; Sato et al. 2011; ADB et al. 2011). As Ngaire Woods (2008: 1220) suggests:

> In Africa and elsewhere, governments needing development assistance are skeptical of [Western] promises of more aid, wary of conditionalities associated with aid, and fatigued by the heavy bureaucratic and burdensome delivery systems used for delivery of aid. Small wonder that the emerging donors are being welcomed with open arms.

However, these recipient/partner countries, and more specifically consumers, workers, sectors, citizens and civil society groups within them, are also cautious. The emerging powers bring problems and challenges as well as opportunities. As long ago as 1965, while welcoming China's growing relationship with Kenya, President Jomo Kenyatta said, '[i]t is naïve to think that there is no danger of imperialism from the East. In world power politics the East has as much design on us as the West and would like us to serve their own interests' (quoted in Larkin 1971: 138). Contemporary concerns about the impacts of growing economic competition, rising prices, land grabs, environmental damage, poor labour conditions, and support for authoritarian and violent regimes are being voiced within poorer countries, as well as by the 'traditional' donors. Many commentators argue that ultimately the issue of whether or not the emerging powers will enhance global development will come down to whether the leaders of recipient nations can or will assert themselves in their people's interests (e.g. Alden 2007; Kaplinsky and Farooki 2009; Kornegay and Landsberg 2009; Cheru and Obi 2010; Naidu 2011; Saidi and Wolf 2011). Quite how this might happen will depend on the confluence of many factors, not least whether ordinary people and civil society organizations have the ability and capacity to hold their governments to account in both recipient and donor countries (Mohan 2012).

Some academic commentators have written about non-Western donors and development partners for years (e.g. Dietz and Houtcamp 1995; Bräutigam 1998), but for the most part both mainstream and critical development scholars have tended to focus on North–South relations, if with very different perspectives and assumptions. As we shall see below, this situation is changing, and researchers are increasingly engaging with the rapidly changing map of development actors (Schmitz 2007). This has implications for how the international relations and political economy of 'development' are understood and theorized. It is also challenging dominant development imaginaries, including long-standing binary constructions of 'North' and 'South',

'East' and 'West', 'developed' and 'developing', and 'First', 'Second' and 'Third Worlds' (Sidaway 2012).

This book aims to examine these changes through a critical assessment of the histories, modalities and agendas of the (re-)emerging foreign aid donors and development cooperation partners. It is aimed at students and scholars within anthropology, development studies, geography, international relations and politics. The analytical focus of the book is on the official bilateral (state) development cooperation activities of the emerging powers, although their relationships with non-state actors, multilateral organizations and the private sector are also discussed. This statist focus therefore regrettably does little justice to the ordinary people who are the face and the capillary agents of these emerging relations, whether as representatives of official institutions, labourers and workers, or small shopkeepers and migrants (Mohan and Tan-Mullins 2009).[2]

The term 'emerging powers' is discussed in more detail in Chapter 1, but for the purposes of this book it is widely conceived to take in states in Africa, Asia, the Caribbean, Central and Eastern Europe, the Middle East and Latin America. I concur here with Scott et al. (2010), who argue that we need to go beyond the major emerging powers (usually taken to mean China, India and Brazil) to look also at the impact on global development of a second tier of smaller but still significant actors (see also Sato 2007; Jaffrelot 2009; Schulz 2010a).

Terms and definitions

It is impossible to write on this subject without running into something of a definitional morass, as the somewhat awkward use of 'foreign aid donors' and 'development cooperation partners' in the discussion above has already hinted. All of the terms for the countries that are the focus of this book have problematic omissions or associations. *Emerging donors* invokes the term 'emerging markets' or 'emerging economies', denoting countries which are sites of risky but potentially lucrative investment as they transition from 'developing' or former socialist status to becoming more industrialized and/or more regionally and globally integrated through trade and investment (Sidaway and Pryke 2000; Lai 2006). The phrase also calls to mind the idea of the 'emerging powers', a concept that extends attention beyond their growing economic strengths to consider wider geopolitical and in some cases military profiles. In this register, becoming an aid donor is symbolically pegged to the notion of a shift to a more advanced and dynamic economic and political status, with implications for the balance of regional or even global power.[3] However, the terms *emerging* or *new donors* can promote the misleading impression that the turn to development cooperation is recent in origin. While some countries are embarking upon development assistance programmes for the first time, many others have a significant history of development partnerships, in some cases stretching back to the 1950s. As we shall see in later chapters, historical contexts and experiences of being donors (and often recipients at the same time) continue to have strong legacies in terms of specific development ideologies and discourses, and contemporary claims and practices must be understood with reference to the past. The terms 'new' or 'emerging' – or even *non-traditional donors*, which is also sometimes used – are therefore problematically dehistoricizing.

A different option is *post-colonial donors*, which is attractive because it explicitly transgresses the dominant geographical imaginaries of who gives aid to whom, disrupting Orientalist binaries which set up the 'North' as giver and the 'South' as receiver (Kothari 2005, 2007; Six 2009; Sidaway 2012).[4] However, the term is not universally accurate in describing some of the countries we are concerned with here. Although China was forcibly subordinated to external trade interests in the nineteenth century following the Opium Wars of the 1840s–1860s, it was never formally colonized, and nor was Thailand. Moreover, it is not a term that would typically be applied to Russia or the formerly socialist European states which are also re-engaging with development aid. If we were going to use the term 'post-colonial donors' should Ireland, or for that matter Australia, New Zealand and the United States, be included (Gilmartin and Berg 2007)? Post-colonial theory offers a powerful analytical lens for critically evaluating the (re-)emerging development partners, but the label 'post-colonial donors' has only partial validity.

A more accurate term is that of *non-DAC donors*, which explicitly locates these states outside of the Development Assistance Committee (DAC) of the Organisation for Economic Co-operation and Development (OECD). The OECD is essentially a club for higher-income countries, which now has thirty-four members following the most recent expansion in 2010, when Chile, Estonia, Israel and Poland were admitted. Of these, only twenty-three are members of the DAC, together with the European Union, which is a member in its own right. It is notable that with the exception of Japan (which became a member shortly after DAC was founded in 1960) and very recently South Korea (since January 2010), all members of the DAC are Western countries. As we shall see in Chapter 1, the DAC is a hegemonic node within the global aid governance architecture that regulates by far the largest global share of bilateral foreign aid (Manning 2008; Carey 2011). Members are expected to subscribe to DAC norms and standards regarding aid definitions, report data annually, and engage in regular peer reviews (Mahon and McBride 2009). However, although *non-DAC donors* (NDDs) is a technically accurate term, it is a residual category which defines these countries by what they are not. As Kim and Lightfoot (2011) suggest, whether they are judged positively or negatively, this is a vantage point that implicitly sets up the DAC as the reference point against which the non-DAC countries are measured. This is problematic because it acts either to normalize the centrality and power of the DAC or to repudiate it, and because it sets up too strong a sense of unity within the DAC, and too stark a divide with those development partners who fall outside of it (Sato et al. 2010).

It is not just the first half of the terminology which is disputed, whether new, emerging, post-colonial or non-DAC. Many of the countries (re-)engaging in development assistance are cautious about the label of *donor*, and some firmly reject it. For a number of Southern states in particular, the term is burdened with associations of paternalism, hierarchy and neocolonial interference. At worst, bilateral foreign aid has helped keep autocrats in power, funded conflict, and leveraged deeply controversial and often damaging economic policies (Sogge 2002; Stiglitz 2002). For many critics, foreign aid continues to mask the ongoing failure to address global structural inequalities, notably with regard to trade (Langan and Scott 2011) and global governance (Reisen 2010). Beyond these economic and political impacts, for many critics, Western foreign aid is inherently demeaning and humiliating, founded as it is on a set of colonial and post-colonial hierarchies that assume the superiority of 'Western' ideas, models and norms, and the right to intervene (Gilman 2003; Kothari 2005, 2007; McEwan 2009; Six 2009; Amar 2012). Recent mainstream foreign aid reforms, including initiatives to encourage more effective donor coordination, recipient country ownership, mutual accountability and more inclusive governance regimes, have not answered the charges of many critics; they are perceived as not going far enough or as suffering implementation deficits, or more fundamentally they still work within a framework of and promote Western-dominated neoliberal globalization. Finally, as we shall see, the concept of 'foreign aid' does not encompass many elements of the wider field of 'development cooperation' relations deployed by some (re-)emerging partners.

For these reasons, and building on a set of historic idioms that are discussed in Chapter 2, while some of the NDDs actively embrace the identity of *foreign aid donors* and seek to move (selectively) closer to a Western/DAC model, others refer to *international, horizontal* or *development cooperation* (or *assistance*), and to themselves as *partners* rather than *donors*, in a conscious promotion of a discourse (if not always a reality) of mutual benefit, non-interference and respect for sovereignty between them and their partners/recipients. In the rest of this book I try to use the appropriate term for different actors – Poland and Saudi Arabia use the language of foreign aid and are comfortable with the label of 'donor', while India insists that it is a development cooperation partner. Interestingly, there is some evidence that the DAC donors are starting to prefer the discourse of development cooperation to that of foreign aid (Glennie 2011b), a discursive shift that is in part a response to the influence of the (re-)emerging development actors. We return to this observation later in the book.

By the same token, the terms used to label the *mainstream, traditional* or *Western* development community are also problematic. *Traditional* implies others are 'non-traditional', despite long-standing genealogies in some cases, while *mainstream* implicitly centres Western and (Western-dominated) 'global' actors and institutions, arguably validating their ideologies and activities as legitimate (rather than dominant) norms within development. The label *Western* excludes Japan (and now South Korea), which at one time was the largest single supplier of bilateral foreign aid and a DAC member that has brought distinctive aid practices and ideologies to the table (Scheyvans 2005; Potter 2008; Tsopanakis 2011). Just like the 'non-DAC' equivalents discussed above, these terms (DAC, traditional, mainstream, Western and so on) can also imply an undue homogeneity, whereas Japan, Portugal, Sweden and the United States, for example, are very different foreign aid actors in their size, capacities, organization and ideological inclinations (Lancaster 2007). Kondoh et al. (2010: 6) point out that '[a]lthough DAC is often assumed to be a like-minded group with convergent interests, the standardised DAC aid model is neither unequivocally articulated nor shared'. Indeed, many analysts find more similarities across the DAC/non-DAC divide than within these groupings, an argument that is taken up throughout this book.

However they are labelled (and problematic terms can be surprisingly hard to avoid, as the title of this book demonstrates!), I argue that we need to critically interrogate the claims, identities and groupings that these terms imply or assert, rather than take them at face value.

The importance of the (re-)emerging donors and development partners

The growing numbers, activities and impacts of non-DAC development actors are starting to raise a series of questions, challenges and opportunities:

1   What impacts are the (re-)emerging donors/development partners having on economic growth, political and governance structures, poverty reduction, environmental sustainability, and social and cultural well-being among poorer people and in poorer countries? In other words, what impacts are they having on development, in its many guises?

2   What impacts are the (re-)emerging donors and development partners having on the current architecture and ideologies of foreign aid and development – the dominant institutions, practices and norms of the 'mainstream' DAC donors, multilateral institutions and civil society actors?

3   What part is foreign aid and development cooperation playing in the wider economic and geopolitical changes that are taking shape globally? In other words, where does aid and development cooperation fit into the agendas and strategies of the emerging powers, individually and more broadly, and in the changing geographies of wealth and power?

4   What challenges do the rise of the (re-)emerging donors and development partners pose for theorizing development, both in terms of longer-term and deeper processes of change, and in relation to the policies and practices of intentional development?

Recent years have witnessed a surge of analysis, commentary and policy response as these questions have started to exercise politicians, policy-makers, development agencies and institutions, development NGOs, publics, the media and scholars around the world. However, this level of interest has not historically been the case, and with a few exceptions, the presence, roles and impacts of the non-DAC donors and development partners had barely registered within most Western debates on foreign aid and development. Lawson (1987) observed that there has been relatively little scholarship on Soviet aid, and this was mostly from Soviet Studies – it did not draw on or contribute to the insights or approaches of development economics or development studies (see also Roeder 1985). As recently as 1998, Deborah Bräutigam noted that although China had been a development assistance partner to many African countries since the 1950s, almost no Western development

8

textbook even mentioned China. The Declaration that emerged from the 2003 High Level Forum on Aid Effectiveness in Rome confidently stated that the 'international development community' had reached broad agreement, despite the absence of Brazil, Russia, India, China and Turkey, among others (Chandy and Kharas 2011). As we shall see, while there is now considerably more awareness of the role of various non-DAC donors, their omission from media, scholarly and other analyses of aid is far from fully redressed, as the example of the 2010 Haiti earthquake suggests (Box 0.1).

This neglect of the non-DAC donors and development partners is powerfully revealing about the dominant psychology and representational regime of 'development' in the West (Kothari 2007; Kapoor 2008; Mawdsley 2008; McEwan 2009; Six 2009). Uma Kothari argues that Western development imaginations are set up around essentialized dichotomies of North/South, developed/underdeveloped, First/Third World, modern/traditional, which act to 'provide the rationale and justification for the practice of some people intervening to develop others and thus also shape those who give assistance and those who must be grateful for it' (Kothari 2007: 37). The dominance of Western donors in (Western) constructions of aid has even led to the relative occlusion of Japan. Copestake (2010) notes that even though Japan has been a DAC donor since 1960, and at times the largest single bilateral contributor of foreign aid, there is far less academic research on its donor values, ideologies, agendas and practices compared to its Western peers. Copestake speculates whether this can be attributed to a parochial complacency in the understanding of foreign aid as an essentially Western virtue. The emergence and/or new visibility of Southern, Gulf and formerly socialist countries as development donors and partners disrupts these persistent Orientalist binaries of North/South, West/East, superior/inferior, donor/recipient; as the changing geographies of aid are harnessed to newer territorial claims and imaginaries (Drazkiewicz 2007; Six 2009; Gray 2011).

Several factors explain the rapid growth of interest and analysis in the (re-)emerging donors and development partners in recent years. First, leaving aside for the moment the major problems surrounding defining and measuring aid and development cooperation flows (see Chapters 1 and 3), non-DAC partners are increasing their aggregate foreign aid contributions in volume and share. Chandy and Kharas (2011) suggest that at present the NDDs provide around 10–12 per cent of global aid flows, and Park (2011) calculates that this could double in the next five years. However, the current share of NDD development

Box 0.1 Cuba's aid ignored by the media?

Among the many donor nations helping Haiti, Cuba and its medical teams have played a major role in treating earthquake victims. Public health experts say the Cubans were the first to set up medical facilities among the debris and to revamp hospitals immediately after the earthquake struck. However, their pivotal work in the health sector has received scant media coverage. 'It is striking that there has been virtually no mention in the media of the fact that Cuba had several hundred health personnel on the ground before any other country,' said David Sanders, a professor of public health from Western Cape University in South Africa. ... Before the earthquake struck, 344 Cuban health professionals were already present in Haiti, providing primary care and obstetrical services as well as operating to restore the sight of Haitians blinded by eye diseases. More doctors were flown in shortly after the earthquake ... However, in reporting on the international aid effort, Western media have generally not ranked Cuba high on the list of donor nations. ... Richard Gott, the *Guardian* newspaper's former foreign editor and a Latin America specialist, explains: 'Western media are programmed to be indifferent to aid that comes from unexpected places. In the Haitian case, the media have ignored not just the Cuban contribution, but also the efforts made by other Latin American countries.' Brazil is providing $70mn in funding for 10 urgent care units, 50 mobile units for emergency care, a laboratory and a hospital, among other health services. Venezuela has cancelled all Haiti debt and has promised to supply oil free of charge until the country has recovered from the disaster. Western NGOs employ media officers to ensure that the world knows what they are doing ... Cuban medical teams, however, are outside this predominantly Western humanitarian-media loop and are therefore only likely to receive attention from Latin American media and Spanish language broadcasters and print media.

Source: Tom Fawthrop, 16 February 2010, english.aljazeera. net/focus/2010/01/20101319551487o782.html, accessed 10 January 2012

assistance is not historically particularly high – in 1978 the OPEC donors alone accounted for 30 per cent of global aid (Manning 2006). So, while the increased financial contributions and development activities of the non-DAC donors have raised their profile, it is not a particularly strong explanation for the sudden visibility and the interest in them.

More important perhaps are the individual countries behind the headline figures, and most particularly China. The rapidly expanding scale and scope of China's development assistance around the world (Bräutigam 2009), and debates about the role this is playing in its economic and geopolitical rise, are attracting huge levels of attention. This has spilled over into greater awareness of and interest in the wider phenomenon of (re-)emerging donors. To some extent, Venezuela's foreign aid policies are also having this effect, especially in the USA. Unlike China, which largely plays down any revisionist intentions, Venezuelan President Hugo Chávez has explicitly challenged US hegemony in Latin America and beyond. Furthermore, the events of 9/11 in Washington and New York resulted in Islamic assistance coming under renewed scrutiny (Kaag 2008; Benthall and Bellion-Jourdan 2009). Although mostly concerned with private flows through individuals, charities and foundations, several commentators have called for more transparent official flows from the Gulf states, although this is generally framed in terms of the need for improved accountability and coordination (Villanger 2007; World Bank 2010). Again, these countries have been official aid donors since the 1960s and 1970s, but they have rarely figured much within Western development textbooks and discussions, despite in some cases very substantial contributions: at one point in the 1970s Saudi Arabia was the third-largest donor in the world, and in 2011 it provided more official development assistance (ODA) than fifteen of the twenty-four DAC donors. The claim that China, Iran, Saudi Arabia and Venezuela constitute 'rogue donors' (Naím 2007) will be critically evaluated later in this book, but these assertions have done much to catapult the changing politics of aid and development cooperation to public, media and policy attention.

The enlargement of the European Union (EU) in 2004 and 2007, bringing in ten new member states, has also helped raise the visibility of (re-)emerging donors and development partners (Grimm and Harmer 2005). The EU requires that new member states adopt common laws, standards, policies and regulations. This includes a commitment to certain levels of foreign aid funding, as well as expectations about its monitoring and reporting, and particular modes and standards of delivery. Negotiations over the volume and nature of these foreign aid programmes have been the subject of domestic debate within the new member states, and within European Union institutions (Light-foot 2010). This has helped prompt a wider awareness among DAC members, dominated as it is by EU members, of the (re-)emerging donors (Grimm et al. 2009).

More broadly, the North is waking up to the profound global trans-itions being driven by the emerging powers (Narlikar 2010). Develop-ment cooperation constitutes a modest element of the overall foreign and economic policy agendas of the emerging powers, but it is playing some role in what are significantly changing geographies of world power. The rise of the emerging powers is being reflected in heated debates over the composition of the United Nations Security Coun-cil, in terms of the balance of voting rights in the World Bank and the International Monetary Fund, and in relation to global trade and financing debates that are now discussed not by the G8 but by the G20.[5] The economic recession, the euro crisis and the downgrading of the USA's credit rating are just some of the pressing contexts within which the older industrial nations are watching a new configuration of global economic power emerge.

Recipient or 'partner' countries are also making their voices heard within this new configuration, articulating their priorities and inter-ests (e.g. Kagame 2009), although this is where research-led analysis remains weakest. They are using various forums and bodies within the United Nations, as well as the spaces that are opening up with the mainstream aid architecture, to welcome the NDDs, but also to try to ensure that their engagement is a positive one (Davies 2008; Carey 2011). For example, a group of partner countries released a position paper in advance of the Busan High Level Forum on Aid Effectiveness (PCPP 2011), which assessed progress towards aid effectiveness, and identified key needs and priorities from the perspective of the recipient states. Among other things, the authors of this document pointed to the opportunities and challenges presented by the (re-)emerging donors for themselves and for the wider aid architecture.

The (re-)emerging donors and development cooperation partners are therefore very much on the agenda, and not before time. Within mainstream development circles we are currently witnessing paradigm shifts within the dominant aid institutions, the creation of new insti-tutions for managing development cooperation, and a stronger voice for recipient countries and the (re-)emerging donors in international forums and meetings. Thus, to take just one 'traditional donor', in 2011 the British minister for international development announced a new policy agenda of working cooperatively in and with the emerging powers in development (Mitchell 2011), a decision that reflects a turn within UK foreign policy more broadly.

A number of themes and arguments run through this book. First, I suggest that it is important to go beyond China, which is currently soaking up the vast majority of attention directed towards (re-)emerging development cooperation partners. While China is unquestionably a singularly important actor within international relations, too Sino-centric a focus narrows our understanding of the new geographies of aid and development. Widening the remit to look at the complex, diverse and highly differentiated field of (re-)emerging donors and development partners in Central and Eastern Europe, in the Gulf and across Asia, Africa and Latin America helps us identify and analyse broader trends and patterns, and indeed to provide a critical vantage point from which to better analyse China's development cooperation ideologies and practices.

Second, as well as the material politics and practices of development assistance, this book is concerned with the symbolic politics and ideational realm of development cooperation. Many of the NDDs assert and enact rather different claims around development cooperation to those of the 'mainstream' donors. Among other things, analysing these symbolic gestures and discursive claims requires us to histori-cize the (re-)emerging donors and development partners. While global contexts and individual country trajectories and circumstances may have changed significantly, their historical experiences as recipients and donors continue to have a legacy – whether in reality or rhetoric, principles, policies or practices. I will argue that notwithstanding the strategic agendas that unquestionably drive the realpolitik of aid, the symbolic claims of alternative partnerships are not merely a discursive veneer, but have a profound purchase on the development imaginaries of the diverse range of (re-)emerging states and their publics.

Third, while rejecting any blanket criticism or simplistic call to abandon aid altogether, the analysis proceeds from a critical evaluation of the dominant structures and practices of Western-dominated foreign aid. That said, I argue for an equally critical stance towards the (re-)emerging donors and development partners as for the 'mainstream' donors. In particular, I ask whose interests are being served within both 'donor' and 'recipient' countries. Masked under the language of solidarity and benevolence in the new geographies of aid and develop-ment are class-based, sectoral and national interests that need to be identified and investigated (Prashad 2008; Taylor 2009). I argue that the demand by some of the emerging powers for greater equality and justice *between* states within global development governance regimes is not necessarily inflected inwards to support a more progressive or just politics *within* states.

The fourth theme is that of recipient perspectives, experiences and agency. What do different groups and interests within the 'partner countries' of non-DAC development assistance make of these flows and activities? At present the empirical evidence base is rather limited (although see Kondoh et al. 2010; Sato et al. 2011), something that impacts on the analysis presented here, but the book seeks to be attentive to this question throughout.

Finally, this book is founded on a critical understanding of 'development'. Liberal reformers have sought to wrest the concept away from those who see it as simply economic growth to include a focus on basic needs and services, gender, environmental sustainability, human security, social justice, the ability to make choices, and the right to representation and a voice within families, societies and governance systems (e.g. Sen 2001; Nussbaum 2011). Post-colonial, feminist and more radical critics have focused on the discursive power of liberal models of 'development', and contest the claims to hegemonic histories, cultures and knowledges that are imbued within Western-led ideologies, practices and institutions (Escobar 1995, 2004; Ferguson 1994, 1999; Li 2007; McEwan 2009). I draw on these rich literatures in examining the impacts and implications of the (re-)emerging development actors; but also ask whether and how more mainstream and critical development theories need to respond to the more complex development geographies that are emerging in the twenty-first century (Schmitz 2007; De Haan 2011; Sidaway 2012).

Chapter outline

Chapter 1 sets out the main empirical and theoretical underpinnings for the rest of the book. It first sketches out the significant shifts that are taking place in global economic and political power with the rise of the 'emerging powers'. The Asian Drivers framework is discussed here as an analytical tool for understanding the complex impacts that the emerging powers are having on poorer peoples and countries. The chapter then turns to the main debates over the history, nature and impacts of 'mainstream' foreign aid. It outlines briefly the major theoretical approaches to foreign aid before examining the emergence of the 'new aid paradigm' in the late 1990s and new millennium. Disquiet about the effectiveness and foundations of the new aid paradigm is a critical backdrop to the growing voice and assertiveness of many (re-) emerging development partners.

Chapter 2 looks at the diverse historical lineages of the main groups of donors and development actors, although with the strong caveat that there is great variation within these somewhat artificial groupings of states. It is structured around five (sometimes overlapping) drivers or contexts: socialism(s), the Non-Aligned Movement, the United Nations South–South Cooperation initiatives, the oil price rises of the 1970s, and European Union expansion. India and Taiwan provide case studies of specific drivers of development cooperation. Notwithstanding important changes in current ideologies, capacities, interests and contexts, these historical discourses and positionings continue to shape NDD development assistance rhetorics and policies – whether they are sanitized, suppressed or celebrated.

Chapter 3 picks up the NDDs in the new millennium. It discusses the issues confronting the definitions, measurement and monitoring of foreign aid and development cooperation, and it analyses current estimated volumes, the share of national income, the division between bilateral/multilateral channels, and humanitarian contributions. The chapter then examines how foreign aid and development cooperation are institutionally managed within the various NDDs. This focuses on official bilateral arrangements, but includes relations with civil society, the private sector and the military. It finishes with a discussion of transparency and accountability, and the current debates over whether and how (re-)emerging development partners should report their development assistance flows.

Chapter 4 first analyses what is revealed by the choice of recipient or partner countries for different (re-)emerging development actors. It then turns to the modes of NDD assistance – loans, grants, lines of credit, debt relief, technical assistance and so on. Drawing especially on the essential insights of Deborah Bräutigam (2009), the chapter critically evaluates the ways in which South–South development cooperation in particular is (mis)construed by being simplistically compared with foreign aid, with implications for how it is debated in media, policy and political circles. The final section picks up on two central debates – the blurring and blending of 'aid' and 'development assistance' with commercial relations and agendas; and the rejection of conditionalities accompanying aid flows by many of the (re-)emerging development actors.

Chapter 5 changes tack to evaluate the symbolic politics of development cooperation among selected donors and groupings of development actors. The first section focuses on South–South development cooperation partners, with examples drawn from China and India especially, and focuses critically on their claims to mutual benefit, respect for sovereignty, and solidarity. The second section examines the relationship between national identity politics and donor status in the case of Poland. Here we analyse the ways in which being a donor may augment the construction of 'Western modernity'. The final section examines the pursuit of political capital by Venezuela, a donor that is admired by some and excoriated by others. The chapter argues that a critical appreciation of the contested symbolic and performative politics of foreign aid/development cooperation is essential to understanding the new politics of aid.

Chapter 6 analyses the tensions and shifts taking place within the international aid architecture as the (re-)emerging donors and development partners cooperate with and challenge the DAC, the Bretton Woods institutions (notably the International Monetary Fund and the World Bank), the United Nations and other nodes and norms of global development governance. It explores the growing role of different (re-)emerging development actors in international forums and debates, and the emergence of new institutions. The series of meetings that have driven the Paris Agenda (the new millennial aid paradigm discussed in Chapter 1) are particularly interesting in this respect, and capture the major shifts that are taking place within the global development community. The most recent High Level Forum (HLF) in this process was held in Busan, Korea, in November 2011, and is discussed in this section. An emerging arena of potential collaboration between Northern, multilateral and Southern donors, Trilateral Development Cooperation, is explored in detail. The chapter finishes by scaling down to look at country-level relationships between DAC and non-DAC donors and development partners.

The Busan HLF may well have marked the beginning of the end for Western-dominated global development governance. In Chapter 7 I discuss the role of the (re-)emerging development donors and partners in what may well be a paradigm shift from 'aid effectiveness' to 'development effectiveness', and the paradigm shift taking place in the international aid architecture and norms.

1 | Contexts: the rising powers and mainstream foreign aid

This book is about the opportunities and challenges raised by the growing numbers and visibility of a diverse spectrum of official foreign aid donors and development cooperation partners. In order to understand the changes that are reverberating through the aid and development sectors, and the extent to which these are impacting beyond these arenas, we need to set them within their wider contexts. The first part of this chapter therefore sketches out some of the epochal shifts in global power being driven by the emerging powers – trends that are predicted to deepen over the next years and decades, even if their exact contours remain uncertain.

The second half of the chapter examines contemporary patterns and trends within 'mainstream' foreign aid, focusing on those elements that are especially relevant to the rise of the (re-)emerging development partners. After an overview of the ways in which aid is formally defined and theoretically positioned, we examine the new millennial aid paradigm, or Paris Agenda as it has come to be known. Initially DAC-led, this rapidly became a wider process intended to improve the effectiveness of foreign aid in achieving monitorable development outcomes. However, as we shall see, the Paris Agenda appears to have had limited success to date, and for this and other reasons the 'global consensus' is presently in a state of considerable flux. The 'rise' of the non-DAC donors and development partners is one of several factors contributing to uncertainty and change in contemporary aid governance.

Changing global geographies of wealth and power

In 2003 Goldman Sachs released a startling set of predictions about how four emerging economies – catchily termed the BRICs (Brazil, Russia, India and China) – would compare to those of the G6 (France, Germany, Italy, Japan, the UK and the USA) over the next few decades. They calculated that by 2025 the BRIC economies would be over half as large as those of the G6 combined, and by 2040 they would have overtaken them (Goldman Sachs 2003). While Goldman Sachs analysts were by no means the first to project tremendous shifts in economic power, their intervention was particularly effective at catching world attention. These claims have of course been extensively reviewed and critiqued. Like all scenario modelling they rely on assumptions and calculations that can be teased apart and queried, while events like the most recent global financial crisis will impact on the predicted tends (Copestake 2010). Analysts have pointed to underlying weaknesses within individual BRIC countries, such as India's enormous burden of poverty and China's ageing population, and the fact that behind the convenient label, Brazil, Russia, India and China have very different resource endowments, political systems, demographic futures and strategic interests (Armijo 2007). As with any grouping of countries, their agendas may clash and their futures diverge. Åslund (2010), for example, argues that Russia should not be included within this grouping given an older and declining population and a less dynamic economy (see also Scott et al. 2010).[1] In the meantime, the formal grouping has expanded – South Africa was invited to the third BRICs summit in China in 2011. But while the degree of change may be debated and future scenarios are certainly open to discussion, the vast majority of commentators across the world recognize that the pattern of Western domination that emerged in the eighteenth century and which prevailed over the nineteenth and twentieth centuries is being challenged. To take just one example:

> Trade between developing countries, and between them and the BRICS, is rising twice as fast as world trade. Even more strikingly, while growth has headed south, debt has headed north, the opposite of what happened in the 1970s and 1980s, when poor countries ran up vast debts. Gross public debt in the rich countries is rising, from about 75% of GDP at the start of the crisis in 2007 to a forecast 110% by 2015, says the IMF. Public debt in emerging markets is below 40% of GDP and flat.
> (The Economist 2010: 69, cited in Sidaway 2012)

The BRICs are central to this shift but they are by no means alone. In 2009, Robert Ward of the Economist Intelligence Unit coined the acronym CIVETS (Colombia, Indonesia, Vietnam, Egypt, Turkey and South Africa), identifying them as second-generation emerging powers with young populations, decent growth rates, emerging middle-class consumer markets, diversified economies, and reasonably robust financial systems. In a discussion that is pertinent to the more specific focus of this book, Schulz (2010a: 1) suggests that the CIVETS constitute a 'third wave' of development players, noting that they bring 'a new wave of development partnerships that go beyond the rich-poor logic and promote South-South knowledge exchange and peer-to-peer learning'.

Other countries that have been described as emerging powers include Argentina, Chile, Hungary, Malaysia and Poland. As we might expect, then, there is no consensus on which countries constitute the rising or emerging powers. Political scientists, international relations theorists, military strategists, credit rating agencies, financial institutions, investors and private sector firms all have different and varied criteria (Jaffrelot 2009). The more powerful of these countries, which despite low per capita incomes have large and rapidly growing economies, are at the leading edge of the challenge to Western dominance, including in the field of development cooperation. Many smaller countries are providing numerical weight and more voices in the struggle, although the positioning of individual governments depends on the issue at hand. Arenas include the various bodies of the United Nations, the World Trade Organization, the IMF and the World Bank (Woods 2010). In a speech given to the newly established China–Africa Cooperation Forum (FOCAC) in 2000, the Chinese president Jiang Zemin critiqued the uneven experience of globalization, and asserted that developing countries (with which China somewhat problematically identifies itself) must therefore act together to:

> strengthen co-operation and consultation on multilateral institutions such as the UN and the WTO, so as to safeguard the common interests of the developing countries ... [and] co-ordinate positions on reforming multilateral economic and trade regimes and formulating new rules, with a view to increasing the collective bargaining capacity of developing countries and make efforts towards the democratisation of international relations and the establishment of a just and equitable new international economic order ... The Ministers agree to work for the reform of the United Nations and particularly the UN Security Council that will be geographically representative.[2]

This is not the first time that alliances of weaker countries have attempted to contest and restructure world power relations. The Non-Aligned Movement, with its origins in the 1950s (discussed in more detail in Chapter 2), has sought to create a collective platform from which 'Third World' and other countries could assert their right to economic and political sovereignty. The call for a New International Economic Order (NIEO) in the 1970s was another attempt to correct the excessive dominance of the industrialized nations, and in particular improve the terms of trade and the value of primary commodities for the poorer countries.[3] As well as these more defined movements and moments, throughout the course of the twentieth century Southern and Gulf nations have sought to influence global governance regimes as best they can, with variable success, to shape a world order that better reflects their interests (Braveboy-Wagner 2009; Alden et al. 2010). More recently, Central and Eastern European states have been actively engaged in attempts to reorient European Union agendas, priorities and approaches 'eastwards', with notable successes in some contexts (Lightfoot 2010).[4]

What has changed in the new millennium is the growing economic leverage behind the emerging powers (Nel and Stephen 2010). For the first time in the post-war period, some have enough economic weight to demand rather than request change, and more so when they act together. However, there are still many hurdles to confront – including resistance from Western states, the concerns and suspicions of smaller countries, and the substantial barriers to working cooperatively (Taylor 2009). Moreover, in some contexts and on some issues the leading emerging powers are increasingly aligning with the existing power structures, sometimes at the expense of their solidarity with less powerful countries. As we shall see in Chapter 6, the superseding of the G8 by the G20 signals the reality of a more multipolar economic world, but the inclusion of the large emerging economies doesn't necessarily mean that the interests of the majority of poorer countries are assured. Just as the emerging powers don't share the same interests and agendas with each other, so too the relationships between the emerging powers and poorer states are not necessarily aligned in all matters. For example, notwithstanding the various claims by some of the large Southern states to leadership and solidarity with other low- and middle-income countries (articulated in Jiang Zemin's statement above, for example), in fact they represent a variety of opportunities and threats for poorer and smaller countries. Moreover, it is critical to distinguish between poor countries and poor people. The latter are present, if in different proportions, in all countries. The USA has the highest poverty rates in the OECD; and although the G20 countries account for 90 per cent of the world's GDP (Fang 2010), they also house 58 per cent of the world's poor (Sumner 2010; Wissenbach 2010; Glennie 2011a). Alliances and strategies that may suit the governments and elites of poorer countries are by no means guaranteed to suit different poor and marginalized groups within them (Prashad 2008; Taylor 2009). Finally, notwithstanding the major shifts under way, we should be careful not to exaggerate the degree of change – Nye (2011) observes that the West still commands military dominance, but also a substantial share of global trade, capital and multinational firms (see also Frynas and Paulo 2007).

To help analyse these complex interrelations we can draw upon the Asian Drivers framework (Institute of Development Studies 2005). Although this framework was originally formulated to examine the regional and global impacts of the Indian and Chinese economies on poorer countries, we can extend its analytical approach to the broader resolution of the emerging powers (although we should note that the sheer size and power of China and India make them distinctive global actors). As well as the other Southern emerging powers (such as Brazil and South Africa), for the purposes of this discussion I include the powerful Gulf states, Russia and Central and Eastern European donors.

The Asian Drivers framework The emerging powers are now effectively the engines of global economic growth, as investors and markets, and as producers of goods and services (Goldstein et al. 2006; Aycut and Goldstein 2007; Kaplinsky and Messner 2008), and this economic muscle is underpinning growing global influence in the structures of power. But while there has been considerable discussion and analysis of the implications, opportunities and risks for the industrialized economies, researchers at the Institute of Development Studies have sought to address the neglected question of the impacts for the rather differently situated poorer countries of the world.

In order to get a stronger analytical purchase on these emerging patterns and trends, the Asian Drivers team devised a framework which addresses four key vectors of impact: production and trade flows; financial flows; environmental spillovers; and global and regional governance. They then disaggregated the impacts across two axes: direct/indirect and competitive/complementary. Direct impacts arise from bilateral economic flows and political relations between two countries. These include, say, the import of affordable consumer products from China; a growing market for commodities and resources in India; or investment in bauxite mining or agricultural processing. Indirect impacts, on the other hand, are experienced in third-country or global settings. They arise from the broader reverberations that the rapid growth of India and China are having around the world. For example, the extraordinary competitiveness of the Chinese manufacturing sector has changed the conditions for domestic manufacturing for many other countries, rich and poor (Kaplinsky 2005). Many textile and garment manufacturers in Kenya, for example, find themselves in competition with China in selling to the EU, and often can't match its economies of scale and other advantages (although alternative opportunities may also open up in Chinese markets for Kenyan textiles: Kamau and McCormick 2011). Another indirect impact is on commodity producers of oil, minerals, timber, biofuels and food crops – exporters are profiting not only through demand from surging emerging economies themselves, but also from the higher world prices driven by the economic dynamism of the Asian Drivers/emerging powers.

As these examples suggest, both the direct and indirect impacts of the Asian Drivers/emerging powers can be complementary or competitive to other countries and groups within them. This constitutes the second axis of the framework. Thus, consumers may benefit from affordable Chinese manufactured goods, but workers may lose their jobs as manufacturing units and investment relocate to Special Economic Zones in Guangdong province. Some states may feel they benefit from India's strong line on climate change in international negotiations as it demands that the West take up a full and fair share of its responsibilities; whereas more vulnerable island states and many drought-stricken African countries may wish for a more cooperative approach which focuses on rapidly addressing greenhouse gas mitigation efforts. Urban elites may benefit from accelerated resource extraction, energy infrastructure and investment opportunities, whereas small farmers and pastoralists may lose their lands, or suffer from the pollution and environmental degradation that all too often accompanies industrial growth.

The Asian Drivers framework is helpful to this analysis of the (re-)emerging development actors because it captures some of the complex dynamics of changing international relations, pointing to plural and heterogeneous impacts for different sectors and social groups within and across different countries and contexts. Specifically, it can be extended to think through the direct and indirect impacts of the new geopolitics of aid and development cooperation, and how these may bring opportunities but also costs and challenges for different countries, sectors and groups. As we shall see in future chapters, certain elements of development cooperation have direct impacts in recipient settings, for better or worse: building roads, dams and energy infrastructure can assist mobility, support energy needs and stimulate economic growth; but they can also lead to displacement, environmental damage and growing inequality. As with all such developments, costs and benefits tend to be shared unevenly between rich and poor, urban dwellers and small farmers and so on. But the (re-)emerging donors and development partners will also have indirect impacts through their influence on mainstream ideologies, practices and governance of foreign aid. As we will see in Chapter 6, the NDDs are playing a significant role in current debates over the role of aid in promoting economic growth (which might erode or indeed support the poverty reduction agenda) over the legitimacy and effectiveness of aid conditionalities (which may improve country ownership or undermine anti-corruption efforts), and on the coherence of the aid architecture and the survival of agreed norms. All of these will have impacts on recipient countries. Although the book is not formally structured around the vectors and axes of the Asian Drivers model, it does aim to reflect its insights in recognizing the complex and multidimensional interplay of risks and opportunities that the non-DAC donors and development partners will bring for different countries, sectors, communities and individuals; countering simplistic narratives of non-DAC donors as 'good' or 'bad' (of which more later).

Although 'development cooperation' has important differences with 'foreign aid' (as discussed in detail in Chapter 3), Ngaire Woods (2008) rightly argues that any evaluation of the non-DAC actors must be grounded within a critical reflection of mainstream foreign aid. Some accounts of the NDDs rely on a complacent understanding of the roles and agendas of Western-dominated foreign aid, assuming benign intents even if they admit that the outcomes are not always effective. Many others, although more aware of the complexities of DAC aid and non-DAC aid/development assistance in discourse and practice, still rely on a number of unspoken normative assumptions about the 'proper' conduct and role of foreign aid, fundamentally arbitrated by the 'traditional' aid community. In order to set up a critical and reflexive analysis of the non-DAC donors and development partners we need to turn next to the main debates around the politics, agendas and institutions of foreign aid. The focus is on official bilateral aid (that is, financed and managed through state–state relations), rather than flows of aid through multilaterals, NGOs or foundations, although these are also discussed briefly.

Foreign aid

Foreign aid has been theorized within a number of different disciplines and from a variety of ideological viewpoints, while its politics, actors and impacts have been examined at different scales, in different time periods and across geographical contexts. Here we first very briefly sketch the dominant international relations theories, and then turn to some other ways of approaching aid, including through critical development geography and anthropology.[5]

International relations (IR) theory offers four main schools of thought for understanding the nature and purpose of foreign aid. The oldest and arguably most traditional international relations theory is *realism*. Realists view the world as an anarchic place in which states, which are understood to be the primary legitimate actors in international politics, must struggle with each other to survive and prosper in what is essentially a zero-sum game. Foreign politics is understood as the realm of power play between states, each of which acts in its own perceived interests. Realists tend to place a particularly high value on military power, as force and the threat of force are considered the key means of expanding and maintaining power. Economic wealth is considered both an end in itself – an expression and measure of power – and as a means to acquiring more military, economic and political power. Realists tend to be suspicious of or even hostile towards international organizations, which they view as attempting to impinge on the sovereign rights of states (Morgenthau 1962; Bull 1977), although many later theorists have nuanced this position within realism (e.g. Keohane 1989).

Within the realist tradition, ethical or moral concern for the plight of distant others is considered an illegitimate rationale for foreign policy action, which should rather be driven by the goals of enhancing national strength and resources (Morgenthau 1962). Here realists divide. For some, foreign aid is positioned as a waste of domestic resources on undeserving peoples and countries, with insufficient benefit for the donor country. Their critique is not a moral one about the failings of aid to achieve development, but the assertion that aid is a poor way of conducting economic and diplomatic statecraft: donors don't get enough back in return. Schaefer and Kim (2010), for example, lament the fact that US aid appears not to translate into supporting votes at the UN, which they suggest therefore renders it ineffective and thus illegitimate as foreign policy expenditure.

However, other realists believe that foreign aid can be used to achieve national goals and therefore can be legitimately deployed as a foreign policy tool. Here foreign aid is considered a means to reward allies, promote trade, build policy orthodoxies which are favourable to the donor economies, support domestic producers and consultants, stabilize potential threats, and project soft power. A classic example of a realist agenda for foreign aid can be found in the Cold War competition between the USA and its allies and communist regimes, notably the USSR and China. 'Foreign aid' budgets helped supply food, weapons and funds across the Third World, helping reward friendly or strategically valuable regimes, cajole possible allies, but also, where geopolitically desirable, promote violence and conflict. Humanitarian and/or long-term developmental considerations were relegated to secondary considerations or actively undermined. Aid was not distributed in the interests of poor people in poor countries, but to the leaders of ally states or movements (Tarling 1986; Griffin 1991; Meernik et al. 1998). In the post-Cold War era, different calculations of strategic benefit have influenced the choice of aid recipients, often also distorting flows away from the poorest and most needy (Alesina and Dollar 2000; Kuziemko and Werker 2006). Thus, although realists may be divided over the strategic value of foreign aid, encompassing both supporters and detractors, they share a foundational belief in the fundamental purpose of aid – to enhance the power and interests of the donor in the power play between states.

The second major IR theory is *liberal internationalism*, which broadly proposes that states benefit from being cooperatively networked within international regimes (Deudney and Ikenberry 1999). In liberal internationalist theory, all states (including the powerful ones) ultimately prosper from a more open, peaceful, interdependent and cooperative world order – although of course it is the powerful states that decide on what constitutes a 'desirable' world order. Multilateral institutions are viewed positively as forums within which states can negotiate and work together towards this (apparently) mutually beneficial world order. As it has evolved over time (Ikenberry 2008), liberal internationalism has encompassed the idea that intervention in other sovereign states is justified in order to help promote a liberal global order of open trade, international cooperation, peace, stability and (more recently) democracy, including – very controversially – through military incursion where it is deemed necessary (Chandler 2004; Bellamy 2005, 2010). Foreign aid is enrolled within liberal internationalism in several registers. In theory, aid helps reduce poverty and accelerates economic growth, contributing to stability and prosperity around the world, and thus reducing various threats such as disease pandemics and migration surges. Foreign aid can promote liberal trade regimes, leading to greater global economic integration; and foreign aid meetings and institutions provide forums within which states learn to cooperate with each other, and through which they develop deepening ties and relations. Foreign aid still serves instrumentalist purposes, but within a different understanding of how power works, and what constitutes a desirable set of relations between states (Stokke 1989).

A third foreign policy approach (although one that some argue is compatible with both realism and liberal internationalism) developed over the 1980s and 1990s (Onuf 1989; Katzenstein 1996; Finnemore 1996; Finnemore and Sikkink 1998; Wendt 1999; Adler 2001). The *constructivist* approach essentially holds that international relations owe more to socially constructed ideas, identities and interests than to simplistic material calculations of military, political and economic might. Constructivists hold that international relations are shaped primarily by contingent ideas and norms: how states construe their identities and interests, what they assume about the identities and interests of other states, and the nature of dominant international norms. These ideas are formed through the inter-subjective construction of what is considered 'proper' or 'deviant'. In their constructivist analysis of the South in world politics, Alden et al. (2010) dissect the politicized and conflictual nature of normative ideas, as well as agency – in particular the constitutive role played by Southern actors in influencing the norms of international relations (including the nature and terms of foreign aid). Two related examples of such global norm-building are the emergence of 'poverty reduction' as the key goal of the international development community over the last thirty years or so (Finnemore 1996), and the creation of the Millennium Development Goals as a 'super-norm' (Hulme and Fukuda-Parr 2009).

Within constructivist theory, foreign aid can be understood as a (contested) norm of 'proper' state behaviour (Lumsdaine 1993). Contingent historical and political drivers, such as the Marshall Plan assistance for the post-Second World War reconstruction of Europe, led to the emergence of modern aid norms and values which over time have been internalized into the international expectation that richer states 'should' give aid to poorer states. Constructivist theory offers a particularly useful set of insights for understanding the changing discourses and agendas of foreign aid and development cooperation (Hulme and Fukuda-Parr 2009; Kondoh et al. 2010). As we shall see later, the emerging powers, large and small, are playing a significant role in challenging the West's discursive as well as material dominance of the aid arena. The language and ideology of aid is changing, both reflecting and leading shifts in policies and practices.

Finally, a rather different way of conceptualizing foreign aid is offered by *world systems theory*. This derives from neo-Marxian critiques of the colonial and post-colonial world order in which foreign aid is understood as a means of securing ongoing uneven capitalist accumulation (Wood 1986; Hattori 2001). World systems theory breaks with other international relations traditions by understanding power not through the lens of competing nation-states but across an international division of labour, as transnational capitalist elites appropriate wealth from the world's workers. For world system theorists, aid assists economic and political elites in (so-called) core, semi-periphery and periphery countries to benefit disproportionately from the financing of goods and services, and from the creation of particular regimes (whether Cold War autocracies or current neoliberal models) that reward the rich and powerful at the expense of the poor. Sogge (2002) details the ways in which foreign aid has been used as a tool within the neoliberal armoury, prising open sovereign decision-making to ensure compliant financial and taxation systems, a 'business-oriented' regulatory environment, and the privatization of land, resources and services. Ironically, world systems critics join with some analysts from the right in wishing an end to foreign aid, although from a very different standpoint (Gulrajani 2011).

What all of these IR theories share is the recognition that aid is political. Altruistic and ethical motives certainly play a role for official actors (although what constitutes 'virtue' may be construed in different ways: see Chapters 2 and 5), but aid must be understood primarily as a tool of foreign policy and thus as subject to the same strategic calculations that are made in other areas. However, this should be seen as distinct from whether or not aid contributes to poverty reduction, economic growth and sustainable societies – these goals may well be considered politically desirable by the donors and be genuinely pursued. Being political does not necessarily make aid ineffective; just as being 'ethical' does not make aid effective. For that matter, being 'effective' does not mean that aid is virtuous.

Foreign aid is also inherently 'political' in the different sense that there is no universal agreement on what constitutes 'development' (Escobar 1995, 2004), or how individuals, communities and economic and political systems should achieve it. For most current policy-makers and practitioners, foreign aid is intended to reshape economies and governance structures towards neoliberal globalization in ways that should promote reasonably sustainable and moderately equitable economic growth, while protecting and promoting the needs of the marginalized (women, children, the disabled, the poor) and the desperate (in humanitarian situations). For these mainstream analysts, the challenge is how to ensure that poor countries and poor people can engage positively with the global economy as they confront hurdles ranging from poor connectivity (the lack of sufficient transport and

ICT infrastructure, or by virtue of being landlocked) to weak and corrupt institutions. Mainstream reformers have been at the heart of the new aid paradigm (the Paris Agenda) outlined below, arguing the need for more aid, and more developmentally effective foreign aid (Sachs 2005; Collier 2008).

Many critics argue that it is precisely neoliberal globalization which undermines efforts to reduce poverty. In their view the benefits of neoliberal growth accrue mostly to wealthy transnational elites while the costs are borne by the poor, marginalized, indigenous and otherwise vulnerable. Under the structural adjustment programmes of the 1980s and early 1990s aid was used to leverage deeply controversial policy changes on recipient countries, with extremely uneven costs and rewards. Southern and post-socialist elites embraced the opportunities for accelerated wealth creation made possible by the economic restructuring, but many ordinary people lost jobs, health and education services, and witnessed wages and public spending being slashed (Stiglitz 2002; Prashad 2008). Overt leveraging through policy conditionalities has changed in the new millennium, but current aid paradigms still work within and support the reformed neoliberalism of the post-Washington Consensus (PWC). For many radical scholars and activists the PWC fails to address poverty as a structural issue, and is still insistent on policies which the developed countries themselves did not follow when they were industrializing, such as protectionism and intellectual property theft (Chang 2002). Its uneven implementation is also criticized, as developing countries are levered open while many Northern economic sectors and interests remain subsidized and protected. Even where the lives of many of the poor have improved, the more rapidly accelerating wealth of the better off has led to rising inequality, a universal phenomenon within and between countries in the neoliberal era. As Wilkinson and Pickett (2009) so effectively demonstrate, this erodes material, social and mental well-being globally.

Bilateral foreign aid therefore has its radical detractors and reformist critics, and both liberal and hawkish supporters. Almost all use the language of values and justice to legitimize their position, whether arguing that aid is a moral imperative, a means of shaping a world suited to powerful interests, a waste of taxpayers' money, essential to poverty reduction and inclusive growth, or a tool of imperial hegemony. Recognizing that all foreign aid is political and that development is a deeply contested concept is an essential basis from which to critically understand and evaluate the roles, agendas and impacts of all donors and development partners.

Other disciplines, including anthropology, development studies, geography and history, have contributed to understanding the political economy of foreign aid, but also offer a range of different lenses through which to observe the histories, cultures and ethnographies of aid and development (e.g. Crewe and Harrison 1998; Wedel 2001; Baaz 2005; Eyben 2006a; Gray 2011; Mosse 2011). Critical scholars have examined the complex interplay of material and discursive power, evaluating identities, ideologies, claims and institutional workings of the development and foreign aid communities. Mosse (2011), for example, takes an ethnographic lens to development projects to reveal how development problems, solutions and strategies are constructed by institutions in culturally and historically specific ways; while Six (2009) is one of many theorists who unpick the Eurocentric assumptions and assertions that sit at the heart of 'international' understandings of aid and development. Six draws on post-colonial theory, which in recent years has provided rich insights into the political and intellectual underpinnings of development principles and practices, and how these have informed the conduct and motivations of foreign aid and hegemonic development ideas (McEwan 2009). Critical social science has exposed the power and politics of foreign aid and development theories, cultures, policies and practices, at different sites and scales. As we will see in Chapter 5, these more ethnographically inspired reflections on practices and cultures of aid have, to date, been largely confined to the dominant Western donors.

In trying to chart this difficult terrain, it is useful to be reminded by Glennie (2008) that foreign aid is far too differentiated and diverse a field – in terms of actors, motivations and impacts – to simply dismiss or defend it, or to find singular solutions to 'fix' it (see also Gulrajani 2011). Glennie urges us to recognize that this is a multidimensional and complex system that defies, or ought to defy, simplistic attempts to demonize or defend it *in toto*. The aid policies and practices of any one official donor tend to be shaped by a variety of contingent and structural factors at any one time, and can rarely be described by a singular 'grand theory' of international relations (Scheyvens 2005). Similarly, the highly complex realities of 'aidland' defy simplistic explanations (Mosse 2011). With that in mind, we turn now to an analysis of the main features of contemporary mainstream foreign aid.

What is 'foreign aid'? The dominant norms guiding the definition, management and monitoring of bilateral foreign aid, or official development assistance (ODA) as it is more formally known, have evolved over the last few decades (OECD-DAC 2006; Manning 2008). They are the result of political contest and negotiation within OECD countries, contingent circumstances, and historical structures favouring powerful actors in deciding on what constitutes desirable or appropriate approaches (Hyden 2008; Hulme and Fukuda-Parr 2009; Carey 2011; Xu 2011). However, as Paulo and Reisen (2010) point out, there are actually very few formal rules governing ODA: most of the formulas, principles and expectations are based on 'soft' agreements, something to bear in mind when various NDDs are accused of 'breaking' aid rules (see also Bräutigam 2010). The DAC defines bilateral foreign aid as:

> Grants or loans to countries and territories on the DAC List of ODA Recipients (developing countries) and to multilateral agencies which are: (a) undertaken by the official sector; (b) with promotion of economic development and welfare as the main objective; (c) at concessional financial terms (if a loan, having a grant element of at least 25 per cent). In addition to financial flows, technical co-operation is included in aid. Grants, loans and credits for military purposes are excluded.[6]

Official flows between governments that do not meet the criteria of ODA are known as 'other official flows' (OOF) and are not formally recognized as foreign aid. This separation underpins a defining feature of mainstream ODA today, which is that it is focused on poverty reduction in recipient countries rather than the political and economic interests of donors. Further enhancing the (apparent) distinction between ODA/OOF, or aid and trade, since the early 1990s the DAC has sought to 'untie' aid by reducing or eliminating the use of financial credits accompanying aid, and by not making ODA conditional upon the purchase of donor goods and services (OECD-DAC 2011b). Although this is far from fully achieved (Flint and Goyder 2006; OECD-DAC 2011b), the focus on separating out foreign aid from other imperatives has been widely seen as a progressive agenda, helping ensure that ODA is clearly directed at beneficiary needs and interests (although see Xu 2011 for a more critical assessment of the motivations and outcomes of untying aid). The UK's 2002 International Development Act, for example, for the first time formally separated aid from trade, completely and with legal underwriting. As we shall see, there are growing pressures to move back towards a more 'integrated' aid and development model, which more organically combines different forms of funding streams around aid, trade and investment, drawing in public and private sector actors. The (re-)emerging development partners are one driver of this potential paradigm shift in mainstream aid ideologies

(Severino and Ray 2009, 2010; Kharas et al. 2011), something discussed at various points in following chapters.

ODA includes longer-term development aid and humanitarian assistance channelled bilaterally (from state to state) and multilaterally (through international organizations like the United Nations agencies and the various elements of the World Bank). It is generally assumed that the stronger a country's commitment to bilateral flows the greater the potential for strategic visibility and leverage; while the stronger the commitment to multilateral avenues, the greater the commitment to being a good world citizen, as multilaterals are often assumed to act in global rather than national interests while being subject to greater coherence and fewer transaction costs (although see Reisen 2010).[7] Over the last fifteen years or so DAC donors have been encouraged to increase the share of aid they are prepared to route through multilateral organizations. The relative proportions vary considerably, but the average has been 30 per cent of total ODA in recent years. This reveals the continued preference for bilateral channels among the DAC donors, by implication prioritizing national policy space and national interest (Saidi and Wolf 2011). Moreover, in the last couple of years there appears to be evidence of the multilateral share of ODA declining further (Kindornay and Besada 2011).

The global development community also includes an enormous variety and number of non-state development actors, including NGOs, foundations, faith-based development organizations, vertical funds and charities. Accurate information is hard to come by, but most estimates suggest that there are several hundred major international non-governmental development organizations (INGDOs). Beyond these are thousands of smaller national and transnational organizations. They vary in their size; their roles (lobbying and advocacy; service delivery contractors for government; facilitating local empowerment); in their ideological leanings and foundations; and in their probity and effectiveness. While some NGOs are little more than employment and profit-making opportunities, others are at the forefront of progressive efforts to promote inclusive development. Within the non-state sector a notable trend of the last decade has been the creation of new foundations, some of them extremely large, such as the Bill and Melinda Gates Foundation (Marten and Witte 2008). Kharas et al. (2011: 14) estimate that private philanthropy has grown from 1 per cent of total aid between 1995 and 1998 to 17 per cent between 2005 and 2008. In 2010 the Center for Global Philanthropy calculated that total private assistance donations in 2008 amounted to US$53 billion, compared with US$121 billion in official development assistance (CGP 2010: 14). Some are now engaging in very active ways with the global aid regime in terms of research and policy directions – indeed, Manning (2008) describes the emergence of the large private foundations as one of the two most important changes within the world of foreign aid in the last decade, the other being the rise of the (re-)emerging development partners.

A trend that bears watching is the growing debate about the role of the private sector in development (Warden 2007; Davies 2011; Nelson 2011). There appears to be increasing interest in thinking about how to leverage the particular strengths and possibilities afforded by the private sector to more formalized development projects and programmes (Bilal and Rampa 2011; Langan and Scott 2011). This is allied to, but goes beyond, debates over corporate social responsibility. I return to this subject later in this book, contending that some of the pressure within the 'mainstream' development community to move in this direction comes from a growing sense of competition with a number of the major re-emerging development partners, who tend to blur their 'foreign aid' with commercial flows and strategies.

This brings us to the debates over aid volumes, but also its quality and effectiveness (Birdsall et al. 2010). In 2002, the UN Conference on Financing for Development was held in Monterrey, Mexico. The major multilateral and bilateral donors present agreed to increase both the volume and quality of ODA. These growing volumes of aid have tended to be on increasingly concessional terms, and almost 90 per cent of DAC bilateral aid is now in the form of grants rather than loans, from less than 60 per cent in 1975. Another shift widely viewed as progressive has been the commitment to channel more funds to the poorest countries, especially within sub-Saharan Africa (SSA). A 2007 IDA Report calculates that sub-Saharan Africa's share of total ODA has risen from just over 20 per cent in the 1960s to a third in 2007 – although many would suggest that this is still too low. Net ODA flows have risen in the last decade, although by 2011 only five countries had honoured the long-standing commitment to provide 0.7 per cent of gross national income (GNI) as ODA.[8]

However, Homi Kharas (2007) is one of many analysts to offer a sceptical analysis of the ODA figures that are bandied about (see also Raffer 1998). He points to discrepancies between reported budgets and actual disbursement, as in the case of the USA's recent flagship programme, the Millennium Challenge Account, which by 2007 had signed 'Compacts' amounting to nearly $3 billion, but which had actually disbursed only $69 million. Susan Roberts (2011) has uncovered the vast proportion of official US aid money that remains within the Washington Beltway as it pays for the services and substantial salaries of a veritable industry of development consultants and contractors. Furthermore, the generosity of DAC loans is questionable because of the discount rate used to calculate their grant element. Richard Manning (2008), former chair of the DAC, notes that the designation of ODA as lending with a grant element of 25 per cent with a 10 per cent discount rate 'is badly out of date as a measure of concessionality in a world of low interest rates', and goes as far as calling it 'indefensible' (ibid.: 5). As it stands, ODA loans are barely distinguishable from commercial lending.

Official ODA calculations often include overvalued commodities and services: food and pharmaceuticals, for example, might be purchased at low cost within a recipient country, but are recorded at Western prices. Aid budgets cover the costs of donor agencies and administration domestically and abroad, which includes the salaries of employees, consultants and researchers: private contractors for official aid agencies may have compensation levels up to three times as large as equivalently qualified NGO personnel (Kharas 2007). Debt forgiveness figures can be manipulated to maximize apparent generosity by adding substantial nominal interest amounts and counting that within the aid budget. The 2007 IDA Report notes that expanded definitions of what constitutes ODA mean that almost a third of ODA flows recorded in 2005 would not have been counted as ODA in the 1970s and early 1980s, and the DAC currently faces pressures from its members to include more expenditures relating to conflict prevention, peace-building and security-related activities (Shah 2011).

Kharas concludes that the value and impact of ODA are grossly inflated, calculating that of the $100 billion in ODA reported by the DAC donors in both 2005 and 2006, as little as $38 billion was left over for 'real development'. Even this remaining amount is then very often subject to extensive leakage within the recipient county. Kharas notes a survey in Ghana, Tanzania and Rwanda by Lindelow et al. (2006) which concluded that of the aid that arrived in-country, approximately half of the overall amount allocated to clinics and hospitals did not actually reach them.

Changing development orthodoxies in the 1990s After the dissolution of the USSR in 1991 'traditional' official foreign aid flows and institutions experienced something of a hiatus,[9] although the outcomes varied considerably by recipient (Easterly 2007). By the late 1990s, however, development orthodoxies were being reoriented, and aid levels started to rise again. This was driven by reformers and advocates within the aid community (e.g. OECD-DAC 1996); by political leaders wishing to project themselves as enlightened and virtuous (Gallagher 2009); and by activists and campaigning organizations supporting a much stronger global poverty agenda, often supported by celebrities (Richey and Ponte 2011). Another driver was the rearticulation of the relationship between development and security, something that was thrust centre stage after the events of 9/11 in Washington and New York.

Historically, poverty reduction has not been the stated goal of most official aid. Under the dominant modernization theories of the 1950s–1970s, aid was (supposedly) intended to promote the conditions for economic growth, with the assumption that once countries had been helped up into a 'virtuous circle' of modern, industrial growth, the benefits would trickle down to poorer groups. Within the neo-liberal orthodoxies of the 1980s–1990s, aid was expected to promote the restructuring of economies along free market principles, which would then stimulate growth and then, in turn, trickle down to the poor. In both, poverty reduction was a desirable but residual expected outcome of economic growth and modernization. Critiques within the mainstream aid community go back decades (e.g. Chenery et al. 1974), leading to some retuning towards the 'basic needs' of poorer people. By the 1990s, however, the aid industry started to more comprehensively reinvent itself, elevating poverty reduction to its core agenda (Finnemore 1996; White 2001; Hulme and Fukuda-Parr 2009), although with variable commitment and success (Riddell 2007; Glennie 2008).

Another major shift within mainstream theories of foreign aid and development has been the rise of 'good governance'. This concept conceives of a capable and effective state working in partnership with an active private sector and civil society, facilitated by robust and accountable institutions, including legal, banking and financial systems under the scrutiny of a free press. Good governance has increasingly been associated with the (contested) view that multiparty democracy is an essential underpinning of functioning states, institutions and societies (Leftwich 1993; Abrahamsen 2000). The good governance agenda therefore supposedly marks two breaks from the past. The first is political – Cold War strategic imperatives had resulted in aid allocation to allies and potential friends regardless of their probity or commitment to the national good. Both the West and the USSR were willing to support dictators and looters of the public purse if they offered political support to the relevant bloc. The mainstream aid community now asserts – not entirely convincingly – that it looks to political leadership and administrative capacity that is intent upon achieving developmental progress. A World Bank paper by Collier and Dollar (1998) was highly influential in making the case for directing aid to those countries where the policy environment was 'right', although their econometric analysis is much debated (e.g. Lensink and White 1999; Hansen and Tarp 2000). Critics have questioned what constitutes 'good policy', noting the bias towards pro-market and trade-oriented regimes, and indeed to allocation choices that continue to be heavily influenced by political and strategic motives rather than the quality of governance, respect for human rights or investment in social well-being (Hout 2004).

Second, the good governance agenda stands in contrast to the earlier phase of neoliberal orthodoxy, which was antithetical to the state in all but its most reduced role. The Washington Consensus of the 1980s and early 1990s centred on a fundamentalist conviction that the free market, stripped of all unnecessary 'interference', would vigorously promote efficiency, healthy competition and economic growth. Doubts about the effectiveness of the Washington Consensus in promoting growth or reducing poverty in Africa and elsewhere grew (Killick et al. 1999; Mohan et al. 2000) and these were amplified by the mishandling by the International Monetary Fund (IMF) of the Russian and eastern European transition, as well as its response to the Asian crisis of 1997/98 (Stiglitz 2002). Critical interventions from 'new institutional economists' (North 1990; Harriss et al. 1995; Lin and Nugent 1995) provided an intellectual framework for a shift towards the reformed neoliberalism of the 'post-Washington Consensus' (World Bank 1997).

Finally, over the 1990s foreign aid institutions had to reorient themselves to the changing security environment of the post-Cold War world. Aid was now argued to be a necessary element in combating a whole range of other non-state-based security issues: drug cartels, disease pandemics, migration, terrorism and climate change. Global poverty and instability, it was argued, constituted threats to the well-being and prosperity of the richer nations, adding strategic rationales to humanitarian motivations (Duffield 2001). These arguments were given a huge boost by the attacks on Washington and the World Trade Center in September 2001. In 2002 the National Security Strategy of the United States of America elevated global development to join defence and diplomacy as one of the three pillars of the 'war on terror', giving it an explicit role in America's security portfolio.

The strategy argued the need to retune the military, intelligence and diplomatic communities to a post-9/11 and (supposedly) 'weapons of mass destruction'-threatened world. Development issues and foreign aid have long been linked with national security in both veiled and explicit ways (Sogge 2002; O'Gorman 2011), but this relationship has been reformulated in the new millennium (World Bank 2011b). Other DAC donors also now articulate a more explicit relationship between security and development, blurring the lines between peacekeeping, conflict resolution, human security, military intervention and national security. The Australian government declared that poverty reduction was now second to security as the rationale for aid; Japan amended its Development Assistance Charter to include 'prevention of terrorism'; while the Canadian International Development agency added 'support international efforts to reduce threats to international and Canadian security' to its mandate. For many commentators, the folding of development into a security paradigm is deeply worrying, blurring the boundaries between military and developmental goals, distorting targets and agendas, and subordinating the needs and interests of poor people to those of local and international defence establishments (Duffield 2007; Bagoyoko and Gilbert 2009; Howell and Lind 2009, 2010).

The aid effectiveness paradigm in the new millennium Building on these new directions and reforms, a distinctive 'aid effectiveness paradigm' started to coalesce within the mainstream donor community at the turn of the century (Craig and Porter 2006; Manning 2008; ECDPM 2011; Murray and Overton 2011; Rogerson 2011a). There are two elements at the core of the new aid paradigm: recipient countries taking greater ownership and responsibility for their development strategies through poverty reduction strategy plans (PRSPs), and the global commitment to tangible target-led development results, notably the Millennium Development Goals.

PRSPs were launched in 1999 and are in theory written by individual recipient countries (White 2001). The ostensible goal is to elevate the agency of recipient countries within the aid relationship. Donors were asked to 'align' with the goals and agendas of the country-led PRSPs, and to work within existing administrative and accounting systems in place within recipient countries. The focus on alignment responded to long-standing critiques of traditional development relationships: that the donors drove top-down agendas which often didn't fit with recipient country conditions; that recipient countries were insufficiently committed to foreign aid agendas; and that the multiplicity of donors imposed excessive transaction costs and undermined state capacity by setting up multiple parallel systems to agree, implement and monitor foreign aid funding activities, rather than working through existing recipient country systems.

Harmonization *between* donors has also been a major reform agenda, given a context of extreme fragmentation of the aid architecture (Kharas 2007; Reisen 2010; Kindornay and Besada 2011). A World Bank (2008) report calculates that the average number of official bilateral and multilateral donors per recipient country increased from twelve in the 1960s to thirty-three in the 2001–05 period. In 2005 a large share of aid to Tanzania was being channelled through more than seven hundred projects managed by fifty-six donor organizations or units; while the government of Tanzania received 541 donor missions, of which only 17 per cent involved more than one donor. The strain on Tanzania's already overburdened administrative capacity was immense, as each donor activity requires specific disbursement accounts and mechanisms, procurement guidelines, reporting structures and so on. An even more concentrated example of this donor pressure can be found in the Pacific island state of Tuvalu, a territory with a population of just 9,000 people. Wrighton (2010) calculates that it receives an annual influx of no fewer than 900 aid workers, consultants and visiting government officials. Not surprisingly, there is clear evidence that donor fragmentation leads to an erosion of bureaucratic quality in recipient countries (Knack and Rahman 2007). Killen and Rogerson (2010) calculate that savings of up to $5 billion/year could be achieved by lowering transaction costs. By promoting harmonization, the new paradigm has sought to encourage donors to coordinate and cooperate better with each other in order to work more effectively. Ideally this would include a greater share of ODA being routed collectively through multilateral organizations, dividing up bilateral activities by country and sector (so fewer donors concentrate their efforts more coherently on specific places and issues), and simply coordinating activities better through the dialogue and information provision.

The aid effectiveness agenda has been pegged to a series of targets, most notably the Millennium Development Goals (MDGs), which followed the Millennium Declaration of 2000. White (2001) argues that targets are important for three reasons. First, they are outcome-based measures, with success being judged by achievement of impact rather than the traditional donor concern with inputs (i.e. the amount spent), or with immediate and short-term effects. Secondly, these targets have expanded the concept of development in that they do not focus on

Box 1.1 Japan's focus on infrastructure and productivity

Japan joined the DAC in 1961 shortly after it was founded in 1960. Japan has always been something of an outlier among the DAC donors, not only as the only non-Western member for five decades, but also in its preference for funding large-scale infrastructure projects (which accounted for 35.6 per cent of bilateral funding in 2001 compared to the DAC average of 13.5 per cent); and deploying a higher share of loans rather than grants (Rix 1993; OECD-DAC 2003). Japan's aid policy formation and delivery have also been much more closely tied to private sector interests than those of most DAC donors (Beaudry-Somcynsky and Cook 1999). As we shall see in later chapters, Japan's 'blended' or 'holistic' approach to development assistance is in some ways closer to many non-DAC donor practices and approaches, especially that of other Asian development partners (Jerve 2007). Over the decades there have been various internal and external pressures to bring Japan more into line with central DAC norms and practices (Castellano 2000; Arase 2005; Scheyvens 2005; Leheny and Warren 2009). Indeed, Kim (2010) suggests that DAC's relationship with Japan in some ways prefigures its attempts to 'reform' the non-DAC development partners today: 'same script, different cast', as she puts it. However, this time around it may well be that more DAC donors start moving closer to the Japanese/Asian model in future years, for reasons discussed later in this book.

income poverty alone: the MDGs, for example, include health markers, gender equality and so on. Third, they have acted as a means of bringing a spectrum of state and non-state actors together, reflecting what appears to be a remarkable consensus on the desirability of these goals. Many of the non-DAC donors and development partners have signed up to the MDGs, including some which are cautious about other forms of cooperation with the international development community, such as China and Saudi Arabia.

Associated with the focus on poverty reduction has been one other trend that should be noted here. DAC aid as a whole has seen a significant shift in sectoral priorities away from economic infrastructure and 'productive' sectors (such as agriculture, industry, energy and transport), towards social sectors (such as health, education and governance). In 1990, 82 per cent of DAC aid was allocated to agriculture, industry, economic infrastructure and the financial sector, but by 2004 health, education and governance accounted for 51 per cent of all aid flows (Harrigan 2007; Saidi and Wolf 2011). In many respects this can again be seen as a progressive move, and a response to the recognition that economic growth does not always 'trickle down' to improve the lives or livelihood chances of the poor; while governance and the provision of health and education are key components to well-being as well as productivity. However, there are concerns that mainstream ODA has gone too far in this direction at the expense of sufficient attention to productivity and growth (Chang 2010). Many of the (re-) emerging development partners, on the other hand, are much more strongly focused on these areas, something that is discussed in more detail later in this book. Interestingly, although a member of the DAC, Japan has also tended to focus more of its ODA on infrastructure investment (see Box 1.1), as has South Korea (Kondoh et al. 2010; Kim 2010; Kang et al. 2011). Some analysts disrupt dominant donor categories by pointing out the approaches that are shared by Asian donors that cross the DAC/non-DAC divide (Jerve 2007).

The aid effectiveness paradigm has been formulated through a series of High Level Forums – Rome (2003), Paris (2005), Accra (2008) and Busan (2011) – and their associated regional and working party meetings. The new paradigm has been codified in two iconic international agreements: the first of these is known as the Paris Declaration (see Box 1.2), and was signed by thirty-five donor countries, twenty-six multilateral donors, fifty-six recipient countries (including many NDDs), and fourteen civil society observers (OECD 2005). The inclusion of DAC and non-DAC actors is discussed in detail in Chapter 6, but it is indicative of a revolutionary change in approach and attitude towards more inclusive and representative forums, away from the DAC/Western-only forums that formerly dominated aid governance. But pointing to an increasingly complex aid landscape, a number of NDDs signed up as recipients of foreign aid without accepting these principles as donors. That said, as Manning (2006) observes, many DAC members are themselves still 'in progress' towards these principles; while Reisen (2010) notes that the aid efficiency agenda has not been meaningfully discussed or extended fully to the multilateral institutions.

The Paris Declaration was followed in 2008 by the Accra Agenda for Action, with the intention of strengthening, building on and

Box 1.2 Summary of the Paris Declaration

Ownership: Developing countries should set their own strategies for poverty reduction, improve their institutions and tackle corruption.

Alignment: Donor countries should align behind these objectives and use local systems.

Harmonization: Donor countries should coordinate with each other, simplify procedures and share information to avoid duplication.

Results: Developing countries and donors must shift their focus to monitoring and measuring development results rather than inputs.

Mutual accountability: Donors and partners are accountable for development results.

accelerating progress towards aid effectiveness (see Box 1.3). It is notable that at this meeting the recipient states had a much stronger voice and visibility, while the journey towards the 2011 Busan HLF also appeared to show greater agency for 'partner' countries (Carey 2011).

Box 1.3 Summary of the Accra Agenda for Action

Predictability: Donors will provide three–five-year forward information on their planned aid to partner countries.

Country systems: Partner country systems will be used to deliver aid as the first option, rather than donor systems.

Conditionality: Donors will switch from reliance on prescriptive conditions about how and when aid money is spent to conditions based on the developing country's own development objectives.

Untying aid: Donors will relax restrictions that prevent developing countries from buying the goods and services they need from whomever and wherever they can get the best quality at the lowest price.

Progress on these goals is now monitored through global surveys, with the baseline survey conducted in 2006. A 2008 interim survey fed initial results back to the Accra forum, and a 2011 survey informed the Fourth High Level Forum (HLF4) held in Busan in December 2011 (Kharas and Chandy 2011). We return to the HLF process and to the outcomes of HLF4 in later chapters.

The aid effectiveness agenda has sought to confront long-standing criticisms of dominant foreign aid – that it is top-down, poorly co-ordinated between donors, tied to donor interests, places excessive transaction costs on recipients, and insufficiently monitors what is successful or not. Many welcome these new development directions, which appear to have won remarkably wide approval and support, and there have been some positive outcomes of the new process and principles. However, problems and criticisms are clearly evident. For many friendly critics, the issue is one of a gap between commitments and actual changes in practices within the process of reform (ECDPM 2011). More radical analysts question the underlying assumptions and goals of the new millennial paradigm, which remains committed to a neoliberal vision of globalization and development without contesting structural inequalities in productive capacity or international govern-ance. We turn next to some of the problems confronting the dominant aid paradigm.

Critical responses to the aid effectiveness paradigm The mainstream aid community has a well-deserved reputation for failing to live up to its promises, and this is a trend that has continued under the new aid paradigm. The 2008 Accra High Level Forum reported some progress with regard to untying aid, coordinating technical cooperation, and improvements in the reliability of recipient governments' financial systems. However, the results were more disappointing in terms of making aid flows more predictable and reliable, encouraging donors to align with recipient country systems, and in enhancing mutual accountability.[10] Interestingly, it appears to be the donors rather than the recipients who are lagging farthest from their commitments (e.g. Monye and Orakwue 2010). There are various technical reasons for this, including the very real difficulties of retuning administrative and financial systems in complex scenarios. Kharas and Chandy (2011) suggest that in order to make better progress, the targets and indica-tors need to be refined, evolving as circumstances change (including the growing role of the non-DAC donors), and as the aid community learns from the monitoring and feedback process. They propose greater sensitivity to context, targeting and sequencing in order to ensure that the aid effectiveness agenda continues to attract support and maintain forward momentum.

However some analysts suggest a more fundamental problem confronting the Paris Agenda is its failure to grapple sufficiently with the political nature of development and foreign aid – a depoliticization that has, of course, a longer history in development (Ferguson 1994). The new millennial paradigm is insistently presented as a consensus among all stakeholders. Political realities are suppressed in this vision of a technical realm in which agents have an agreed set of goals and market-led means to get there, encompassed within the liberal framework of the Millennium Development Goals (Rogerson 2005; Hyden 2008; Hulme and Fukuda-Parr 2009; Unsworth 2009; McGee and Gaventa 2011; Vandemoortele 2011). The *politics* of development – the interests of particular states, sectors and institutions within donor and recipient countries; the fundamental disagreements over the nature of 'development' and the 'right' route(s) to achieving it; and inequalities of power and agency – are invariably bubbling away below the surface of these debates, meetings and forums, but are rarely formally acknowledged within official documentation and pronouncements (for an outstanding analysis of the way in which development was 'rendered technical' in relation to post-communist eastern Europe, see Wedel 2001). Recipient resistance to donor plans and agendas continues to be framed as a lack of capacity or a deficiency of will (attributed to corruption and narrow power politics) rather than alternative definitions, desires and interests within and across developing countries (Eyben 2008, 2010). Structural inequalities in global governance and trade regimes are not acknowledged or contested, while the MDGs do little to promote the sort of value-added industrialization that provided the engine for growth in today's richer nations (Chang 2010; Langan and Scott 2011).

Dijkstra and Komives (2011), for example, provide a detailed account of the progress of the Paris Agenda in Bolivia, Honduras and Nicaragua. They observe that some of the DAC donors working with these countries are not especially committed to the Paris Agenda principles, which certainly inhibits progress. But their study suggested that the main problem is the Paris Agenda itself, which treats poverty reduction as a technical issue rather than an essentially political one. When governments change as part of the normal democratic process, so do priorities, personnel and policies: something the Paris Agenda does not accommodate in its consensus approach to development. Related to this, many commentators are dubious about the extent to which PRSPs genuinely represent country-led views, suggesting that donors often have a heavy involvement in their formulation and writing (Hickey and Mohan 2008). Notwithstanding the language of 'partnership', in which stakeholders are consulted about their priorities in order to ensure country-led strategies, the actual shift in the power to set development agendas has been far more circumscribed. In a study of how the Paris Agenda is being translated into action in Tanzania, Zambia and Mozambique, Odén and Wohlgemuth (2011) identified a disregard for the unequal power relations between donors and 'partners'. Many critical commentators argue that 'participatory' spaces and processes are little more than an exercise in massaging consent, and constitute only a veneer of partnership, beneath which powerful interests are able to manipulate the agenda to their own interests.

Insufficient attention to politics also afflicts the well-meaning and desirable goal of increasing harmonization between donors. The Paris Agenda does not sufficiently acknowledge the fact that donor interests are served through foreign aid (Morrison 1998; Hyden 2008). Foreign aid is a national foreign policy tool for all countries, although it is operationalized around very different notions of what constitutes a desirable foreign policy agenda (e.g. promoting poverty reduction or promoting greater trade integration), and with very different ideas about how this should be pursued (e.g. promoting universal, free primary healthcare and education versus promoting privatization and user fees). The USA and Sweden, for example, both deploy foreign aid as a tool for securing certain foreign policy goals, which for both include strategic, commercial and humanitarian goals – but with rather different emphases and understandings. Under these circumstances, achieving harmonization between donors confronts profound ideological hurdles.

A different set of concerns arises from the use of targets. Targets may lead to distorted policies, with an undue focus on the chosen sectors to the neglect of others. In the effort to meet the targets, states and development institutions may turn to the easy pickings rather than addressing the poorest of the poor, or the most challenging issues and regions (Black and White 2003; Sumner and Melamed 2010). Moreover, current development targets are weakly enforced. It is increasingly clear that the world is unlikely to achieve the MDGs by 2015, but who will be held to account?

Adding to the internal pressures and fractures confronting the Paris Agenda is a large and increasingly complex external development environment. Ironically, it would seem, just as the mainstream aid community has attempted to improve donor harmonization, the sector has grown more diverse and arguably unruly. The growth in the numbers and activities of official and non-state development actors has led to an extraordinary explosion in the number of aid actors and programmes (Worthington and Pipa 2010). As Kharas (2007: 3) puts it:

> The sheer number of aid players, both public and private, has exploded. There are significant benefits to this dynamism: more resources, more innovative solutions, more direct action. But there are also costs. The number of development projects has grown while the average size of a project has declined, burdening weak administrative structures in recipient countries. There is overlap and waste in many studies needed for each donor. Accountability and sustainability are threatened. Mechanisms for information sharing, coordination, planning and scaling up are breaking down. The key issues facing development aid are those that arise from this fragmentation and the accompanying volatility of aid disbursements.

The (re-)emerging donors are just one set of actors who are presently only weakly enrolled in the Paris Agenda, or are dissociated from it, in what is a proliferating wider field. While some of the larger multilaterals are actively involved (including the World Bank, the regional development banks, the European Commission and the Global Fund to Fight AIDS, Tuberculosis and Malaria), the substantial body of smaller multilaterals are not, and nor are some of the very substantial private foundations and NGOs (Kharas and Chandy 2011). The large DAC bilaterals are questioning the costs and demands of the aid effectiveness agenda at a time when it appears that other countries are successfully pursuing their national interests through development partnerships. Moreover, the global financial crisis is hitting hard, and governments are likely to seek to leverage more national benefits from remaining expenditure (Dang et al. 2009).

Kharas and Chandy (2011) argue that the Paris Agenda is an evolving process – it would be unrealistic to demand universal change in a short time frame, or to dismiss it in its entirety because of deficits and shortcomings. However, its internal deficiencies are becoming more apparent, while externally its cooperation and coordination agenda appear to be in danger of being overwhelmed or undermined by a growing tide of other development actors and initiatives. Among other problems, Kharas et al. (2011) note that the current Western-dominated 'international' architecture lacks both legitimacy (it is not representative of poor countries and peoples) and credibility (it has a weak record of achieving development and poverty reduction): 'While the OECD-DAC remains the core of the global aid system, its monopoly of world ODA is eroding with the rise of the so-called new development partners ... Traditional donors that form the OECD-DAC can no longer claim to speak for the world's donor community' (ibid.: 38–9).

Bilal and Rampa (2011) suggest that growing aid scepticism and the increasing pressures of commercial and national interest are pointing towards a turn away from ODA towards a 'development effectiveness paradigm'. Changes in political leadership in a number of DAC countries (notably the UK, Germany, New Zealand and the Netherlands) and the global financial crisis have stimulated a much stronger discourse of national interest and value for money within foreign aid (Banks et al. 2011; Mawdsley et al. 2011b; Noxolo 2011). The costs of aid effectiveness, and the loss of donor ownership that it ought to entail, make it unpopular with a new generation of political leaders. The sense that the rising powers are now serious economic competitors, and that their 'aid' is assisting their economic prowess, is also encouraging a reappraisal of 'mainstream' foreign aid. The shift also reflects the changing landscape of development finance, and the fact that in most contexts foreign aid is taking up a smaller and less important share of available funds.

There is no agreement on what 'development effectiveness' might mean, but the different elements include a renewed focus on economic growth and wealth creation (rather than poverty reduction per se); greater integration between foreign aid and other policy areas, such as trade, investment and migration (rather than separating out ODA and OOF); and a growing role for the private sector (ECDPM 2011). It is important to note that European and American support for the private sector (domestically and in recipient countries) is, of course, not new. Trade for Aid, for example, attempts to assert a poverty-reducing role for deals and investment which promote greater economic integration (for a critical account, see Langan and Scott 2011). What is different is the growing legitimacy of and inclination towards this sort of model, at a time when foreign aid is under attack. Schulz (2010a) talks about a 'post-aid world', and it is clear that development agencies and organizations around the world are rapidly trying to respond to what may well be the next paradigm shift within mainstream development theories and practices (Severino and Ray 2009, 2010). As we shall see in subsequent chapters, many of the non-DAC donors and development partners interweave trade, investment and development cooperation, and this seems to be a model that, while currently criticized, is increasingly attractive to many DAC donors, not only in parallel to foreign aid, but perhaps surpassing and supplanting it. The key challenge of the next decade may well be to harness the developmental benefits of this approach while avoiding a race to the bottom by competing national interests, sacrificing well-being, environmental sustainability and social and political justice.

Before concluding, I will mention one other associated set of debates and initiatives. This concerns the recognition that foreign aid alone cannot be effective if it is being undermined by other policy decisions and directions among the more powerful states; and more positively, that efforts to achieve poverty reduction and development will be far speedier and more effective if foreign aid is able to leverage, catalyse or harness the energies and capacities of other policy areas. In the last decade this has been termed 'policy coherence for development' (PCD), although the essential arguments go back much farther (Picciotto 2005; Droeze 2008; Manning 2008; Hudson and Jonsson 2009). 'PCD' was coined by the OECD and defined as 'working to ensure that the objectives and results of a government's development policies are not undermined by other policies of that government which impact on developing countries, and that these other policies support development objectives, where feasible' (cited in Droeze 2008: 166). These other policy areas include agriculture, trade, tariffs and subsidies, intellectual property rights, investment, labour standards, environmental quality, aid for trade, and so on. In recent years a number of states and organizations have sought to translate PCD more systematically into action, including the OECD (OECD 2005), the European Commission (EC 2007) and the Netherlands (Droeze 2008).

However, commercial and foreign policy agendas have proved difficult to budge in the interests of development agendas, both nationally and within various regional and global governance regimes and institutions. While part of the problem in achieving PCD is technical (information, administrative, legal and so on), a more fundamental problem is competing economic and political interests. EU farmers may support ongoing subsidies, distorting competition and the market for Third World agricultural exports; while pharmaceutical firms may drive strong intellectual property laws, suppressing the production and availability of cheaper drugs to treat tuberculosis or AIDS/HIV in Africa. PCD efforts are confronted by the fact that interests clash between countries, sectors and classes, and arguably the two most meaningful words in the OECD definition above are 'where feasible' (ECDPM, Particip, ICEI 2007).

Conclusions

Bilateral foreign aid flows, policies, ideologies and institutions represent a particularly complex and dynamic field of theory and practice. These official flows and actors intersect with a number of terrains, including changing foreign policy contexts and strategies; and changing economic and political orthodoxies, from modernization theory to neoliberalism(s). But, until recently, the analysis of non-DAC contributions to foreign aid and development cooperation has been almost negligible, at least compared to the enormous amount of research into various elements of foreign aid from the industrialized countries. It has only been within the last few years that the presence, activities and importance of non-DAC development cooperation have become visible to the majority of Western analysts. In this chapter I have suggested that an understanding of the issues and debates raised by the NDDs need to be contextualized within two major arenas: the wider rise of the emerging powers, and shifts within (so-called) 'mainstream' or 'traditional' foreign aid.

The next chapter turns to the non-DAC development partners, focusing on their historical origins and earlier contexts. In the introduction I argued that the terminology of 'new' and 'emerging' donors can act to dehistoricize the discourses, practices and agendas of the various (re-)emerging development partners. But as we shall see, an appreciation of past development agendas, experiences and discourses is essential to a critical understanding of today's politics, policies and practices of development cooperation.

2 | Histories and lineages of non-DAC aid and development cooperation

This chapter charts the various genealogies of different development cooperation partners. The chapter is structured around five historical drivers of and contexts for (re-)emerging development cooperation in the present day. These are socialism(s), the Non-Aligned Movement, the rise of the Organization of the Petroleum Exporting Countries (OPEC), UN initiatives to support South–South cooperation, and the (re)launch of donor programmes by the accession countries that joined the European Union in 2004 and 2007. Two examples of more specific circumstances motivating and shaping the emergence of development cooperation are also set out, using India and Taiwan (the Republic of China) as case studies. Some of these drivers intersected of course – and the sections are not intended to suggest watertight categories. Different socialist blocs courted some of the non-aligned countries, for example, while the oil-based donors included 'Southern' states like Ecuador, Nigeria and Venezuela. The discussion is pitched mostly at the level of the state, and focuses on international relations and geopolitical strategies. However, the history and politics of foreign aid also involve transnational networks of communities and individuals. Intellectual and political understandings and agendas were shaped and experienced not only in the realm of state-led foreign policy but by ordinary people and families. Susan Bayly's (2007) study of the cosmopolitan intellectuals of socialist and post-socialist Vietnam, which is discussed in the section on socialism, provides a rather different perspective on the history of development cooperation. Finally, current non-DAC discourses and practices of development cooperation have also been influenced by the experience (in most cases) of being recipients of foreign aid – whether within COMECON (the Soviet Council for Mutual Economic Assistance), and/or from China, Japan and different Western donors. A short section touches on this issue of recipient experience shaping donor practices.

Cold War geopolitics, fraternity and competition: the politics of socialist development cooperation

In the post-Second World War era a large number of socialist countries provided various forms of development assistance to other socialist countries and 'friendly' regimes, as well as to those they hoped to attract and influence. The most powerful of these donors were the USSR and China, but donors included Cuba, Vietnam and a number of satellite countries in Central and Eastern Europe (CEE). Indeed, within the socialist world, technical assistance, subsidized trade and exchange of material goods were common. In this section we will start with the USSR, briefly comment on the Central and Eastern Europe countries, and then move on to China. In the final part of this section, we draw heavily on Bayly (ibid.) to look at Vietnam's contributions of expertise and assistance to the socialist world.

The USSR[1] Over the course of the 1920s and 1930s the young USSR was engaged in an epic drive towards 'super-industrialization' and had little in the way of economic or other resources to spare. In any case, Stalin was committed to the idea of two separate world economies, and viewed 'Third World' countries as little more than imperial vassals, while Asian and African national liberation movements were derided as bourgeois phenomena (Lawson 1988). Despite earlier commitments to economic aid made in 1917 by the new Bolshevik government, which reflected a Marxist-Leninist commitment to the promotion of socialism through international fraternity and assistance, under Stalin the USSR did not engage in foreign aid. Stalin aimed at self-sufficiency and a high degree of autarchy, blocking any significant trade with the capitalist world, including colonized and newly independent countries.

This situation changed after 1953 when Khrushchev came to power. Khrushchev viewed foreign aid as a potentially valuable instrument in the pursuit of Soviet foreign policy, with the most important aim of encouraging the growing number of decolonizing countries to choose a socialist path (Friedman 2009). As well as augmenting the Soviet sphere of influence it was thought that this would disrupt the trade and resource interests of the capitalist countries, weakening their purported neo-imperialistic economic and political ambitions (Tansky 1966; Cooper and Fogarty 1979; Bissell 1980: although see Roeder 1985 for an alternative account). The context was, of course, the rapidly chilling Cold War and growing competition with the USA and its allies to draw formerly colonized countries into their respective orbits. Studies on the recipients of foreign aid during the Cold War show that both sides used it to reward allies and cajole potential friends, while withholding it from enemies (Griffin 1991; Meernik et al. 1998). In some cases this aid and technical assistance contributed to economic growth and improved livelihoods, but the predominant concern with geopolitical expansion, competition and containment meant that, at the very least, foreign aid was often ineffective and poorly targeted. Aid flows were also complicit in more damaging outcomes for millions of ordinary people, as the Third World became a proxy theatre of the Cold War. Across Asia, Africa and Latin America, the West armed and trained one faction while the USSR armed and trained another, with both deploying foreign aid as part of their 'support' for specific regimes. This resulted in conflict and political repression, the legacies of which persist to this day. However, the 'Third World' countries were not a passive backdrop or simple stage for superpower contests. The 1950s and 1960s were decades of intense anti-colonial activity, transnational activism and rejection of the racialized hierarchies of knowledge and power (Young 2003). The USSR and Western governments were also caught up in internal power struggles and the attempts by various factions, liberation movements and governments of newly independent nations to assert their own place in the world (Chari and Verdery 2009).

In addition to this central and widely analysed political motivation for Soviet aid, another factor in Khrushchev's shift in stance was a reappraisal of Soviet economic theory, with the new generation of leaders keen to move away from Stalin's diarchic schema of two separate world economies. These Soviet leaders sought to develop trade and investment links outside of their immediate sphere of influence, and (just as for the West) foreign aid policy was a means of helping facilitate economic relations. Hindley (1963: 108), for example, notes that in the case of Indonesia, 'trade with the USSR remained virtually non-existent until the first Indonesian–Soviet trade agreement was signed in August 1956, shortly before the first Soviet aid agreement'. After 1959 the USSR exported cheap oil and gas to Cuba, for example, while buying nickel and sugar above the world market price in return. Egypt was a particular focus. Handousa (1991: 202) calculates that between 1958 and 1964 the Soviet Union signed aid agreements worth $750 million, and other eastern European creditors extended up to $425 million.

There were therefore several elements to the role that aid was intended to play in the promotion of Soviet socialism. First, it was a material demonstration of the goodwill and fraternity offered by the USSR – Khrushchev's stand at the United Nations General Assembly in 1960 when he made his 'Declaration about the liquidation of the past colonial system' was one example of the Soviet Union's new assertion of solidarity with the peoples of the global South (Friedman 2009). Second, the ability to provide foreign aid signalled the prowess of the Soviet system. In the ideological competition with Western capitalism this helped boost the image of the USSR's political and economic stature. After the Sino-Soviet split in the early 1960s, ideological competition with China was also a significant driver of Soviet engagement with the Third World, with significant impacts on the nature and goals of USSR foreign policy in Africa, for example (ibid.). Third, some Soviet theorists believed that by encouraging industrialization in the Third World, and thus in theory the growth of an urban working class, aid could contribute to the emergence of a progressive social force which could act as a vanguard for socialist transition. Fourth, as we have seen, aid was intended to support growing trade with the USSR and its satellites. But sometimes these rationales came into conflict with other political imperatives. In the case of Indonesia in the 1950s and 1960s, for example, the USSR cautiously balanced itself between the various power centres – President Sukarno, the army and the communist Partai Komunis Indonesia (PKI). The Kremlin proved quite willing to back the 'national bourgeois' government over the interests of the PKI when it suited them. Indeed, Hindley (1963) suggests that Sino-Soviet aid at this time might have hampered efforts by Indonesian communists to challenge the ruling elites and mobilize the peasantry, helping instead to further entrench Sukarno's power. Realpolitik interests trumped those of ideological conviction – tragically for the hundreds of thousands of Indonesian communists who were massacred in 1965/66. Lawson (1988) also observes examples of Moscow prioritizing its economic needs (in this case the demand for phosphate) over ideological consideration in its dealings with Morocco in the late 1970s.

Soviet aid in this period was strongly oriented towards developing large-scale public sector industrial infrastructure and capacity, often in the form of turnkey projects (facilities which are fully designed, constructed and equipped and then handed over or sold to the recipient). These were directed towards countries whose leaders were considered to have socialist inclinations – India, Egypt, Ghana, Guinea and Mali, for example. Examples include contributions to the Aswan Dam in Egypt, the Bhilai steel plant in India and the East–West Highway in Nepal. Friedman (2009) calculates that in the early 1960s electricity accounted for 23 per cent of Soviet aid projects, metallurgy 21 per cent and machine-building 9.5 per cent. Another classic form of Soviet aid was the provision of 'prestige projects', such as the Asian Games complex in Indonesia, and numerous sports stadiums across Africa.

Under Khrushchev, Soviet optimism about the ability of aid to effect large-scale economic and social change in ways that would contribute to Soviet foreign policy goals mirrored that of Western modernization theorists of the period (Gilman 2003). Like their Western counterparts, the Soviets were to be frequently disappointed (Lawson 1988). Different commentators suggest an array of reasons for this, including the unsuitability of the Soviet model of centralized, technical planning, especially in newly independent Africa; the resentment and rejection of Soviet interference in domestic political affairs; the determination of poorer countries to retain autonomy within world affairs (see the non-alignment section below); and the limits to Soviet aid when compared with the deeper pockets of the Western powers. More systemic analyses would point to the wider problems with the universalistic and linear underpinnings of all modernization theories, capitalist as well as communist, and their failures, or at best very partial successes, in successfully imposing their models on the global South (Peet and Hartwick 2009).

By the time Brezhnev came to power in the mid-1960s the Soviet leadership was more aware of the limitations of aid as a foreign policy tool. In some cases the USSR found itself committed to expensive outlays with little in return. A number of countries it had supported had turned decisively to the capitalist world, such as Ghana and Guinea. The context had also changed – China had broken away from the Soviet Union in the early 1960s and was now a competitor and critic (Friedman 2009); while Western aid to Africa and elsewhere had started to increase substantially as more countries achieved formal independence, but often remained heavily tied to the economies of the former colonizing country. The Soviet Union started to take a more cautious approach to its economic assistance, retreating from countries considered to be wavering or unimportant, and increasingly aware of the limitations of large-scale development projects. Lawson (1988) argues that notwithstanding a rekindling of interest in foreign aid following the Soviet bloc's military intervention in Ethiopia and Angola in the mid-1970s, it became less important as an ideological tool over time.

It appears that during the later 1970s and 1980s the Soviet Union started to develop an increasingly economically pragmatic and less ideological agenda (Valkenier 1979; Roeder 1985). Extracting and developing resources to support the Soviet economy was becoming a major strategic goal, while the choice of recipient countries narrowed further to those that were members of COMECON, or which were considered to be sufficiently friendly and important (such as India, Egypt and Syria) to merit ongoing support (Lancaster 2007). Lawson (1988) examines the nature and role of various aid instruments in this period, and suggests that Soviet loans tended to have a lower grant component and harder terms than counterpart loans from the West. Interestingly, he suggests that the Soviet Union was wary about the idea that its development aid reflected a moral imperative, especially when this translated into an insistence by recipients on aid targets. In the early 1980s Soviet spokespersons stated that it was the former colonial countries and neocolonial powers which were responsible for world poverty, not the Soviet Union, which should not therefore be subjected to the same pressures and calls to increase aid. Lawson suggests that this attitude became a matter of embarrassment on occasions for the USSR when poorer countries demanded higher aid targets, leading the USSR to make (unsubstantiated) claims that it was providing over 1 per cent of its GNP in economic assistance. Most estimates put the Soviet bloc share of global official development assistance at the end of the Cold War at 10 per cent.

This brings us to a short consideration of other members and allies of the USSR during the socialist period. Various forms of aid and cooperation flows were common across the socialist ecumene – Romania, East Germany and Bulgaria were notably active among the CEE states, for example (Lawson 1983). However, Hancilova (2000) suggests that most were rather reluctant donors, their involvement in development assistance being the result of pressure from Moscow, while their aid policies were shaped by Soviet priorities and agendas. As the following excerpt from a paper by Hindley (1963: 107–8) demonstrates, they were nevertheless engaged in development cooperation, here evidently tied into trade agreements.

In 1952, Indonesia and Hungary signed a trade and payments agreement which was renewed in July 1954. In 1954 also, similar agreements were signed between Indonesia and East Germany, Poland, Czechoslovakia, Rumania, China and Bulgaria. Trade between Indonesia and Eastern Europe increased rapidly, even though it remained a minute part of total Indonesian trade … In January 1954 the Czech Consul-General in Indonesia stated that his country was prepared to help Indonesia industrialise by providing complete factories. In September 1954, an East German delegation declared that its country could supply factories, train Indonesians, and grant credit facilities. And in October 1954 both the USSR and Czechs expressed their readiness to supply Indonesia with loans and machinery. During 1955 Indonesia received its first two loans from Communist countries; $9.2 millions from East Germany for the construction of a sugar mill; and approximately

$2 millions from Rumania for the construction of a cement plant. On September 15th 1956, Indonesia was offered a Soviet loan of $100 millions.

Hindley calculates that between 1955 and 1961 Indonesia signed agreements with the USSR and eastern European countries for a total of over $593 million in loans for economic development, and $450 million for arms purchase. Indonesia also received technical assistance and specialists, and the gift of a 200-bed hospital in 1960 from the USSR; while Hungary educated an estimated 6,000 Cuban and 4,000 Vietnamese students during the communist period. Halaxa and Lebeda[2] calculate that Czechoslovakia allocated development assistance to 136 countries in the 1980s, which varied from 0.7 to 0.9 per cent of its GDP (cited in Horky 2011).

Soviet and eastern European aid was changing, complex and varied according to specific bilateral relations, the historical period and contingent circumstances. There are indications of disagreement and debates among USSR academics and policy-makers over the nature and intent of foreign aid, and of course, splits between socialist countries, notably with China, to which we now turn.

China China's aid activities began with ad hoc transfers of grain, medicine, cotton and other industrial material to North Korea during the Korean War of 1950–53 (Park 2011). Under Chairman Mao, foreign aid became a significant means of conducting diplomacy, to the extent that in 1971 China's foreign aid was estimated to be as high as 6 per cent of public expenditure – an extraordinary figure given China's relative poverty at the time, and its own very significant resource constraints (Jerve 2007). In this section I focus on China's past relations with Africa. In part this reflects the depth of scholarship in this field, driven by early field leaders (e.g. Larkin 1971; Yahuda 1978; Snow 1988; Bräutigam 1998) and by a huge surge of interest in Sino-African relations in the present day (e.g. Taylor 2006; Tull 2006; Alden 2007; Alden et al. 2008; Bräutigam 2009; Mohan and Power 2009; Power et al. 2012). However, there are dangers in too narrow a focus on Africa alone, notwithstanding its considerable diversity, and the range of contexts and relationships China has with different African countries (e.g. Vines et al. 2009). China's past relations with Asian, Latin American, Caribbean and Pacific countries have some shared features with its various African relations, but also regional and individual trajectories and specificities too, which may not be reflected in Sino-African analyses. With this caveat in mind, this section outlines briefly the principal directions of China–Africa development cooperation over the past sixty years.

Although there had been some limited contact between the People's Republic of China (PRC) and some African leaders before 1955 (Walter Sisulu of the South African National Congress, for example, visited in 1953), it was the Bandung Conference which initiated more sustained relations (Camilleri 1980). Twenty-nine Asian and African countries adopted the Five Principles of Peaceful Co-existence, which had initially been formulated by China and India in 1954. The main themes and declarations of the conference centred on respect for sovereignty; non-interference in the internal affairs of other nations; economic and technical cooperation; mutual benefit; the needs and rights of developing nations (including investment, and the stabilization of primary product prices); as well as peaceful coexistence. These constituted an explicit rejection of both European colonialism and US–USSR neo-imperialistic superpower rivalry, and asserted the right of self-determination for newly independent states within the global polity and economy (discussed in the section on non-alignment below).

Larkin (1971) argues that Maoist China's long-term goal in Africa was to encourage the spread of Chinese socialism, which was pitted both against Western capitalism and Soviet socialism. In the short to medium term, however, Larkin suggests that these ideological imperatives were translated into the more modest aims of supporting anti-colonial liberation movements, such as the Front de Libération Nationale in Algeria, and the growing number of independent African states in asserting their economic and political autonomy. Similarly, China was supportive of independence movements in the rest of Asia and the colonized world. Of course, these foreign policy relations were also driven more tactically by the need to create allies to help secure the fledgling People's Republic of China. A pressing political factor motivating Chinese interest in Africa was the attempt to displace the Taiwan-based Republic of China (ROC) at the United Nations, something it finally achieved in 1971. Twenty-six of the seventy-six votes in the PRC's favour came from African countries (discussed in more detail below).

China's economic limitations and domestic imperatives meant that solidarity was largely expressed through technical assistance, such as providing doctors, nurses, agriculturalists and engineers, educational scholarships, and diplomatic ties and delegations. But other forms of assistance were also deployed, including military equipment and infrastructural development, most famously the immense Tazara railway linking Tanzania and Zambia (Monson 2009). China also offered loans and grants to various African countries, which, although usually relatively small in scale compared to those of other donors, were often granted on distinctive and very favourable terms:

> In addition to consisting largely of intermediate technology, all Chinese aid projects are given without 'strings', and since 1964 without interest. Chinese workers are paid at the local rates, they train their local equivalents and the general aim is to leave projects in such a way that they can be locally managed, operated and maintained so that even the spare parts could be locally produced. (Yahuda 1978: 13)

However, on other occasions commerce was foremost, and at times economic imperatives superseded and even undermined politico-ideological agendas (Larkin 1971; Taylor 2000). The growing Sino-Soviet rift in the early 1960s also eroded some of the goodwill generated by these policies, as Africa became one of the theatres of Chinese–Soviet rivalry. Diplomatic relations were broken off with some countries that were deemed to be too close to the USSR, such as Angola, while there was clear geopolitically driven competition for the support of others. China criticized the USSR as just another white, imperial power, and argued that the USSR's commitment to peaceful détente with the West undermined any commitment to anti-imperial struggles in the 'Third World' (Friedman 2009).

How did different African movements and states respond to China over this period? Obviously the various political and ideological dispositions, situations and preferences, and the role of specific governments and leaders, all influenced their diverse and changing relations with China (Larkin 1971; Camilleri 1980; Snow 1988; Bräutigam 1998). At times many welcomed the example China provided of national autonomy; its identification with the oppressed nations; its demand for greater equality and justice within the world system; its model of discipline and frugality; and its moral, financial and technical support. But many African leaders were also wary of Chinese ambitions and agendas, particularly during periods like the Cultural Revolution, when Maoist fervour overrode more pragmatic, long-term and sensitive approaches. Moreover some African leaders were unwilling to alienate the USSR, and Sino-Soviet duelling did not improve China's reputation in the continent (Snow 1988).

The late 1970s and 1980s marked a shift in Sino-African relations as Mao's ideological fixations were eclipsed by the more pragmatic approach adopted under Deng Xiaoping. The new aid philosophy was 'giving moderately and receiving a lot', and Jerve (2007) reports that other than in relation to competition with Taiwan, China largely withdrew from the Cold War power game. The emphasis was on economic growth, and during this period China became a recipient of Japanese and Western aid – indeed, for a while China was the largest recipient of ODA. Although trade increased over this period, there was a marked shift away from ideology as a determinant of foreign relations. Taylor (1998: 443) suggests that:

> In stark contrast to China's position in the 1960s and 1970s, exhortations and propaganda grounded in Maoist foundations disappeared, for the 'socialist modernisation' project of Deng Xiaoping demanded economic investment and a non-conflictual approach to international politics. As a result, non-ideological relations with the United States, Western Europe and Japan based in expanding trade links and co-operation took a priority in China's foreign policy formulation.

Overall, Chinese development cooperation flows to Africa declined, as did the number of delegations and visits that acted as a benchmark of diplomatic ties and political solidarity. Taylor suggests that Africa's poor economic situation, which worsened almost everywhere in the continent over the 1980s, and its peripheral place within global politics, further militated against Chinese interest. Snow (1988) observes that although there was still the rhetoric of South–South cooperation and solidarity, the reality was increasingly hollow, and African nations confronted a 'cold new realism' in Chinese diplomacy. China's focus was on its own modernization, and its scarce resources were deployed to that end rather than to assist Africa (Yahuda 1983). Having said that, Bräutigam (1998) notes that China's aid commitments of $258.9 million in 1984 still made it Africa's sixth-largest donor in aggregate at the time.

The most recent phase of dramatically accelerating Sino-African relations can be dated to 1989, when student and trade unionist uprisings in Tiananmen Square were followed by swift reprisal. Taylor (1998), who examines the effect of this event on Sino-African relations in detail, argues that its negative reverberations in the Western world both alarmed and angered China, prompting it to seek political allies. One outcome was a dramatic increase in development cooperation. Taylor points out that of fifty-two countries receiving Chinese aid in 1990, twenty-four were African. However, in the last decade the more enduring driver of change has been the demands of China's booming economy, resulting in a sharp growth in trade, investment and joint enterprises between China and various African countries (World Bank

2011a), some of which are allied to development cooperation activities (Mohan and Power 2008, 2009). Contemporary Sino-African relations are now a subject of intense interest around the world, and various aspects are discussed in the following chapters.

Vietnam The historical lineages of non-DAC foreign aid and development cooperation should not be reduced to the interplay of states alone, or understood solely as the realm of foreign policy and international relations. Individuals, families and communities were also enrolled within transnational networks of state and non-state solidarities and ideas, and helped shape and construct the multiple forms and practices of foreign aid and cooperative relations. In this section I draw extensively on Bayly (2007) to provide a case study of how individuals and families were enrolled in socialist development cooperation.

In a richly textured historical analysis, Bayly examines the distinctive idioms and moral claims of socialist modernity articulated in Vietnam.[3] She argues that these not only framed official government statements on development cooperation, but also the personal biographies, family identities and transnational friendships forged by thousands of Vietnamese experts and skilled workers who travelled, studied and worked across the socialist and socialist-friendly world – including Russia, East Germany, Algeria, Mozambique, Iraq, India, Cambodia and Mongolia. Bayly suggests that overseas volunteering was socially constructed through the reference points and idioms of socialism as a principled and moral project to defeat imperialism and advance scientific progress and modernity. For the individuals involved, Vietnam's contributions to this project, through its victories against the French and then the United States, and its provision of thousands of experts to poor socialist countries, also helped assure its own place within the socialist fraternity, not just as a recipient or client of the USSR and/ or China (a complex three-way set of relationships, of course), but as part of a wider socialist ecumene. She suggests that '[t]he work of "experts" as aid-bringers to that array of other leftist "friendship" partners therefore played a critical role in establishing Vietnam's credentials as a major architect of that wider socialist world, rather than a mere client of the bigger, richer Communist states' (ibid.: 183).

Bayly argues that socialism must be recognized as having had a moral, emotional and even aesthetic disposition. To reduce it to a set of economic and political relations or dry authoritarian ideologies is to miss the far more culturally complex personal convictions and experiences of socialist ideas and relationships. Of course, these discourses and imperatives brought tensions – Bayly explores the ways in which her intellectual friends and respondents negotiated the contradictions of personal versus collective benefits from their service within Vietnam and overseas, for example. But they also brought satisfaction, friendships and fulfilment, and a sense of oneself and one's country being a principled player in the global arena. Vietnamese men and women acted as teachers, technicians, advisers and experts around the world under cooperation pacts signed by the Vietnamese government.[4] Their salaries were paid by the host governments, and while a proportion went to the individuals themselves, most usually went to the Vietnamese government, providing a vital source of hard currency. Bayly argues that the payments for their services brought together two intersecting narratives – that of 'gifts', but also of a moralized socialist marketplace:

> Those [individuals] involved thus place much emphasis on a vocabulary of mutuality and warm-heartedness, of doing the business of international contacts in terms of imparting, sharing and succouring. The key claim is to have performed such acts [the volunteering of expert aid] without calculation of profit or loss ... Where gains are made, they are legitimated by something akin to the moral logic that had exalted the wartime petty trader ... as a contributor to the revolutionary cause, a provider of necessities embodying the love and care of those who nurtured both kin and fellow socialist citizens. It is these qualities of the 'heart' and affect which are said to differentiate bilateral relations of benevolence of mutuality from those involving 'profit' and 'interest'. (Ibid.: 205)

This affective reading of the relationships forged through technical assistance provides a fascinating counterweight to the classic state-centric, realpolitik focus of most international relations and political theories. Critically, and something we pick up on in later chapters, Bayly argues that:

> This language of diplomatic affect should not be dismissed as empty conventionalism deployed as a device to mask the realities of Cold War power politics. For socialist countries, these quasi-anthropomorphic representations of states as altruistic, feeling actors on the international stage can be seen as projections of the Party-state's claims that its actions and judgements embody the heartfelt sentiments of 'the people'. Much as 'the people' were to be seen as righteous arbiters of morality and justice on home soil, it was their will and sensibilities that were held to underpin the generosity and fellow feeling being

shown when their leaders identified the provision of development and military aid as acts of 'co-operation' and 'friendship' between the peoples of interacting states. (Ibid.: 205–6)

However, as Bayly documents, there is an inherent tension in the representation of these experts as bringing the benefits of scientific modernity and advance to needy and less advanced nations, while at the same time seeking to project equality rather than superiority.

> On the face of it, this 'expert' work was in the best tradition of the socialist ecumene, unimpeachable as an enactment of nation-to-nation 'friendship' and improving power of state-managed science. ... [including] irrigation engineers, agronomists and medics in specialities such as radiology and cardiac care. Much pride is taken in the fact that Vietnam, though still [in the 1970s and 1980s] struggling with the daunting economic legacy of the war years and the collapse of aid flows from China and the Soviet Union, could supply 'needy' host countries with trained practitioners in all these sophisticated modern fields. (Ibid.: 204)

Problematically, however, this discourse appears to replicate colonial and post-colonial hierarchies of nations – Vietnam in this case being the provider of superior knowledge to other nations. However, Bayly suggests that her respondents felt confident in their discerning embrace of *modern* – not *Western* – science, industry, philosophy, arts and culture, recognizing those elements which were universal and enlightening (and which they could bring to others), while rejecting Orientalist and Eurocentric accounts of their ownership and origins in a superior West. Bayly explores how official and private discourses sought to finesse the tensions inherent in promoting socialist modernity to 'less advanced' countries with repeated and strong reference to the 'heart'. By asserting a concern for the partner country, the relationship was argued not to exploit or demean the recipient. This was compared to capitalist (and especially US) aid, which was depicted as self-interested and corrupt, not given in the humble spirit and feeling of true partnership.

> Both in official accounts and my informants' personal narratives, *chuyen gia* [overseas/aid expert] work is spoken of as an act of disinterested benevolence, a gift of tutelage and enlightenment given freely and without expectation of return to the peoples of 'needy' and 'underdeveloped' countries. (Ibid.: 183)

So there was nothing demeaning for either the givers or receivers of this aid. Vietnam too was a poor country, but this was because of the costly wars it had fought in defence of its homeland, and as a defender of revolutionary modernity on behalf of all the world's progressive peoples and nations. It was therefore neither problematic nor shameful to receive the payments which African countries were offering in return for the Vietnamese experts' services.

> The former [experts] speak of themselves as humanitarian providers and bringers of advancement to 'backward' African nations, expressing pride in having done work that reflects credit on themselves, their families and their homeland. They speak of themselves as enlighteners and providers ... unlike Western experts and aid workers whose countries are routinely represented as professing humanitarian aims but undertaking such giving merely to acquire strategic clients, captive markets and cheap labour. (Ibid.: 207)

Among other things, Bayly's ethnography reminds us that the socialist world was not static, homogeneous or impersonal. For some nations and individuals, socialism was projected as a defining reference point for both modernity and a moral life of service, friendship and cosmopolitan endeavour towards progressive futures. This moves us beyond the realm of state-led accounts of foreign policy regimes, and also uncovers how deep certain narratives of cooperation and solidarity can run. As we shall see in Chapter 5, these socialist idioms and relationships have found new expression in the contemporary era of capitalist Vietnam, despite very different contemporary contexts.

The Non-Aligned Movement

The Non-Aligned Movement (NAM) came about as a number of countries tried to resist the polarizing pressures mounted by the West and the Soviets in the years after the end of the Second World War. It aimed to promote and project autonomy and solidarity, particularly in the Middle East and the Third World, at a time when imperial and neo-imperial power was being challenged (in different ways and in different contexts) in Latin America, Africa and Asia. The early champions of NAM were the leaders of India, Egypt and Yugoslavia, with other key proponents including Ghana, Burma, Ceylon (now Sri Lanka), Indonesia and Pakistan. The principle of resisting subordination to the Cold War giants and insisting on the needs and rights of the newly decolonizing nations was articulated in 1955 at a conference of African and Asian states held in Bandung, Indonesia (mentioned above). Braveboy-Wagner (2009) argues that this had considerable impact on the international system, which until then had been dominated by top-down 'vertical' relationships between metropoles and colonies (or formally independent but still heavily tied and influenced countries). She states that: 'The "Bandung Spirit" came to signify a time of exhilarating solidarity, a shorthand reference used by global south leaders since then to anchor foreign policies of non-interference and non-alignment' (ibid.: 14).

The NAM was formally established in 1961 at a conference hosted by Yugoslavia. The NAM asserted the rights of non-aligned states to resist subordination to Cold War politics and ideologies, the need for a more just, multilateral world system, and peaceful resolution of conflicts. As well as diplomatic stances and alliances, the NAM encouraged South–South trade and cooperation, and supported initiatives like the New International Economic Order (NIEO), which claimed to seek a more just global economic order. The NAM also engaged with global development debates, and among other things pushed the concept of the UN's 'development decades', and the commitment to the 0.7 per cent GNI target for ODA transfers from richer to poorer countries (ibid.). In his discussion of foreign aid to Indonesia, Hindley gives examples of development assistance specifically framed within the Non-Aligned Movement. He reports that India provided training for air force personnel, while in 1962 Saudi Arabia offered eighteen two-year scholarships to a university in Medina. According to He (2006), following the Bandung Conference, four Egyptian students came to China, four Egyptian scholars went to lecture in China, and one English teacher and seven Chinese students went to Cairo (cited in Nordtveit 2011). The Non-Aligned Movement also encouraged Yugoslavia's aid engagement.

A 'Solidarity Fund for Non-Aligned and Other Developing Countries' was established in 1974, and assistance to developing countries was identified as a priority in the Yugoslav constitution ... The Solidarity Fund had much of what is still considered 'good practice' for aid donorship today: an articulation of principles and goals; a definition of comparative advantage; and clear selection criteria, with the aim of giving at least two-thirds of grants to Sub-Saharan Africa and 20–25% to Asia. As was common in the 1970s and 1980s (and still is for some DAC donors), all grants were tied to 'goods and services of Yugoslav origin'. Humanitarian assistance explicitly included resources for 'liberation movements', and for countries suffering 'foreign aggression'. (RCCDC 1983: 52–3, cited in Harmer and Cotterrell 2005: 11)

But despite its achievements, the NAM's rhetoric of solidarity out-paced reality and it has always struggled to overcome weaknesses and divisions. A number of members were (and are) bitter regional rivals (India and Pakistan, Iraq and Iran, for example), and the inclusion of both oil- and non-oil-producing states meant that members had critically different interests at the time of the oil price rises of the 1970s (see below). Divides also surfaced between some Islamic and non-Islamic members when the Soviet Union invaded Afghanistan in 1979. Western powers, for the most part, sought to exploit these fault lines in order to weaken Third World solidarity. However, the NAM continues to this day, having survived the loss of its Cold War rationale. It now has 120 members (and seventeen observer states) and claims to act as a platform for the countries of the global South to voice a commitment to multilateralism, equality and mutual respect, particularly within the UN system (Braveboy-Wagner 2009).

Foreign aid was never a major theme within the Non-Aligned Movement, but as we shall see in later chapters, the calls for non-interference and mutual benefit have become core stated principles for a number of non-DAC development actors, and they continue to echo strongly in the present day for many Southern states. Socialism was far more potent at the time, but perhaps with the exception of Cuba, few countries would now frame their foreign aid or development cooperation activities in the language of socialist fraternity. While the NAM was a much weaker institution, its South–South *discourses* (if not always practices) have weathered the decades better, and act as a strong rhetorical framework for many of the NDDs. One forum in which they found purchase was the United Nations, to which we turn next.

The United Nations: formalizing South–South cooperation

South–South cooperation (SSC) refers to the exchange of resources, personnel, technology and knowledge between 'developing' countries – a loose definition that can cover almost any form of interaction from South–South foreign direct investment by Asian, African and South American multinational firms (Aycut and Goldstein 2007), to diplomatic meetings and agreements, to the provision of technical experts. It has multiple lineages, including formal initiatives like the Colombo Plan[5] and the Bandung Conference/Non-Aligned Movement, as well as individual bilateral relations between formerly colonized countries. Key events in the emergence of a more formalized recognition of SSC include the 1962 Cairo Conference on the 'Problems of Economic De-velopment', which led to the formation of the Group of Seventy Seven

(G77) at the United Nations, as well as to the creation of the United Nations Conference on Trade and Development (UNCTAD) in 1964. UNCTAD was the first UN agency to assert the need to promote greater economic integration and cooperation between developing countries as part of its regular work programme, and during the 1970s it was a key vehicle in the attempts to forge a New International Economic Order (NIEO).

In 1978, UNCTAD's Buenos Aires Plan of Action for Promoting and Implementing Technical Cooperation among Developing Countries was adopted by the UN General Assembly. Vaz and Inoue (2007) suggest that for Brazil, as for many other developing countries, this conference was a landmark event, signalling a confidence in and commitment to the idea that Southern states could find their own development solutions. Although Brazil had previous development cooperation arrangements, its involvement expanded rapidly after 1978. The concept received formal support from the UN General Assembly in 1978 when, following lobbying by the G77, the United Nations established the Unit for South–South Cooperation to promote South–South trade and collaboration within its agencies. It is hosted by the United Nations Development Programme (UNDP), which has the mandate to promote, coordinate and support SSC and triangular development cooperation,[6] discussed in Chapter 6.

For a small minority of Third World leaders, SSC was positioned as part of an explicit rejection of Western imperialism. For most, although greater autonomy, influence and power within the international sphere were certainly goals of SSC, this was seen as complementary to North–South relations rather than substituting for them. North–South aid was argued to be an obligation of richer countries, many of which had been previous colonial powers; whereas South–South cooperation was not a product of such moral and historical responsibilities, but a fraternal exercise of solidarity and support. The traditional powers rather marginalized and neglected the meetings, agendas and achievements of SSC over this period, although the G77 were able to advance some of their interests in promoting SSC through the UN (Alden et al. 2010). However, in recent years SSC has become highly prominent within mainstream development institutions and discussions. UNCTAD (2010: 1) defines South–South cooperation as 'the process, institutions and arrangements designed to promote political, economic and technical co-operation among developing countries in pursuit of common development goals'. In 2003 the G77 stated that developing countries see SSC as '... an imperative to complement North–South cooperation in order to contribute to the achievement of the internationally agreed development goals, including the Millennium Development Goals' (G77 2003). The Paris Declaration had this to say about SSC:

> South–South co-operation on development aims to observe the principle of non-interference in internal affairs, equality among developing partners and respect for their independence, national sovereignty, cultural diversity and identity and local content. It plays an important role in international development co-operation and is a valuable complement to North-South co-operation. (OECD 2005: para. 19e)

As we shall see in later chapters, SSC now constitutes a very powerful language, concept and set of developmental principles, and the 'traditional' donors are engaging much more closely with it, while many of the (re-)emerging Southern development partners are pushing it strongly. Importantly, it encompasses a far wider range of flows and relationships than 'foreign aid' alone, and includes investment, trade and diplomatic initiatives. These categories and distinctions are discussed more fully in Chapters 3 and 4.

The creation of OPEC and the Gulf donors[7]

Official Gulf state aid agencies and foreign aid activities date back to the 1960s, including the Kuwait Fund for Arab Economic Development (established 1961) and the Abu Dhabi Fund for Development (established 1971), while several Arab countries gave aid to Egypt, Syria and Jordan after the 1967 Arab–Israeli War (ODI 1980). Following the Khartoum Agreement of 1968, Saudi Arabia, Kuwait and Libya pledged grants of $250 million per year to compensate Egypt for the loss of the Suez Canal revenue and the Sinai oil fields (Handousa 1991: 206). These activities remained relatively small – until 1973 total OPEC aid came to less than 5 per cent of global ODA, and all of it went to Arab countries. However, by 1976 OPEC countries were providing no less than 25 per cent of global ODA.

The defining event that expanded Gulf aid was the substantial and coordinated increases in oil prices in 1973/74 managed by the recently established Organization of the Petroleum Exporting Countries (OPEC). The reverberations of these and later rises were felt around the world as real oil prices quadrupled. In the OPEC countries the 'petrodollars' rolled in and state revenues surged. The increase in foreign aid was a response to the needs and demands of poorer non-oil-producing countries, which were hit hard by the oil price rises and which were struggling to raise funds through commercial channels. The OPEC donors were concerned that this would cause divides within the Middle East and among Third World countries more generally, weakening solidarity and therefore geopolitical strength (Hunter 1984). There were also concerns that the economic hardship caused by the oil price rises would lead to declining markets. Harmer and Cotterrell (2005) note that in addition to these common concerns there were more specific motivations for individual donors. They suggest that Saudi Arabia's aid in the 1960s and 1970s was partly designed to help contain the spread of communism, with support being provided to anti-Soviet forces in Afghanistan after the invasion of 1979, and to Oman and North Yemen in the effort to contain South Yemen. Harmer and Cotterrell (ibid.) report that the Saudi government also gave financial support to anti-Soviet governments and movements in Somalia, Zaire and Angola in the 1970s.

Saudi Arabia is the biggest OPEC bilateral by far, followed by Kuwait and the United Arab Emirates (UAE): together they currently account for 90 per cent of Arab ODA (World Bank 2010). Unlike smaller Arab donors, such as Algeria and (formerly) Libya, these three donors have dedicated aid agencies through which grants, loans and technical assistance are administered.[8] These are the Kuwait Fund for Arab Economic and Social Development (founded 1961); the UAE's Abu Dhabi Fund for Arab Economic Development (founded 1971); and the Saudi Fund for Development (founded 1974). However, while these agencies handle the flows and activities they count as 'foreign aid', their respective ministries of finance are the dominant channels for concessional loans, which constitute far more substantial sums (Neumayer 2003a, 2003b; Villanger 2007). A question discussed in Chapters 3 and 4 is whether or not these are or should be considered 'aid' or 'commerce'.

In addition to these bilateral donors, a number of regional multilateral organizations also emerged at this time. These are the Arab Fund for Economic and Social Development (founded 1974); the Arab Bank for Economic Development in Africa (founded 1975); the Islamic Development Bank (founded 1975); the OPEC Fund for International Development (founded 1976); and the Arab Monetary Fund (founded 1976). Unlike the bilaterals, which also deal in grants and technical assistance, these multilaterals focus almost entirely on soft loans, some of which are compliant with sharia rules of lending. Responding to some of the problems that followed the rapid creation of all of these agencies, in 1975 the Coordination Secretariat for Arab National and Regional Development Institutions was also founded. It acts very much as DAC does for the OECD, although it is not as detailed or transparent in monitoring or reporting on aid flows. Nonetheless, the various Arab donors do appear to exhibit a relatively high degree of coordination, including co-financing of some projects.

Arab states rapidly became significant donors – indeed, by the late 1970s Arab aid was almost 50 per cent of that supplied through DAC. Moreover, when their contribution was calculated as a share of GNI, Arab donors proved to be extremely generous – significantly more so than DAC donors at the time (see Chapter 3). However, these amounts and shares of aid, while remaining very substantial, were heavily influenced by oil revenues, which tend to be volatile, and Neumayer (2003a) has shown how the declining prices of the 1980s correlated with contracting aid budgets. Even so, when calculated in aggregate, between 1974 and 1994 Arab donors were responsible for 13.5 per cent of world ODA, and Saudi Arabia remains one of the biggest bilateral donors today (Villanger 2007).

One aspect of Arab aid that will be discussed at more length later in this book, and which constitutes a particularly interesting claim to distinctiveness among a large number of the non-DAC donors, is their rejection of conditionalities and other forms of 'interference' in the sovereign affairs of recipient nations. This is reflected in the fact that during the 1970s and 1980s the Arab bilaterals tended to offer grants rather than loans, and there was an emphasis on unconditional giving that they claimed reflected an Islamic philosophy of charitable giving without an ulterior motive. Moreover, unlike with the DAC donors of the time, and most of the Southern development partners today, there was almost no tying of aid, although this may now be starting to change. More problematically, the lack of transparency of many of these large concessional official flows elevates concerns about the role of some Gulf states in 'land grabbing' across the world, but especially in parts of Africa.

The 'new' EU states

The discussion of the 'new' European Union donors in this chapter differs from the other sections in a number of ways. First, the period in question (from the accession preparation that started in the mid-/late 1990s, and post-2004 and 2007 in terms of formal membership) is more recent than the other historical drivers under discussion. Second, most of these countries had previously managed foreign aid programmes during the socialist period (the exceptions are Cyprus and Malta, which are new member states but do not share the socialist background of the other accession countries: I focus here on the post-socialist states). After the fall of the Soviet Union much of the Central and East European (CEE) region experienced severe economic decline and restructuring, and almost all of the formerly socialist countries ceased foreign aid flows and operations (the Czech Republic, formerly part of Czechoslovakia, is the only country that maintained some continuity over the whole period). So we are looking at the same countries in two reasonably distinctive periods and cultures of donor activity. Third, a dominant driver of the return to donor activities for the CEE states has been external: it has not solely reflected domestic political choices, priorities or agendas, but has been strongly driven by the desire to join the European Union, and therefore the necessary compliance with the *acquis communautaire* (Horky 2011). This is the term for the entire body of European law, including all treaties and EU legislation on policies, standards and regulations. Among a vast array of other more prominent elements (trade laws, production standards, procurement procedures, labour laws and so on), EU membership includes a commitment to being a foreign aid donor (Arts 2004; Carbone 2004; Lightfoot 2010). Additionally, new members were required to sign up to a number of international documents such as the Cotonou Agreement (2000), the Monterrey Consensus (2002) and the United Nations Millennium Declaration, together with the Millennium Development Goals (MDGs). The new states have been given a graded target in terms of the GNI share of ODA, starting at 0.17 per cent of GNI by 2010 and rising to 0.33 per cent by 2015; although the global economic recession may reduce the likelihood of meeting these targets. An additional driver for some of the CEE states has been the desire for OECD membership, which also promotes norms of donor activity. The Czech Republic joined in 1995, Hungary and Poland in 1996, Slovakia in 2000, and Estonia and Slovenia in 2010.

Although important, the role of EU expectations should not be overstated in explaining the return of the CEE states as donors. Grimm and Harmer (2005) argue that the accession countries were also motivated by the strategic benefits of foreign aid, particularly in terms of contributing to their regional security and stability; and, as for other NDDs, by the international status that accompanies a donor identity. The Balkan conflicts of the 1990s also played a role in stimulating the revival of foreign aid activities, stimulating public support for official aid, driven both by humanitarian concerns and anxieties over regional stability (ibid.; Drazkiewicz 2007). Harmer and Cotterrell (2005) observe that the latter was especially important in the case of Slovenia, a country in close proximity to Croatia and Bosnia. The influx of refugees in the early 1990s prompted Slovenia to ratify the Geneva Convention and Protocol on refugees and to accede to other international refugee treaties. A UNHCR presence was established in Slovenia in 1992 at the request of the Slovene government to assist in the response to the massive influx of refugees into the country (ibid.).

Other external actors have also played roles in this process. The UNDP, for example, has helped facilitate the (re-)emergence of these states as donors by retuning its regional offices away from their earlier role as in-country development agencies assisting the CEE states in their own transition, towards helping them develop their own donor architectures and policies (e.g. Vittek and Lightfoot 2010). The UNDP has also engaged in promoting public awareness of development, encouraging 'civic development education' (Drazkiewicz 2011). Harmer and Cotterrell (2005: 30) report that in 2004:

> UNDP Poland and the Polish [Ministry of Foreign Affairs] jointly launched a public campaign called 'Millennium Development Goals: time to help others!' This was the first UN-driven campaign in Central Europe in support of the MDGs. The goal of the campaign was two-fold: to familiarise Polish society with the MDGs, and to draw public attention to the needs of people living in poorer countries; and second, to initiate a public debate in Poland on the country's role and responsibilities as a donor of development assistance (with the longer-term objective of building support). UNDP has also established a Regional Trust Fund to promote development cooperation between emerging donor countries and recipient states, with a special focus on south-east Europe and the Commonwealth of Independent States (CIS).

Individual DAC donors have also redefined their relationships to the CEE states in response to their emerging donor profiles. Canada, for example, moved from being a donor to a number of CEE countries during the 1990s to helping certain CEE countries set up their own aid institutions and policies, including establishing twinning programmes for development assistance in poorer countries (Grimm and Harmer 2005). Individual member states took on 'mentoring' roles, including the UK (Richelle 2002), Ireland (O'Neill 2007) and Austria, Belgium and Germany (Biesemans 2007). Moreover, coalitions of European development NGOs provided advice and forums for discussions with CEE counterparts and governments.[9]

Grimm and Harmer (2005) report that the aid policies and programmes of the new EU members remain in flux as they adjust to their new responsibilities. They point to important differences in contexts, priorities and mode of engagement between the different CEE states, and rightly observe that they should not be assumed to share attitudes or aptitudes (see also Lightfoot 2010 for a detailed analysis). Nonetheless, they identify a number of features and trends that are broadly shared. These include stronger inclinations towards humanitarian rather than development aid among leaders and citizens; and towards 'higher visibility' bilateral aid rather than contributions to multilateral funds. They also note strong recipient selectivity, with a clear preference for directing foreign aid towards weaker countries within the region, which are potential sources of problematic migration flows, and/or which are potential sites of regional instability, such as Belarus, Ukraine, Moldova and so on (discussed in more detail in Chapter 4). Richard Manning (2006), the former chair of the DAC, suggests that the new EU member states are expected to increasingly comply with DAC standards, and to eventually become members of the DAC. However, he also notes their resistance to untying aid, and their concerns about maintaining national 'visibility', and therefore lack of enthusiasm about multilateral routes in which their absolute contribution is likely to be very small. Both of these may slow down or hamper alignment with DAC norms.

Finally, an observation that several commentators have made about the return to foreign aid among the CEE countries concerns a notable reluctance, both domestically and within the European Union more broadly, to acknowledge their past donor activities, institutions and relationships during the socialist era (Drazkiewicz 2007, 2011). By and large, these countries have not sought to highlight their earlier experiences or build upon prior institutions, personnel or practices. 'Western' EU politicians, policy-makers and publics tended to assume the superiority of their model, and constructed the accession states as 'blank slates' on which to write EU standards, norms and practices (Wedel 2001). Although there were negotiations over the timing, sequencing and financing of implementation, accession to the EU effectively demanded one-sided compliance with the existing *acquis communautaire*. This erasure of the CEE's socialist past was also embraced by many eastern European leaders and publics eager to shed their past subjugation by the Soviet Union and socialist identity, including within the field of foreign aid and development cooperation. It is noticeable that there is little or no acknowledgement within current emerging institutions and policy formation of former ties, experiences and expertise. Instead, the 'memory' of foreign aid is centred on the experience of being a recipient of Western solidarity and support during the heady days of the 1980s (ibid.). This is something explored further in Chapter 5.

Specific drivers for emerging donors

All donors and development partners have specific domestic and international historical contexts and motivations driving their foreign aid/development assistance ideologies, policies and practices (see Kondoh et al. 2010). These may interweave with one or more of the rationales described above, but are also shaped by other considerations and more specific country circumstances. Two examples are offered here: continuities and changes in India's development cooperation ideologies and approaches; and the ways in which competition with the People's Republic of China (PRC) for diplomatic recognition has been a major driver of aid from the Republic of China (ROC), based in Taiwan. Many other examples could be found, but these help illustrate more country-specific drivers.

India India achieved Independence from Britain in August 1947 under the charismatic leadership of Prime Minister Jawaharlal Nehru, later one of the founders of the Non-Aligned Movement. India was targeted by both the USA and the USSR as a potential ally, although over the succeeding decades the USA was to turn much more strongly to Pakistan. Both offered substantial amounts of aid to India and it became one of the largest aid recipients in the world. Despite this, India rapidly took on a donor mantle, and was one of the original signatories of the Colombo Plan in 1950. Many Indian nationalists, and notably Nehru himself, had a strong sense of India's manifest destiny as a great nation and as a champion of the formerly colonized nations and ongoing independence movements (Oglesby 2011). Indeed, even before independence, Indian nationalists offered solidarity and support to anti-colonial liberation movements in Africa. After independence, this solidified into various forms of development cooperation.

Nepal was one of India's earliest recipients or partners (Price 2005). India's first tranche of assistance in 1951 (a mere four years after its own independence) was to help build Kathmandu's Tribhuvan Airport. India also helped fund the construction of the East–West Highway and other significant infrastructure projects like the Kosi Dam. In the early 1960s India also started providing development assistance to another northern neighbour, Bhutan, helping finance its First Five Year Plan in 1961. Price (ibid.) notes that India was the sole contributor to Bhutan's Second Five Year Plan, and it remains a key contributor to

Bhutan's economy. As well as large-scale investment in big infrastructure projects in these Himalayan neighbours, a strong focus of India's development assistance was the provision of technical experts in a wide range of fields to partner countries. Despite budget constraints, Nehru was determined that India would invest in science and technology, and to that end he made sure that universities and research institutions were funded and supported. These institutions have often been actively enrolled in India's development assistance programmes. The National Research and Development Corporation, which was founded in 1953, for example, has been involved in projects in Senegal, Egypt and Angola. In 1964 India created the Indian Technical and Economic Cooperation (ITEC) scheme and the Special Commonwealth African Assistance Programme (SCAAP), both of which aimed to enhance development cooperation with India's regional neighbours and beyond. ITEC comprises four elements: projects and project-related work, deputations of experts, study tours, and (its main focus) providing training programmes in India in areas as diverse as small and medium enterprises, rural credit programmes, food processing, textiles and women's entrepreneurship. In more recent times information technology and communications skills have come to represent an increasingly large share of the training available and in demand. Between 1964 and 1989, ITEC provided training to over ten thousand men and women from partner countries, and Agrawal (2007) calculates that there are now some forty thousand ITEC alumni around the world. The scheme now runs in 156 countries, and through it the Indian government offers about four thousand placements a year. Price (2005) calculated that about one third of ITEC placements are offered to African governments. Partner governments are free to nominate their own candidates, usually bureaucrats and officials, who are then funded by the government of India to undertake the relevant training within Indian institutes, organizations and the higher education sector. The Indian Council of Cultural Relations also promotes an array of cultural interactions and tours.

What explains India's early entry into donor activities? One reason was energy demand: the early and ongoing focus on hydropower projects helped produce much-needed power for itself and its Himalayan neighbours. Bhutan, for example, currently exports almost 80 per cent of its electricity to India (Kondoh et al. 2010). More broadly, India wanted to create regional goodwill given the hostile embrace of West Pakistan (now Pakistan) and East Pakistan (now Bangladesh) following Partition in 1947. India looked to secure regional allies, and foreign aid played some part in that. India also had an interest in promoting strong and stable buffer states between itself and China. The transport infrastructure built in the 1950s, for example, was driven more by concerns following China's move into Tibet than Nepalese development interests. Security concerns were amplified following the 1962 Himalayan border conflict between China and India. Shrivastava (2009) argues that the shock of China's surprise invasion had reverberations for India's development cooperation relations beyond those with its northern neighbours. Nehru was deeply disappointed by the failure of other members of the Non-Aligned Movement to condemn China's incursion into Indian territory, with only the (former) United Arab Republic openly supporting India. As well as taking steps to improve its military capacities and establishing ITEC, the event led India to reappraise its foreign policy as whole. Shrivastava (ibid.: 125) suggests that '[t]hese programmes heralded an era of economic diplomacy and selective engagement with African nations, replacing the treatment of Africa as a bloc'.

A third motivation for development cooperation was India's desire to take its place in the world not just as a regional hegemon, but as an international power. The indignities of British colonial rule had been thrown off and India looked forward to establishing itself as a great nation. Within the context of the Cold War and of the independence movements across Africa and Asia, India was an active international player, notably in co-founding the NAM, but also striving to play a leadership role (although not always with full sympathy or support) for the 'Third World' within the 'global' institutions, such as the UN. Being a development cooperation partner helped build relations of solidarity with other newly independent countries, and its own net recipient status notwithstanding, signalled India's aspirant status to international stature.

Until the later 1980s and 1990s, economic incentives played a relatively limited role in India's development cooperation decisions. Ideological and political agendas were dominant, while India's rather inward-looking economy meant that there was not in any case a strong export drive. However, the accelerated neoliberalization of the economy in the 1990s and the new millennium, ongoing competition with China and sea-changes in foreign policy approaches to India's own diaspora and to the United States have all encouraged a much more pragmatic and economically oriented approach to foreign policy more broadly, including development cooperation (Beri 2003; Raja Mohan 2004). At the same time, India's booming economy has enabled it to develop a growing portfolio of concessional loans, lines of credit and sovereign lending and investment, while expanding its long-standing technical assistance programmes. Moreover, signalling a major shift from recipient to donor, in 2003 the government of India insisted that all but its six largest donors cease their official foreign aid flows, and it paid off some $1.6 billion in outstanding debt to fourteen bilateral donors (Sinha 2010). The government of India also announced debt relief to seven African countries, the establishment of the India Development Initiative, and in 2005 refused external assistance in dealing with the Indian Ocean tsunami, and indeed provided $22.5 million in emergency aid to other affected countries. India has also sought to gather diplomatic support through its development cooperation activities, in support of its objectives in the World Trade Organization, the United Nations and other international forums and meetings. As we shall see in later chapters, India is an increasingly significant non-DAC development cooperation actor, perhaps less so in the size of its aid programme (although in some cases this is significant) and more in its challenge to the mainstream. As Oglesby (2011: 30) nicely puts it:

> India's earlier overseas assistance programmes reveal important elements of an Indian model of aid that has longer and more significant roots. This removes India from a narrative in which its economic rise has recently allowed it to break the glass ceiling into an existing donor club, and allows instead India's aid activities to be understood as part of an alternative trajectory to that of traditional donors.

Diplomatic recognition: Taiwan/the Republic of China The origins of the Republic of China's (ROC) foreign aid activities are highly specific to its competition with the People's Republic of China (PRC) for diplomatic recognition, but they also reflect its achievement of rapid and very successful industrial development and economic growth, and the view that it has valuable experiences to share. In 1949, after a bloody civil war, the Chinese Communist Party prevailed over the governing Nationalist Party. The Nationalists fled to the island of Taiwan and declared that the PRC was a renegade state that was illegally occupying mainland China.

Until 1965, Taiwan was a recipient of aid, receiving substantial support from the USA, the World Bank and the Asian Development Bank in particular. According to Chan (1997), Taiwan received a total of $1.5 billion in economic and technical aid, and $2.4 billion in military aid from the USA. By 1965, Taiwan's spectacular economic growth had created a sufficiently solid financial base for the USA to cease its aid flows. Taiwan had become a donor in 1959, sending a team of agricultural experts to Vietnam, and in 1961 it started sending agricultural experts to Africa (Baker and Edmonds 2004). But the PRC was starting to issue a much stronger challenge to Taiwan, and had been courting support across Africa and beyond for a shift in their diplomatic recognition of 'China' at the UN (see above). Chan (1997) cites the views of Lin Bih-jaw, the former director of Taiwan's Institute of International Relations, who suggested that it was this competition with China which prompted Taiwan to start trying to consolidate support at both the governmental and the non-governmental level in Africa – albeit ultimately unsuccessfully. The Republic of China held China's seat at the United Nations until 1971, when it was displaced by the People's Republic of China.

The struggle continues to this day, with foreign aid a key tool for both the People's Republic of China and the Republic of China (Taylor 2002). According to a PRC official (cited in Bräutigam 2009: 67), PRC aid commitments in 1990 rose by 68 per cent as a result of a diplomatic spat with Taiwan. Chan (1997) reports that the major recipients of Taiwanese aid are (a) those countries that have diplomatic relations with Taiwan, and (b) those with which Taiwan does not have diplomatic relations but which still allow official Taiwanese representatives to operate under the title of 'Republic of China'. Others include those who have substantive cultural or trade links, those who are trying to improve their relations with Taiwan, and those who are not hostile to it. Some countries, such as Chad, Burkina Faso and the Gambia, have 'flipped' from Taiwan to China and vice versa, losing aid from one but gaining from the other.

As always, however, a single narrative cannot capture the complexities of aid motivations or agendas. Chan (ibid.) argues that the political imperative of diplomatic recognition sometimes clashes with economic and other interests, and that in implementing Taiwan's foreign aid policy a compromise between the Ministry of Foreign Affairs and the Ministry of Economic Affairs is often necessary. In recent years, and especially following the establishment of the International (formerly 'Overseas') Economic Cooperation Development Fund (IECDF) in 1988, other rationales for foreign aid have been articulated. These include humanitarian and moral reasons, as well as political and economic incentives, although Chan argues that the latter remain far more important. Moreover, Taiwan has come under pressure from some Western donors to increase its foreign aid to a level that accords with its advanced economic status and high national income levels. In 1989, for example, the United States urged Taiwan to contribute to Third World debt relief plans. Taiwan was also encouraged to make large contributions to regional development banks, and by 1995 had increased its share of multilateral funding to 16.3 per cent of the IECDF total, amounting to some $86.6 million.

Experiences as recipients

All of the current (re-)emerging donors have been recipients of foreign aid and development assistance, and most still are.[10] Horky (2006) points out that in 2004 the Czech Republic was still receiving two and a half times more aid than it was giving. The circumstances and factors shaping their individual experiences vary enormously, and in different ways and to different extents these historical and ongoing experiences as recipients have contributed to contemporary ideologies, policies and practices as donors and development partners (Wedel 2001). For some, foreign aid has (all or in part) provided welcome expertise and resources, while for others it has been associated with interference and ineffectiveness. Factors include (changing) donor profiles over time – from the 'superpowers' (the West and/or Soviets); to different DAC donors (Japan is a rather different actor to, say, the Scandinavian countries, for example); and whether the relationship is in continuity or not with former colonial ties. Different donors have their own motivations, cultures of aid, approaches, agendas and so on, all with implications for the impacts on recipient economies, polities and psychologies. Numbers also matter – one reason why aid was relatively successful in building up Taiwan's economic base is widely thought to be the fact that the USA was by far its biggest donor, allowing the Taiwanese government to focus their negotiations effectively. As we have seen, the Tanzanian government, on the other hand, is besieged by unmanageable numbers of donors and aid channels, undermining its capacity to exert a leadership role. Recipient experience may also vary by sector (social protection, infrastructure, good governance, for example), and by channel (budget support, UN-based, bilateral and so on). Kondoh et al. (2010) report that in the 1950s grant aid to South Korea was recognized as having worsened rent-seeking and corruption, while concessional loans for economic infrastructure, such as power plants and roads, effectively supported Korean economic development during and after the 1960s.

Recipient experiences of foreign aid will also be shaped by a host of domestic contexts, including national histories, cultures, ambitions and fears; and by a country's sense of its status and positioning within the world.[11] To take one example, Korean policy-makers and aid agencies are strongly inclined towards a pragmatic approach to economic development and loans for economic infrastructure in their foreign aid to developing countries – which Korea experienced as a successful intervention – and construct their aid as 'knowledge sharing' (Kim 2010). Similarly, China's positive experience of Japanese resource-backed loans in the 1980s (described in Chapter 4) have encouraged it to deploy this modality with its own recipients (Bräutigam 2009). However, China is also frequently careful to assert that it does not see itself as promoting a 'model' of development, and is insistent that individual countries must shape development strategies and paths that are appropriate to them. This contrasts, of course, with the dogmatic approach of the IMF and other traditional actors and their ideological certitude and that there is a single, superior model of development – from the modernization theorists to the neoliberals (Fukuyama 1992; Gilman 2003).

Conclusions

Many of the non-DAC development partners have a long-standing presence in international development, and their renewed, enhanced or simply newly visible contribution to the field is not an extraordinary phenomenon. Rather, they have for various reasons been unduly neglected by most (Western) scholars and foreign aid policy-makers and analysts. The current vigour of the NDDs is in some respects a return to older patterns rather than a new departure. Nonetheless, there have been profound shifts within the domestic profiles of many NDDs (including expanded EU membership; massive economic growth in the BRIC countries and other emerging powers; and the transition from socialism), and very profound changes in the external landscape in the new millennium (including changing neoliberal orthodoxies, the new aid paradigm, the War on Terror, and the global financial crisis). The diverse domestic and international factors that shaped the early emergence of many of the NDDs that have been outlined in this chapter can continue to be traced in the contemporary era – the legacies of their origins and experiences persist to some extent in the institutions, languages and practices of development cooperation (e.g. Bayly 2009). But, as the next chapters show, there are also fundamental shifts within and beyond NDDs and the field of foreign aid, all which have a powerful bearing on future trends and debates.

3 | The (re-)emerging development partners today: institutions, recipients and flows

Having outlined some of the historical contexts for the (re-)emerging development cooperation partners, this chapter moves to the present. It starts with the thorny question of data and definitions: what is defined as 'foreign aid' or 'development cooperation' by different (re-)emerging development partners? This is a deeply complex and inherently political issue which has a strong bearing on current debates about the roles, impacts and implications of the NDDs (Tan-Mullins et al. 2010). Indeed, we return to it with a longer discussion about tied aid, export credits and the blending of aid, trade and investment in Chapter 4. Having established the problems confronting the comparability and credibility of some of the data and reporting in this area, the chapter turns cautiously to the various calculations that have been made about the absolute amount and relative share of foreign aid and development assistance provided by individual (re-)emerging development actors and in total. This section also includes estimates of the breakdown between bilateral and multilateral contributions, and between developmental and humanitarian assistance. The next section then looks at the institutional actors and structures through which the various non-DAC actors manage their development assistance. Shorter commentaries on the military, civil society and donor public perceptions follow. The chapter concludes with a discussion of trends within transparency and accountability across the aid and development sectors.

Definitions and data

An issue of much debate and often very considerable confusion arises from the variation in definition and reporting on 'foreign aid', and where and how this sits within the more loosely constructed concept of 'development cooperation'. Saidi and Wolf (2011) suggest that we should think of these as two (complementary) philosophies: 'international development assistance' (the charity philosophy articulated by the DAC) and 'international development investment' (investing in the productivity and capacity of the partner country in pursuit of mutual benefit). Of course, these categories overlap and interweave in many ways, and they are discussed in detail in this and later chapters, but in the first instance they help us think through the debates about definitions and data that follow.

The DAC has worked hard to formulate definitions and measurement criteria for bilateral foreign aid (or ODA) for its members, and their calculations have become an authoritative technique of aid governmentality. DAC members must provide annual data on the volumes, type, nature, quality and destination of their aid, under the classifications and detailed headings of the DAC Creditors Reporting System (CRS). However, although it is relatively robust, discrepancies in DAC aid reporting do persist (Easterly and Phutze 2008; Birdsall et al. 2010; Sinha and Hubbard 2011). Different member states may have different budget and financial monitoring processes, different political timescales, and even different constitutional requirements which affect their ability (or willingness) to report comprehensively and to the requirements of the CRS system. Moreover, there is considerable non-compliance within DAC as regards some of its norms and expectations, including the goal of a 0.7 per cent GNI contribution, and in terms of tied aid.

Twenty-one non-DAC countries also report their ODA figures to the OECD-DAC (see Table 3.1), although generally not in ways that can be fully entered into the disaggregated CRS categories. Other than Chile and Mexico, these include all of the non-DAC members of the OECD (the Czech Republic, Estonia, Hungary, Iceland, Israel, the Slovak Republic, Slovenia, Poland and Turkey), as well as Cyprus, Kuwait, Latvia, Lichtenstein, Lithuania, Malta, Romania, Russia, Taiwan, Saudi Arabia, Thailand and the United Arab Emirates. Although this allows for reasonably meaningful comparison there are still inconsistencies that affect their foreign aid reporting. The World Bank (2010), for example, finds that Arab aid is underestimated within the DAC dataset by some 5–8 per cent because of various differences in reporting structures and measurements between the various institutions (see also Shushan and Marcoux 2011). Smith (2011: 21) provides a detailed example of data inconsistency with another aid database – the Financial Tracking Service (FTS) of the UN Office for the Coordination of Humanitarian Affairs (OCHA), which monitors humanitarian aid:

> Turkey's humanitarian aid is reported to the FTS and the OECD DAC, and while the patterns [over time] are similar, the volumes differ vastly. In 2005, Turkey reported US$179 million to the OECD DAC compared with US$78.7 million to the FTS, and in 2006 its humanitarian aid was US$115.7 million as reported to DAC compared with US$11.4 million to

the FTS. The reverse is true for the UAE; in 2009 significantly more was reported for the country through the FTS (US$352.6 million) than via the OECD (US$134.8 million).

TABLE 3.1 The 2011 figures for non-DAC countries reporting to DAC Net ODA disbursements: other providers of development cooperation (current $US million)

	2004	2005	2006	2007	2008
EMERGING DONORS					
EU members					
Cyprus[1]	15.2	26.0	34.9	37.4	–
Czech Republic[2]	108.2	135.1	160.9	178.9	249.2
Estonia	4.9	9.5	14.1	16.2	22.0
Hungary[2]	70.1	100.3	149.5	103.5	106.9
Latvia	8.3	10.7	11.9	15.9	21.9
Lithuania	9.1	15.6	25.0	47.6	47.9
Poland[2]	117.5	204.8	296.8	362.8	372.4
Romania					122.9
Slovak Republic[2]	28.2	56.1	55.1	67.2	91.9
Slovenia		34.7	44.0	54.1	67.6
Non-EU					
Iceland[2]	21.2	27.2	41.5	48.2	48.4
Israel	83.9	95.4	89.9	111.0	137.9
Liechtenstein				19.7	23.3
Turkey[2]	339.2	601.0	714.2	602.2	780.4
PROVIDERS OF SOUTH–SOUTH COOPERATION					
Chinese Taipei	421.3	483.0	513.0	514.0	435.2
Thailand			73.7	67.0	178.5
ARAB DONORS					
Kuwait	160.9	218.5	158.0	110.1	283.2
Saudi Arabia	1,734.1	1,004.8	2,094.7	2,078.7	5,564.1
United Arab Emirates	181.4	141.3	218.8	429.4	88.1
TOTAL	3,288.4	3,153.2	4,687.1	4,861.4	8,679.0[3]

Notes: 1. The following note is included at the request of the Turkish government: 'The information in this document with reference to "Cyprus" relates to the southern part of the island. There is no single authority representing both Turkish and Greek Cypriot people on the island. Turkey recognizes the Turkish Republic of Northern Cyprus (TRNC). Until a lasting and equitable solution is found within the context of the United Nations, Turkey shall reserve its position concerning the "Cyprus issue".' 2. OECD member 3. Note that two thirds of the increase since 2007 is due to the large increase in Saudi Arabian aid.

Source: OECD-DAC statistics; from Smith et al. (2010)

Of those (re-)emerging development partners who choose not to report to the DAC, not all use the term 'foreign aid'. India, for example, talks only of 'development cooperation', although it certainly engages in flows and practices that would fall within DAC definitions of aid, including grants, concessional loans and technical assistance. Other NDDs, such as China, do have some recognized 'foreign aid' component within a larger concept of development cooperation. By and large, this tends to consist of a similar set of flows and activities to those that comprise DAC ODA: grants (including food aid and humanitarian assistance), concessional and development-oriented loans, debt relief and technical cooperation. In some cases, however, non-DAC donor national definitions and reporting structures do not include activities that would be defined as ODA by the DAC within their 'foreign aid' reporting and accounting. Shushan and Marcoux (2011) point out that the main Arab donors do not include their debt forgiveness figures – which can be very considerable – in their aid reporting. China's calculations of its foreign aid do not include debt relief or the cost of scholarships for overseas students studying in China (Bräutigam 2011); while India does not include the various costs associated with hosting refugees – some of which would be included by DAC donors as a part of its development cooperation budget. Thus, while broadly parallel, 'foreign aid' is often somewhat differently constructed, institutionalized and measured by different partners. Rogerson (2011b), for example, refers to 'ODA-like' sources and terms.

The more complex category is 'development cooperation'. Different actors use the term in a range of ways, and there is no agreed or single definition. It usually includes whatever individual partners define as 'foreign aid' and/or aid-like activities (as outlined above), but also a range of other official funding flows and relationships. These can include various forms of joint ventures, support for foreign direct investment, non-concessional loans and export credits, which under OECD definitions would count as other official flows (OOF). Beyond these material transfers, 'development cooperation' also often describes a wider relationship that is discursively constructed in terms of the principles of mutual benefit and solidarity. Diplomatic events and cultural exchanges are a recognized and valued part of such relationships. The key point is this: judging (re-)emerging foreign aid and development cooperation on 'mainstream' terms often leads to problematic expectations, conclusions and comparisons with ODA. Rather, they should be judged on their own terms – what they claim to be, to promote and to achieve.

A variety of factors have therefore contributed to considerable confusion over the definition, nature and purpose of non-DAC foreign aid and development cooperation. The first is that the non-DAC donors and development partners are so diverse. China, for example, makes a distinction between its foreign aid (which is similar, but not identical, to DAC ODA), and official support for economic and development cooperation, much of which blurs with more commercial decision-making and agendas, and which it does not call or claim to be 'aid'. India, on the other hand, has to date abjured the term 'foreign aid', and tends to refer to all categories of official support as 'development cooperation', from grants and technical assistance to concessional Lines of Credit (see Chapter 4).

Second, information has tended to be scarce, a situation that has not encouraged greater understanding or accuracy among external commentators, or more transparency and accountability generally (discussed below). The domestic auditing systems of many countries are not expected to differentiate between ODA and OOF (as defined by the DAC). They are, after all, not 'natural' categories, but the product of very particular historical debates, interests and contingent politics among the dominantly Western nations that constitute the DAC. Further complications may arise from the number of government agencies and departments engaged in development cooperation with little or no overall coordination. For example, Braude et al. (2008: 7) make this observation about South Africa (although the likely creation of a dedicated aid agency in 2012, which is discussed later, should ameliorate some of the problems they identify):

> South Africa has no systematic database to track the country's development assistance; no separate financial reporting lines for development projects; no overall government strategy to direct aid; and no generic operating guidelines (outside of the ARF [African Renaissance Fund]) to facilitate the overall provision of aid. This apparent gap exists despite the fact that dozens of departments, agencies, and parastatals are involved in providing assistance to other African states.

Brazil is another case in point. John de Sousa (2010: 2) reports that:

> Like most other non-DAC development actors, Brazil does not systematically report its outgoing financial flows for development cooperation and there is no evaluation of its development cooperation budget. Thus, the volume of Brazilian aid is difficult to assess. Nevertheless, several officials have confirmed that such systematization is being worked at; the Brazilian Cooperation Agency is expected to publish a

report by the beginning of 2010. Thus far, several estimates of Brazilian aid volumes have been published based on different sources of information. According to the most often-cited approximation of development cooperation disbursements (ECOSOC 2008), the total volume in 2006 was estimated at US$ 345 million, which represents 0.04% of the Brazilian GNI. ... Yet, it is important to recall that these numbers are estimates with a high margin of error. According to the Brazilian Cooperation Agency, the amount could be rather around US$ 1275 million.

Concerns about transparency and reporting constitute a particular concern about and criticism of many of the (re-)emerging development partners. According to Nonneman (1988) and Van den Boorgaerde (1991), Saudi Arabia, for example, has actively kept large sums of official financing secret, as has Kuwait (Villanger 2007; Shushan and Marcoux 2011). For some critical commentators, this is proof of rather sinister or at least unworthy economic or political motivations (Naím 2007), but even more considered analysts express concerns about limited transparency. However, in some cases governments are cautious about publishing how much they spend abroad because they fear a domestic backlash. Given the acute politics of domestic poverty in South Africa, for example, many ordinary people might resent government spending on peacekeeping or economic infrastructure development in other countries (Yanacopolos 2011), something that may also inhibit Chinese government reporting on the full range of its official financing (Bräutigam 2011). Smith et al. (2010) suggest that another reason for limited reporting and transparency is that some smaller donors fear that by revealing their full development cooperation flows they would become ineligible to be recipients, a concern they suggest is a misconception.[1]

Generally, though, it is not 'aid' figures that are being suppressed, but other official development financing figures that are more commercially sensitive. Park (2011) observes that the Chinese Ministry of Finance makes public its grant aid budgets annually as part of its financial statistics: in 2008, for example, it reported a total of $1.9 billion to developing countries. However, 'information on concessional loans is only provided on a piecemeal and occasional basis' (ibid.: 42). Park estimates that in the same year, these preferential loans and credits came to about the same sum of $1.9 billion. The Chinese position – like that of many other non-DAC actors – seems to be that it is willing to disclose information about more ODA-compatible funding streams, but not more commercially oriented official financial arrangements. In this regard it does not differ much from most Western

Box 3.1 Chinese 'aid' to Africa[2]

One of the myths that circulates widely ... comes from a much-criticized report on Chinese aid prepared by the US Congressional Research Service. According to the *Japan Times*: 'A U.S. congressional report last year quoted research showing that total Chinese aid in 2007 was $25 billion. Aid to Africa in the 2002–2007 period was more than $33 billion.' ... [T]hese estimates are so preposterous that they should simply be treated as amusing, a funny story, except that they were presented to the US Congress as serious. Here's the inside story: what was the 'research' quoted by the CRS report? A background paper on 'Chinese aid' done as a class project by *a group of graduate students from NYU*. The students, perhaps encouraged by the researchers, decided to count every media report of a flow of finance from a Chinese entity into Africa, Latin America, or Asia as 'aid'. They lumped together grants, official and commercial bank loans, export credits, supplier finance, foreign direct investment, and so on. As long as it had some link to the Chinese government (i.e. it was from a state-owned bank or company) they added it to their database and called it 'aid'. This methodology has two obvious problems. First, investment, export credits, supplier finance, etc., [are] not 'aid' but commercial in nature, and should not be counted as official development assistance. Second, the fraction of projects mentioned in the media that actually go forward is small, no matter who is financing them. This overstates the size of Chinese engagement. While the CRS report claimed that China gave $25 billion in 'aid' to Africa in 2007, by my estimates, the real figure of official aid disbursed in 2007 was less than 5 percent of that.

countries, which are similarly reluctant to disclose details about their export credits and guarantee financing (Bräutigam 2010). There is a case to be made that these should be open to scrutiny, but as trade, investment and business relations, not aid. What seems to confuse many analysts is that some of the (re-)emerging donors choose to 'blend' different activities, packaging up grants, concessional loans and technical assistance with, say, market-based loans and export credits, in support of particular projects or a suite of projects. As we shall see later, this more 'integrated' approach is argued to be a more effective strategy than the DAC's well-intentioned inclination to largely separate out ODA from commercial flows. Notwithstanding the significant criticism directed at China and others for their integrated 'bundling' approach, the pendulum may in fact be swinging in their direction, including among the DAC and other 'traditional' donors (Japan and South Korea, of course, have always been closer to other Asian and Southern partners in this regard).

The last factor behind the disputed and confused definitions and estimates is weak scholarship and sloppy reporting, even within prominent think tanks, government bodies and multilateral organizations. This is powerfully exposed in Bräutigam's forensic examinations of how certain figures and stories circulate about Chinese 'aid' to Africa. The sheer numbers of distorted cases that she documents suggest that credulity is often enhanced by pre-existing prejudices, as the excerpt from her indispensable blog, 'China in Africa: the real story', suggests (see Box 3.1).

These cautions and caveats about the definition and then the calculation of foreign aid and development cooperation are essential to a critical reading of various estimates and projections that are made. Bearing this in mind, we turn to various estimates of non-DAC 'foreign aid' (recognizing the malleable nature of this term), and touch on wider estimates of development cooperation financing.

How much do the NDDs contribute to foreign aid volumes?

Based on figures reported by the twenty donors listed above, and on calculations drawn from national budgets of non-reporters, the OECD Development Cooperation Directorate calculated that in 2009/10 the non-DAC donors/development partners contributed almost $11 billion, or 8 per cent of total global foreign aid (Zimmerman and Smith 2011). This refers to flows that are broadly equivalent to DAC definitions of ODA from the twenty-one countries that report to the DAC, plus estimates for the BRICs (so not all of the NDDs). By 2010, Park (2011) put the figure at $14 billion, and estimated a 10–12 per cent share of global foreign aid, and it appears that a striking trend of non-DAC aid and development assistance over the past decade or so has been the very significant increase in volumes.[3] Park (ibid.) suggest that this upward trend will continue, and that non-DAC contributions are likely to double over the next five years, to the extent that he calculates by 2015 they will account for 20 per cent of total global foreign aid.

Among both DAC members and non-DAC actors there is a substantial range in terms of individual absolute contributions. In 2008 Saudi Arabia reported foreign aid flows of $5.6 billion (making it a larger contributor than fifteen DAC donors that year); China is estimated at $3.8 billion (a contribution larger than that of eleven DAC donors); and Turkey $780 million (larger than four DAC donors) (ibid.). Some of the smaller development partners provide almost negligible cash sums of aid in loans and grants, but as we shall see in later chapters, are able to contribute in symbolically and materially meaningful ways to technology transfer, training, education and other cooperative arrangements.

Aid as a share of national income Both DAC and non-DAC development partners vary significantly in the proportion of their national income directed towards foreign aid. The new EU donors are, in theory, committed to the EU's goal of achieving 0.7 per cent of gross national income (GNI).[4] However, recognizing the realities of transition and domestic constraints, they have negotiated a gradual process, pledging to increase ODA levels to 0.17 per cent GNI by 2010, rising to 0.33 per cent by 2015. The available calculations suggest that for development partners like India, China, South Africa and Turkey and so on, GNI shares are very low. But given their far lower GDP per capita and higher shares of domestic poverty, this does not seem unreasonable. The Arab donors, on the other hand, have at times been exceptionally generous. Drawing on calculations by Van den Boogaerde (1991) and Neumayer (2003a), Villanger (2007) reports that between 1973 and 1978, Arab aid averaged 4.3 per cent of their combined GNI (with peaks of 12 per cent for the UAE and about 8.5 per cent for Kuwait and the Kingdom of Saudi Arabia: World Bank 2010), and from 1974 to 1994 it was 1.5 per cent (the DAC average over both periods was 0.3 per cent). This has fallen more recently: from 1995 to 2004 the figures are Saudi Arabia 0.43 per cent, Kuwait 0.59 per cent and UEA 0.7 per cent. Shushan and Marcoux (2011) suggest that aid as a share of national income (although not in absolute terms) is continuing to fall for various reasons, including a stronger focus on domestic expenditure.

Bilateral and multilateral shares On average DAC members direct just under 30 per cent of their aid flows through multilateral organizations, although this figure disguises wide variations among them and is exaggerated by including the share that goes to the EU from its members, which then acts as an individual bilateral and a member of DAC. How do the NDDs compare? Kharas et al. (2011) calculate that the overall multilateral share of the new development partners comes to 18 per cent of their total foreign aid, but as with the DAC donors there is a wide spectrum of activity. The Arab donors, for example, are strongly bilateral in orientation – Zimmerman and Smith (2011) report that in 2009 Saudi Arabia provided a total of $209 million, or 6 per cent of its ODA, to multilateral bodies; while the World Bank (2010) calculates that from 1995 to 2007, only 11 per cent of Saudi ODA was directed multi-laterally. For many of the NDDs, and especially the Southern and Arab partners, the multilateral development institutions lack both credibility (they have a rather poor record of promoting development, economic growth and poverty reduction) and legitimacy (they continue to reflect Western ideas and dominance). In 2006 the Venezuelan government, which is particularly critical of US hegemony, announced that it would switch its multilateral funding from the World Bank's International Development Agency (IDA) and the Inter-American Development Bank to Southern-led institutions, such as the Banco del Sur and the OPEC Fund for International Development (Harris and Azzi 2006; Chahoud 2008; Muhr 2011). While few others would fully subscribe to this action, many share reservations about the main multilaterals.

The 'new' EU donors are in a rather different position. Under their accession agreements they are required to direct a large share of their foreign aid to the EU itself, sometimes leaving them with very small sums to deploy bilaterally (Lightfoot 2010). This reduces the attractiveness of ODA as a policy tool through which these states can help support domestic economic interests (by promoting trade and investment under the auspices of aid); pursue geopolitical strategies (for example, by helping fund studentships and democracy initiatives within their eastern and southern neighbours); and exert soft power and garner international status (by, for example, being visible as a donor in humanitarian crises, or 'doing good' in Africa). Given these imperatives, the new EU states (like their DAC counterparts) have in some cases resisted the pressure to direct too much of their ODA to multilateral bodies.

However, in some contexts and for some development partners, support for certain multilateral organizations can provide considerable advantages. It can raise the profile of a country within the region and the international community, and it is a means by which the emerging powers can start to influence the policies and practices of these institutions. Chahoud (2008) reports that South Africa channels around 75 per cent of its development cooperation funds through multilaterals; while in the last five years Brazil has directed some 75 per cent of its development funding to international organizations, mostly those regionally oriented within Latin America (Chandy and Kharas 2011). In 2007 India was the second-largest troop contributor to the UN (Shrivastava 2009), and like other emerging powers, India is also now a net contributor to the World Bank and the IMF, and makes contributions to the Asian Development Bank, to the African Development Bank, to UN organizations, such as the UNDP, and to multilateral bodies, such as the World Food Programme (WFP), the Global Environment Facility and the Afghanistan Reconstruction Trust Fund (Kondoh et al. 2010). Increasing contributions to global organizations are being accompanied by demands that the emerging powers should have more voice, exercised through stronger voting rights, within these institutions. This growing presence and voice within bilateral forums and multilateral organizations is discussed in detail in Chapter 6.

Humanitarian aid Within mainstream development norms, policies and institutions, a distinction is generally made between longer-term development aid aimed at socio-economic transformation, and aid to alleviate human suffering in humanitarian crises, usually following natural disasters or human-made conflicts. Smith (2011) suggests that most of the non-DAC donors and partners don't make this conceptual distinction, seeing it as an artificial divide – something she points out may well be a more realistic and constructive understanding of the often closely integrated reality of humanitarian development needs. Definitions aside, most of the NDDs are certainly engaged with and committed to various forms of what the UN would define as humanitarian assistance (ECOSOC 2008; Smith 2011; Amar 2012). Indeed, the smaller and more sporadic development partners tend to engage only in humanitarian gestures. To take an extreme example, the government of the Democratic Republic of Congo offered $2.5 million to Haiti following the 2010 earthquake, a gift that caused some domestic controversy (Ori 2010). Gabon, Tunisia and Equatorial Guinea also made contributions to Haiti. Harmer and Cotterrell (2005) note that no fewer than ninety-two countries made pledges of support following the 2004 Asian tsunami (which translated into eighty-four actual contributions). They recognize that this is a crude measure of non-DAC involvement, but suggest that it is revealing nonetheless of a new plurality and dynamism within the humanitarian aid sector. By their calculations, the non-DAC partners account for some 12 per cent of humanitarian assistance, a figure similar to the estimated share of their total ODA contributions.

Humanitarian aid is one realm in which some non-DAC donors and development partners are high in the 'generosity' rankings measured by aid as a share of per capita income (a different measurement from GNI). Calculated this way, Liechtenstein, Monaco, Kuwait and the UAE have all ranked in the top ten most generous donors (2007–09) according to Smith (2011). Indeed, she reports that 'in 2009 the UAE's humanitarian aid per capita was US$77, ranking it third, and therefore higher than Sweden and Denmark' (ibid.: 10). In terms of GNI rankings, in 2008 Saudi Arabia was the single most generous humanitarian donor. As ever, though, these estimates must be treated with some caution for all of the reasons suggested above, while uncertainty is amplified further because of the difficulty of valuing the goods in kind and the role of personnel and logistics that often make up a substantial proportion of a humanitarian package.

While the absolute share of global humanitarian assistance remains low, in some contexts specific non-DAC donors provide very substantial shares of humanitarian assistance – for example, Gulf state contributions to the West Bank and Gaza (World Bank 2010), and China and South Korea's provision to North Korea. Saudi Arabia and Brazil were the largest donors to Haiti after the earthquake in 2010 (US$50 million and US$8 million respectively), while India made the largest single contribution following the 2010 Pakistan floods, with US$20 million (Smith 2011). As well as specific geographical and cultural motivations for humanitarian assistance, Harmer and Cotterrell (2005) suggest that a number of Asian donors especially are motivated to respond to specific natural disasters, having considerable empathy given their own experiences of flooding, earthquakes and tsunamis; as well as expertise in responding to them. Indeed, they suggest that the 2004 Indian Ocean tsunami marked a pivotal moment for a number of nations in conceiving of themselves as donors rather than recipients, and in realigning their institutions accordingly (Meier and Murthy 2011; Oglesby 2011). As we saw in Chapter 2, the humanitarian crisis provoked by the Balkan wars of the mid-1990s and the conflict in Chechnya did much to provoke public support for official and NGO aid programmes in Central and Eastern European states. Two of the largest development NGOs in the CEE region were established as a result of these events: Polish Humanitarian Action, and the Czech People in Need Foundation. Both have been influential in encouraging public and governmental engagement in development. Interestingly, Smith (2011) notes that, in 2008, China was the largest recipient of humanitarian aid from other non-DAC partners following the earthquake that hit the Sichuan region. As she says, 'this dual role demonstrates the blurring of lines between donors and recipients and the complexities within this group' (ibid.: 17).

With the exception of the CEE partners, most non-DAC donors have tended to keep their distance from the dominant multilateral humanitarian aid infrastructure (although there are exceptions, as we shall see shortly), and by and large the non-DAC partners tend to respond bilaterally to specific events rather than regularly help replenish international humanitarian funds (Harmer and Cotterrell 2005).[5] In part this distancing reflects administrative costs and hurdles. But it is also located in the different development cooperation lineages and ideologies, in which solidarity is articulated in specific ways, and which frequently reflect a historical critique of Western hegemonic ambitions and strategies, and their dominance of 'international' institutions and arenas (Amar 2012). Harmer and Cotterrell (2005) identify four issues which have tended to limit cooperation and engagement by the non-DAC donors in mainstream humanitarian regimes and organizations. The first of these is the concept of the 'responsibility to protect' (R2P), which emerged after the 1994 genocide in Rwanda, and which has a strong bearing on contemporary mainstream humanitarian principles. In essence it is proposed that where a state fails to protect its citizens, or is itself committing mass atrocities, the 'international community', under UN sanction, has the right to intervene, including if necessary through breaching territorial and state sovereignty (Chandler 2004; Bellamy 2005, 2010). Controversial 'humanitarian action' in the Balkans, Darfur, Afghanistan and Libya have all been justified with recourse to the notion of R2P. This has provoked considerable debate and has many critics, not least those who feel that it is mobilized by the powerful nations only when it suits them to depose an 'undesirable' regime. Many Southern countries have a strong historical commitment to state sovereignty, given a history of colonial and post-colonial interventions by the West, and this position is bolstered by considerable distrust of the motivations and outcomes of this sort of humanitarian intervention among many of the (re-)emerging development partners (Amar 2012). However, in some cases there has been broader support for certain R2P interventions (e.g. from the African Union), and there is certainly no unity among the emerging powers on individual issues.

Related to this is a second concern about the growing integration of security and development agendas within the mainstream aid community, including within humanitarian contexts. While some commentators suggest that a more coordinated approach is necessary given the frequently close relationship between conflict, reconstruction, humanitarian need and development, others are highly critical of the blurred boundaries, and argue that humanitarian and development agendas are distorted and even perverted by being subordinated to military objectives (Duffield 2001). A number of studies (e.g. Doty 1996; Orford 2003, 2011; Mamdani 2010, 2011) have examined the ways in which the merging of developmentalism and securitization has been legitimized by 'the blending of discourses of humanitarianism and human security with neo-colonial metaphors of tutelage and protection' (Amar 2012: 3). A third issue for some development partners centres on distrust of some of the NGOs through which the UN channels elements of its humanitarian funding; and the final difference that Harmer and Cotterrell (2005) identify is the desire of many of the Southern donors especially that there should be a stronger UN focus on natural disasters, both in terms of preventing them (e.g. through early warning systems) and responding to them. At present conflict and post-conflict humanitarian situations tend to be at the top of the agenda, arguably reflecting the concerns of the United States and its allies.

That said, there are some events and contexts within which there has been considerable non-DAC engagement with mainstream humanitarian institutions and processes. Harmer and Cotterrell (ibid.) note that in an unprecedented move, China directed $20 million out of the $60 million in total that it spent following the Indian Ocean tsunami to the UN. Again marking a real national and international transition, India joined Australia, Japan and the United States as one of the four countries coordinating the 2004 tsunami response, while rejecting offers of external assistance in dealing with the impacts on its own shores. Harmer and Cotterrell (ibid.) also note the strong support among many non-DAC partners for the WFP. Interestingly they suggest that in part this is because the WFP has handled intelligently the non-DAC partners, recognizing and incorporating their strengths, concerns and particular interests in creative and effective ways (see Box 3.2). This contrasts with some of the early 'outreach' efforts by the UN's OCHA, for example, which initially simply tried to squeeze more contributions from the emerging powers without seeking to justify the role of multilaterals, or offer them more voice within the institutions.

Harmer and Cotterrell (ibid.) suggest that the mainstream

Box 3.2 The (re-)emerging partners and the UN World Food Programme

The World Food Program (WFP) is perhaps the most advanced [multilateral organization] in terms of non-DAC dialogue, breadth of support and range of networks. Between 2002 and 2003, 23 low-income countries contributed to WFP, to a value of $56 million; as a result, WFP set itself the goal of securing contributions from all 191 members of the UN. Its strategy to achieve this – 'New Partnerships to Meet Rising Needs' – was released in 2004. The agency has also decentralised its donor relations offices, and plans to open new offices in Riyadh, Saudi Arabia, and other regional locations. The WFP has been more adaptive and innovative in the way in which it supports and matches contributions from non-DAC donors, not only in the provision of goods and services, but also in in-kind aid.

WFP also encourages twinning arrangements, whereby it matches cash and commodity donors (the latter often being non-DAC) with a specific appeal or development project. Debt swaps have also been piloted; in 2004, for example, Italy agreed to forgo debt from Egypt on the condition that Cairo invested in domestic development projects … In 2004, WFP and the League of Arab States signed their first Memorandum of Understanding for future cooperation. This underlines the two organisations' common interest in improving food security in the Middle East. It also reflects the fact that Arab League countries are increasingly important donors to WFP: Algeria gave $10 million in 2003, while Saudi Arabia contributed $3.3 million and Jordan $44,000. In early 2003, the WFP held a conference on 'Expanding Partnership: New EU Member States and WFP' to highlight the agency's emergency response capacity, and to discuss areas of potential cooperation. In China, the WFP has aimed to build internal capacity. The WFP is the only UN agency with which China has completed the transition from recipient to donor. From 2006, WFP's office in Beijing will become a liaison office, focusing exclusively on building up the agency's relations with the Chinese government, primarily for fundraising.

The WFP recognises that the tendency for non-DAC donors to channel their giving bilaterally is a challenge. In analysing this, WFP's strategy notes that the political imperatives behind donorship are similar to those of the DAC donors. On this basis, WFP has committed itself to providing donors with publicity and press coverage; it makes a commitment to solicit aid for countries in which these donors have a political interest, and which are plausible recipients geographically and logistically. WFP has also suggested that countries may enhance their standing in the UN on the basis of WFP contributions.

Source: Harmer and Cotterrell (2005: 30–1; parentheses added)

humanitarian institutions now recognize the need for more sustained partnerships with the non-DAC actors, and the value of supporting South–South and regional mechanisms (see also Oglesby 2011). Smith (2011) suggests that many non-DAC partners are moving closer to aspects of the 'mainstream' humanitarian infrastructure. She notes that in 2010 Brazil became the thirty-sixth member of the Good Humanitarian Donorship group, committing to its '23 Principles and Good Practices'. To date, though, Brazil is the only non-European NDD – the other twelve are the former CEE states, which are not yet members of the OECD and/or the DAC. However, the section on the military below offers a more critical reading of the emerging power's past and present engagement with the humanitarian security arena.

The institutional organization of non-DAC development assistance

Most of the (re-)emerging development partners are in a process of institutional flux as they seek to launch, strengthen or reform their development cooperation systems and structures (Davies 2010). Some are relatively new to foreign aid and development cooperation, such as Thailand, but even those with longer histories of donor activity are responding to changing strategic contexts, expanded development cooperation flows and activities, and relatively new domestic and external scrutiny. The administration of foreign aid and development cooperation requires trained personnel, legal frameworks, budget lines and management, monitoring and evaluation systems and so on, both at headquarters and at partner country level. The management of external assistance also requires attention to the balance of responsibility and power between different domestic institutions, and the coordination of their relevant activities. In some countries foreign aid and development cooperation budgets, policies and flows are conducted under the close eye and critical gaze of civil society organizations, parliamentarians, the general public and the media; as well as external analysts and commentators. In other countries, development cooperation institutions, flows and activities are relatively insulated from domestic and external scrutiny, and take place in the spaces of national elite power and decision-making (Kondoh et al. 2010; Mawdsley et al. 2011b). The consensus among most commentators is that most if not all of the non-DAC donors, other than the main Arab donors, are institutionally rather weak (Kondoh et al. 2010; Lightfoot 2010). Most have insufficient numbers of trained personnel; they are constrained by path dependency and struggle to reorient themselves to new development contexts and agendas; and development cooperation departments and agencies tend to lack power relative to other parts of government. Even South Korea, which has invested significantly in its development cooperation activities, identity and institutions, and which joined the DAC in 2010, suffers from a variety of institutional shortcomings (Kondoh et al. 2010).

The major Arab donors are something of an exception among the non-DAC partners in that they are reasonably well institutionalized bilaterally and regionally. The Coordination Group of Arab Aid Agencies was established in 1975 and now has nine members – the three national agencies of Saudi Arabia, Kuwait and the UAE, and six Arab multilaterals, with the Arab Fund holding the secretariat. Its stated aim is to:

> increase the efficiency of Arab aid, help beneficiary countries obtain the required funding for their high priority projects, avoid overlapping and duplication of donor efforts, increase the efficiency of utilization of resources, coordinate project evaluation activities, apply unified rules and procedures at the project implementation stage, exchange information and data relating to projects and developing plans, and coordinate interventions with international and regional financing institutions. (Arab Fund [2006], cited in Villanger 2007: 22)

The outcome appears to be a relatively high degree of harmonization of operational procedures, the exchange of information, co-financed projects, joint proposals, and standardized loan agreements – all goals of the Paris Agenda aid effectiveness paradigm. The complex array of Arab aid and financing bodies demonstrate some division of labour under the umbrella of pursuing social and economic development.

Some are focused on Arab countries alone (e.g. the Arab Fund for Social and Economic Development and the Arab Monetary Fund), while others are mandated to provide assistance to a wider range of countries. The OPEC Fund for International Development focuses on encouraging cooperation among oil exporters and non-oil-exporters; the Islamic Development Bank aims to foster the principles of Islamic financing; and the Arab Monetary Fund promotes monetary stability, financial integration and trade flows. The Arab Gulf Programme for United Nations Development Organizations (AGFUND) is reported as having the most direct focus on sustainable human development (World Bank 2010).

Different bilateral development partners manage their foreign aid and development cooperation policy-making and projects through a wide range of domestic institutions. The most concentrated model is one in which a nodal agency has pre-eminent (but rarely sole) responsibility for ODA management. DAC equivalents would be Canada's International Development Agency (CIDA), or DANIDA, the Danish International Development Agency. The UK's Department for International Development (DfID) is exceptional in having ministerial status – more commonly national agencies are located within ministries of foreign affairs, some of which are co-responsible for trade, as with New Zealand and South Korea. Agencies of this nature are being established in the 'new' EU member states. In all cases, they are located within the Ministry of Foreign Affairs (or equivalent), and are still evolving their structures and procedures. There also appears to be a growing trend towards creating dedicated development agencies in other non-DAC countries in the last few years, although quite what does or would come under the remit is varied. In 2008 the South African cabinet approved the creation of the South African Development Partnership Agency (SADPA), due to be established in mid-2012 (Glennie 2011b).[6] International Relations and Cooperation Minister Maite Nkoana-Mashabane, who launched SADPA in Nairobi in October 2010, stated that the agency 'will not only enhance our contribution in institutional and capacity building on the continent, but also ensure that our post-conflict reconstruction and development efforts are centrally co-ordinated'.[7] The new agency will eventually absorb the African Renaissance Fund (ARF) and all its activities in order to reduce bureaucracy and duplication, although some of the decision-making is also informed by internal rivalries within the African National Congress (ANC).

In some cases, aid agencies and institutions are well established. The Turkish International Cooperation and Development Agency, for example, was established in 1992, has offices in twenty partner countries, and is the principal administrator of Turkish ODA. Brazil's Agência Brasileria de Cooperaração (ABC) was set up by the federal government in the late 1980s within the Ministry for External Relations (although its development cooperation relations go back to the 1960s: Vaz and Inoue 2007). ABC acts as the coordinating agency both in terms of Brazil's recipient status and for its own donor activities. According to Abdenur (2007: 6), ABC was coordinating eighty-six South–South projects, of which 'approximately 50 per cent were in Latin America, 25 per cent in Africa, and 25 per cent in East Timor'.

Notwithstanding these older and newer dedicated agencies, most of the Southern development partners tend to have rather fragmented aid and development cooperation infrastructures. For example, a remarkable number of India's ministries, agencies and official research bodies have individual development cooperation programmes, often long-standing in nature. To take one example, Dak Bhavan (India's postal ministry) has various bilateral cooperative programmes with peer organizations in Asia and Africa. It provides technical assistance to help partners modernize and reform their postal services, often with leading-edge communications technologies, but also with skills and experience tuned to similar contexts, including poor transport infrastructure, low literacy levels, dispersed rural populations, and dense informal urban settlements in some areas. China delivers its aid programme, including grants, zero-interest aid loans, youth volunteer schemes and technical assistance, through the Department of Foreign Aid within the Ministry of Commerce, in cooperation with the Ministry of Foreign Affairs. The Ministry of Commerce also oversees the EXIM Bank's concessional foreign aid loan programme, in which aid works as the subsidy that softens the loan (Bräutigam 2010). In addition to these major conduits of financing and assistance, the Ministry of Education runs scholarships; medical teams are provided through the Ministry of Health; multilateral donations come from various ministries; and sectoral projects (in transport, agriculture, industry and so on) through relevant ministries. Thai ministries engaged in bilateral development cooperation (mainly in the form of training, seminars and study missions) include those for Energy, Public Health, Agriculture and Cooperatives, Education, Higher Education, Natural Resources and Environment, and Social Development and Human Security (Kondoh et al. 2010).

The non-DAC donors are not unusual in such official decentralization and fragmentation – the USA has a similar array of bilateral aid relations managed by various government bodies, while Japan has an exceptionally fragmented aid system (OECD-DAC 2003). While this can lend diversity and dynamism to the aid sector, such administrative plurality can undermine policy coherence and development impact. As well as technical issues of cooperation and coordination, Mohan and Power (2008) observe examples of inter-ministerial rivalry and competing departments seeking to capture budget lines, postings, travel and status.

Institutional assemblages evolve over time. India demonstrates the ways in which changing domestic agendas and external contexts can lead to shifts in structures and mandates. India's long-standing engagement in development assistance has historically been coordinated principally by the Ministry of External Affairs, as one might expect given its positioning within a political discourse of 'Third World' solidarity and the Non-Aligned Movement. Over the last decade or so, as its geostrategic and commercial ambitions have shifted focus and increased in scale, the Ministry of Commerce and the EXIM Bank have taken on larger roles in managing concessional financing agreements (some of which it would count as development cooperation, blurring into more clearly commercial arrangements). In July 2011 India announced that it intends to establish the Indian Agency for Partnership in Development, something that has been mooted since 2003. This is indicative not just of the growing scale of India's development assistance flows and activities, but also the intent to manage them more effectively and strategically, including in terms of public diplomacy – building India's image around the world.

Many of the (re-)emerging donors and development partners are investing in a rapid increase in foreign aid and development cooperation flows and activities, with agendas, partners and modalities that have sometimes shifted significantly from their historical moorings. South Africa now finds itself in a profoundly different relationship to other sub-Saharan African countries in the post-apartheid era. (Re-)emerging donors like Russia and Turkey are discovering or rediscovering aid in new ways and changing geopolitical contexts. One outcome of the rapidity and rearticulation of development cooperation with changing foreign policy interests and agendas is often an aid bureaucracy that is struggling to keep up. These changes require changed attitudes and approaches among bureaucrats, different forms of training and promotion structures, new legislation and finances, political and administrative leadership, and understanding and support from other power-holders and institutions. This has implications for the full scale and spectrum of foreign aid and development cooperation.

At the country level, embassies are very often the nodal agencies for non-DAC aid and development assistance because of fewer or no dedicated development agencies with country offices. Embassy staff can find themselves at the operational end of dynamic and expanding aid and development cooperation relations. Nordtveit (2011) describes staff in the Chinese embassy in Cameroon being swamped by the growing volumes and channels of foreign aid and development cooperation, even as they carried on with their consular and other diplomatic duties. He notes that this is one reason why monitoring and coordination levels are often quite low. This can lead to frustration for Cameroonian officials, who were sometimes unable to manage development cooperation relations more effectively with Chinese counterparts, but also for the Chinese embassy staff. Casting some of the transparency and aid effectiveness debates in a slightly more sympathetic light perhaps (see below), Nordtveit quotes a harassed Chinese official:

> Our statistics services are not very good, and we have not yet established a very good data system ... Chinese aid and cooperation with Africa have been hindered by a lack of transparency, and a lot of the documentation on prior projects has been lost. The new strategy of aid to foreign countries is important for us, and we are currently reviewing old projects and practices, to learn for the future. (Ibid.: 105)

Most Arab donors also have limited in-country presence. For the most part their aid agencies have a core staff working in the headquarters, supplemented by consultants, with few external offices or representatives (the Islamic Development Bank is something of an exception). This can be interpreted as a positive feature of their aid architectures – a World Bank report (2010: 20) notes that this means that these agencies must 'depend on beneficiary country officials to identify and design operations that fall within wider organizational mandates': a key goal of the Paris Agenda.

State-owned enterprises and private firms An issue that we pick up in more detail in subsequent chapters, but which must be noted here, is the very significant enrolment of public and private sector firms by many of the non-DAC donors and development cooperation partners. These may be directly contracted by their donor government to undertake projects, or in other ways benefit from tied aid. As discussed in more detail in the next chapter, many of the non-DAC partners insist that a proportion of their grants and concessional loans must be spent on buying their own goods and services, benefiting public and private firms and other providers in the donor country. Technical assistance – the provision of expertise – is also inherently beneficial to donor providers, whether these be state agencies, private sector firms or universities and training institutes. To give just one example here, Bijoy (2009: 71) reports that:

> The government of India is keen to emphasize the benefits that accrue to India with its external assistance [grants, concessional loans and technical cooperation]. The boosting of India's business is showcased as a result of such assistance. Companies such as Tata Motors (US$19 million World Bank tender to provide 500 buses to Senbus, a transport company in Senegal), the state-owned RITES (sale of locomotives to Sudan Railways and other involvements in Tanzania, Ethiopia and Uganda), and oil companies such as ONGC Videsh (oil assets in Sudan costing US$750 million) and Indian Oil Corporation Ltd. (IOC) are cited.

However, the differences with DAC donors should not be over-stated. As discussed in various places in this book, domestic firms and consultancies within the DAC member countries are often the beneficiaries of substantial shares of their ODA budgets. Interestingly, as one part of the move from 'aid effectiveness' to 'development effectiveness', the DAC donors seem to be increasingly interested in engaging with the private sector. The OECD-DAC held its first informal meeting on the role of the private sector and aid effectiveness in 2010,[8] and has also commissioned a paper on the subject (Davies 2011). We return to this in Chapter 7.

Civil society and the (re-)emerging development partners How do the different (re-)emerging development partners view the role of development NGOs and other civil society organizations (CSOs) in their development assistance programmes? Those (re-)emerging donors seeking to move closer to mainstream norms and approaches have tended to take a more inclusive approach. The 'new' EU donors provide support for a range of national NGOs, which in some cases are playing a proactive role in shaping official development policies, institutions and practices. In Poland, for example, development NGOs are lobbying the government, providing advice and support, and attempting to encourage greater public legitimacy for official aid and private giving. Polish civil society organizations argue that they played a key role in their own transition to a democratic society and free market economy, and that this is a skill and insight that they bring to their discussions with the Polish government and public, and in terms of development work in other countries, whether their eastern neighbours or in sub-Saharan Africa. The Polish government (and specifically the Ministry of Foreign Affairs) recognizes the role that NGOs play in informing and encouraging support for its emerging donor identity from wider Polish society, the contribution that Polish NGOs can make to policy-making, and their value in terms of delivering aid projects and programmes. As in all NGO–state relations, there are sometimes tensions and disagreements, although Drazkiewicz (2011) suggests that these are often not between NGOs and the government, but across these boundaries, between those in both settings who share particular views on the appropriate recipients and modalities of aid, and those who want to deploy aid in different ways.

Other (re-)emerging donors, notably Brazil, have also turned to their own vibrant civil society organizations active within the domestic sphere, contracting them to undertake projects abroad (Schläger 2007). Humanitarian work may be one sector where more non-DAC partners are likely to turn to civil society organizations. The major Arab donors route a share of their humanitarian aid through the Red Crescent Societies (Benthall and Bellion-Jourdan 2009; World Bank 2010: 19). Smith (2011) calculates that overall some 15 per cent of non-DAC humanitarian assistance is channelled through Red Cross and Red Crescent societies. Other development partners, however, have chosen not to work through their own CSOs or with recipient/partner country CSOs. China's own highly circumscribed civil society and explicit commitment to state primacy and sovereignty militate against engagement with CSOs. India, on the other hand, has a sizeable and proactive domestic CSO sector working in a wide range of fields, but to date it has rarely sought to make particular use of its own or partner country NGOs as a channel for development funding and assistance, or in other ways engage civil society in its development assistance policy planning or activities. Oglesby (2011) identifies a number of examples in humanitarian contexts, but these are the exception rather than the rule:

> Medical supplies worth [US$74,326] for the 2001 floods in Cambodia were provided through the Cambodian Red Cross ... and a cash contribution of US$5million was made to the American Red Cross following Hurricane Katrina ... Relief worth US$1million was made through the Catholic NGO Caritas for the January 2011 floods in Sri Lanka ... which is particularly surprising given India's long history of bilateral

assistance to Sri Lanka. Overseas aid has also been provided through Jaipur Leg, an Indian NGO providing artificial limbs; the MEA reports describe the NGO being 'deputed' in Afghanistan and Sri Lanka, although it is not clear whether the funding was provided by the Indian Government. (Ibid.: 35)

Equally, to date, India's vibrant civil society sector has not sought to scrutinize India's development cooperation activities in other countries (Mawdsley 2011). In a similar vein, Kondoh et al. (2010: 36) note that:

Despite a latent but growing awareness of human rights, the environment, and public heath, Thai civil society has not yet concerned itself with the foreign aid issue. Our enquiries could identify no NGO or civil organisations involved in foreign aid, nor any scholars working specifically on this topic. Asked about the accountability of aid agencies, staff of the Thailand International Cooperation Agency (TICA) replied that on certain occasions, when the Foreign Affairs Minister gives a press conference, questions on ODA are raised.

This may start to change. Penny Davies (personal communication, 2012) notes that some Thai organizations linked up to the overall CSO consultations and preparations ahead of the Fourth High Level Forum in Busan in 2011, and there are of course very strong Asian NGO networks like Ibon, which work on aid effectiveness issues and which are increasingly turning their attention to the emerging powers.[9]

From a different perspective, an issue that is critical to the developmental impacts of the (re-)emerging donors and development partners is the role of ordinary people and civil society organizations within recipient/partner countries. These include people expressing their views and concerns as voters, demonstrators and consumers, through trade unions, watchdog organizations, NGOs and so on. In this context we might also add the rights and abilities of journalists and academics to research and report freely on the agreements and outcomes of development cooperation projects, as well as their influence on wider issues of politics and governance. These debates tend to transcend the distinction between 'aid' and commerce (both trade and investment), partly for the reasons of problematic category error explained in the opening to this chapter, but also because development cooperation is sometimes bundled – infrastructure projects may be funded and supported through both 'aid' and commercial loans.

Obiorah (2007) argues that the commitment of China and other Southern and Gulf donors to a development model which puts the importance of economic growth and productivity first and foremost raises different and difficult questions about rights, standards and well-being. While this may ultimately contribute to poverty reduction, the needs and rights of ordinary workers, citizens and others can in some cases be poorly recognized or addressed. Many recipient/partner states have relatively weak civil societies, and for political and structural reasons it may be harder to hold their states to account. In some contexts, political and administrative elites may have little reason to pursue more transparent or accountable development cooperation relations with the (re-)emerging donors. An optimistic scenario might suggest that as aid and development cooperation relationships expand and deepen, recipient country civil society organizations will be able to respond, working out tactics and strategies to ensure better developmental outcomes. This may be taking place in several African countries where CSOs have taken action and tried to engage with emerging donors.[10] A less positive scenario discussed by Mohan (2012) is that the 'new' development partners will further entrench the power of unaccountable political elites. They may in fact harness this to more effective growth in some sectors and areas, and in this respect, GDP figures for poorer countries may improve. But the question that remains is whether this will translate into wider benefits for the population at large, or eventually to more accountable domestic governance. Any analysis of this question needs to be located within a wider recognition of global shifts in financial and corporate accountability, and the historical accountability deficit of all donors and development banks downwards to the peoples most affected by their policies, projects and programmes.

The military and development cooperation Many (re-)emerging development actors provide police and military personnel to UN peacekeeping operations, and other multilateral efforts supporting security and stability in partner countries (e.g. Bullion 1997, 2001; Beri 2008); and bilaterally as part of specific development cooperation programmes and links (e.g. Muhr 2012). As we have seen in Chapter 1, this is a contentious but growing dimension of development activities and foreign aid budgets. It can include active missions, or help train and equip the security forces of partner countries in-country or by providing scholarships and training programmes domestically. Military personnel, logistical support and equipment may also be used to assist in humanitarian emergencies. The Indian armed forces, for example, played a prominent role in delivering assistance after the 2004 tsunami:

navy engineers were dispatched to the Seychelles, for instance, to assist with the reconstruction of bridges and roads. Oglesby (2011) notes that the National Disaster Response Force (NDRF), a paramilitary force mandated to respond to disasters within India, was deployed overseas for the first time in Japan in 2011 to assist in search and rescue operations following the earthquake and tsunami.

At present, most analyses of bilateral and multilateral military commitments for humanitarian and development purposes tend to be framed within realist international relations and mainstream policy-oriented security and peacekeeping literatures. However, a remarkable collection edited by Amar (2012) draws on a range of critical theories, including global studies, gender and race studies, critical security studies and so on, to set out a powerful analysis of the ways in which 'emergent powers in the global south ... are transforming and deploying distinct internationalist security and militarized humanitarian development models' (ibid.: 5). The contributors to this volume share an interest in the identities and subjectivities of peacekeeping troops and other public and private security personnel, and their insertion into global hierarchies of labour, race and post-colonial identity (ibid.: 6). The collection is rich, and cannot be reprised here, but some of the key arguments are that critical analysts cannot be utopian about the new kinds of internationalism articulated by the Southern emerging powers in security-humanitarian contexts. Newly assertive humanitarian interventionism by Turkey (Bayar and Keyman 2012), Nigeria (Hill 2012), Kenya (Bachman 2012), Indonesia (Agensky and Barker 2012) and Venezuela (Muhr 2012) demonstrates a range of subjectivities, agendas and impacts. In some cases there is an active engagement with reshaping global security-humanitarian norms, but there is no certainty that this will lead to a greater democratization of global governance, or improved response, behaviours or outcomes on the ground.

One of the few authors to specifically address the relationship between development ideologies and peacekeeping is Suzuki (2011), who asks why China (which is the fifteenth-largest supplier of military and police personnel to UN operations) participates in what he calls 'intrusive peacekeeping', given its strong stated commitment to non-interference in sovereign states. Suzuki observes a number of strategic rationales for China's engagement, including enhancing its image as a great power, as a demonstration of its commitment to the UN, to acquire valuable overseas military experience and technical skills, and to project its own interests in host states. However, Suzuki suggests that these realist rationales are insufficient to fully explain or understand the apparent breach of apparently fundamental principles of foreign policy. Suzuki suggests that many Chinese elites and ordinary people share a 'modernization discourse' of development that shares many attributes with Western models – a teleological understanding of evolving economies (from agriculture to industry to knowledge revolutions) and societies (from inferior to superior). Like past and present Western models, these are often suffused with racial notions of ethnocentric hierarchy. Controversially, given official Chinese statements of sovereign respect and equality between nations, Suzuki argues that this discourse provides a paternalistic justification for legitimate intervention in 'inferior' nations. As in the example of Vietnamese development ideologies discussed in Chapter 2, Suzuki analyses the tensions between competing claims and agendas of superiority and fraternity. He suggests that contradictory statements about whether or not China can provide or demonstrate a non-Western 'model' of development to developing nations are evidence of these tensions. Suzuki's paper is a short one, the evidence base is limited, and it does not include much detail on the role and style of Chinese military contributions in order to augment his argument. Nonetheless, like the authors noted above, Suzuki demonstrates the importance of critical approaches to the emerging development partners.

Public perceptions and attitudes The dominant perceptions of Western, Japanese and now South Korean publics regarding the 'developing' world, the nature of development, and the role of foreign aid are shaped by a whole variety of experiences, information and imageries (Said 1978; McClintock 1984; Lutz and Collins 1993; Myers 2001; Mahadeo and McKinney 2007). Most DAC donor governments have a strong interest in monitoring and shaping the 'public face' of foreign aid and international development (Smith and Yanacopolos 2004), and have invested in national and cross-national surveys to understand how people perceive 'development' and the 'less developed' world more generally (Foy and Helmich 1996; Darnton 2007; Diven and Constantelos 2009). Publicly stated rationales may reflect or depart from the realpolitik concerns driving elite decision-makers, but DAC donor governments have to convince an array of voters, parliamentarians, journalists and civil society watchdogs that ODA is a just and effective expenditure.

To date there has been far less research into public perceptions of aid and development cooperation among the non-DAC development partners. The exceptions are the CEE donors, where a number of studies have examined public responses within these countries

(Eurobarometer 2007; Lightfoot 2010; Drazkiewicz 2011). NGOs and governments (in some cases with the assistance of external agencies like the UNDP) have been keen to raise awareness of global development issues and promote public support for their (re-)emerging roles as development actors. Other non-DAC partners are also keen to publicize their activities to domestic audiences, albeit selectively. Like many donors, Russia, for example, gave considerable domestic coverage to the role of its response in the aftermath of the 2010 Haiti earthquake (Gray 2011). Heroic and humanitarian actions are almost universally more palatable to domestic audiences than many other forms of development activity and expenditure.

In the case of most of the Southern development actors there has been little or no analysis of what their various publics think about their foreign aid/development cooperation activities. Two exceptions are Kondoh et al. (2010), who pay attention to public perceptions as one of the domestic factors shaping aid patterns in China, India, Korea and Thailand; and Mawdsley et al. (2011b), who conducted research into public perceptions of aid and development cooperation in China, India, Poland, Russia and South Africa.[11] Among many of the Southern partners, public awareness of development cooperation activities tends to be low. In part this is because development cooperation has historically been the domain of political and bureaucratic elites, who have seen little need for public consultation or approval: India is one example of this (ibid.). For some partners, of course, poverty levels at home may mean that support for other countries would prove controversial, an issue identified in South Africa and China, for example.[12] But there are some pressures towards greater transparency and accountability. Shobokshi, for example, suggests that greater foreign aid regulation 'is not only a political decision. It is also a social decision on behalf of a lot of Saudis, who want to know where the money goes' (cited in Harmer and Cotterrell 2005: 28).

Obviously in each donor country there are different publics (rich and poor, educated and uneducated, of different political views, and so on), and changing political dynamics, all of which shape the contexts for public awareness and perceptions. While aid and development cooperation tends to have a lower profile in many non-DAC countries, it is by no means invisible, and it is likely that media and public attention will grow as activities and flows expand. Lumsdaine et al. (2007), for example, chart the growing but also changing civic attitudes to foreign aid in Korea. Understanding public debate will call for detailed historically, culturally and politically contextualized analyses.

Recipient institutions and politics Are there differences between the DAC and non-DAC donors in terms of how they shape and are shaped by the domestic political and governance regimes of recipient countries? It is obvious that there is too much variation in the rich range of bilateral and multilateral relations within and across all categories of donors and development partners to answer this question in any singular way. Turkey and Taiwan operate differently as donors, while Ecuador and East Timor are distinctive as partners/recipients. Detailed case studies provide evidence of a range of outcomes and interplays that are contingently shaped by particular contexts, personalities, actors and events (see, for example, Vittorini and Harris 2011a, who analyse how different domestic contexts within Ghana and Liberia have shaped rather different relationships with and outcomes of Indian development cooperation).

Mohan (2012) steps back from individual studies in a review paper examining the effects on domestic governance and politics of Chinese development cooperation within its African partner states. He identifies a number of characteristic (but not universal) aspects of how African states and elite actors manage development relations with China, and vice versa. These include the creation of institutional 'enclaves' within recipient states as a way of organizing these inflows, which tend to be elite-based and bypass regular accountability mechanisms. Mohan also argues that in Sino-African relations recipient states tend to favour the needs of inward investors over domestic regulations on the environment and labour; while domestic civil society is relatively weak to contest these relationships and outcomes – although where it has some power it can ensure greater developmental gains from the relationship. Mohan concurs broadly with Davies (2008: 12–13), who notes that:

> Partner countries have voiced concern that South–South cooperation agreements are often made at the highest political levels of government and are not always aligned with national planning and management systems on a more technical level ... Coupled with weak local capacities, such arrangements can become a 'recipe for rent seeking'.

Mohan (2012: 1) argues that 'recipient states are crucial in brokering the entry strategies and developmental gains of these new flows of aid and investment' – in other words, that there is clear evidence that states (or rather, the different elements that comprise 'states') can exercise agency in shaping the terms of the relationship. But as noted above, the question is to what extent political elites will pursue strategies that have wider developmental benefits. Elite-negotiated, enclaved activity can lead to greater corruption, contribute to the erosion of the rights of marginalized groups affected by change, and distort the internal power politics of particular individuals and parties. Essentially, the concern is that the non-DAC donors will undermine good governance – democratic accountability, institutional fairness, judicial independence and so on (Obiorah 2007). However, drawing on a range of studies and annual indices, Saidi and Wolf (2011) suggest that in the case of sub-Saharan Africa the evidence to date does not support concerns that the growing presence of the (re-)emerging development partners is leading to increasing corruption or worsening governance scores.

Clearly this is something that needs ongoing assessment. Mohan concludes by observing that a major gap in current research into the rising powers is how they impact on and are impacted by domestic politics and governance regimes. I would agree that, as in other areas of analysis of the rising powers, the focus tends to be too strongly directed towards China and Africa (important though this is, it tends to overshadow other players), and too little attention is paid to recipient actions and agency.

Transparency and accountability

Running through all of the discussions above is the question of transparency, and thus the means to ensure accountability. Transparency and accountability are core elements of the aid effectiveness paradigm, and are championed as a means of addressing both democratic deficits and development failures (Klingebiel 2011; McGee and Gaventa 2011). Transparency and accountability initiatives range in scale from participatory budgets, citizen report cards and social audits to national freedom of information campaigns and international attempts to improve the monitoring and recording of aid data. Different actors within the aid arena have varying rationales and motivations for pursuing greater transparency and accountability (Barder 2011). Taxpayers and parliamentarians in donor countries want to ensure that their contributions are effectively allocated and spent (in whatever way they deem to be 'effective'). Citizens of recipient countries may want to ensure that aid is being put to publicly beneficial purposes: donor and government transparency enables democratic scrutiny and oversight. Data transparency is also essential to donors seeking to better coordinate their efforts. They need to know what other countries are doing and where (see Chapter 6); while without access to data, academics and development professionals cannot assess success or failure. Official aid players are also keen to ensure that other actors are playing by the 'rules of the game'.

As we have seen, at present twenty non-DAC states choose to report their ODA volumes to the DAC annually (Zimmerman and Smith 2011). The majority of the Southern development partners, however, do not report to the DAC, although they do release figures wholly or in part on their aid and development cooperation flows within annual budget reporting. In the case of the Arab donors, Shushan and Marcoux (2011) suggest five reasons why aid flows tend to be opaque (although they note that these differ considerably between Arab donors), some of which are more widely relevant. They are: little or no domestic pressure to reveal aid data; hidden, unpopular or problematic agendas of aid; little exposure or socialization into mainstream transparency norms; a politico-cultural heritage of dynastic rulers who blend public and private finances; and Islamic precepts which frown upon publicizing charity.

Some of the rising powers unquestionably see the push for greater transparency and accountability as intended to 'clip their wings' (Barder 2011). Puri (2010) certainly interprets attempts to impose transparency as part of a wider attempt by Northern partners to co-opt the Southern donors into the international architecture to help mitigate the burden on Northern countries. Nonetheless, the direction of movement appears – for the moment – towards greater transparency, although in multiple forms and not necessarily on DAC terms. For example, in 1999 only nine non-DAC partners reported to the FTS of the OCHA (Harmer and Cotterrell 2005), whereas by 2010 it had risen to no fewer than 127 nations (Smith 2011). In 2011, China published a White Paper on Foreign Aid, and it is suggested that one motivation was to counter suspicions about its activities through more open reporting on its spending. Smith (ibid.: 2) suggests that '[t]he launch of China's White Paper is a massive step for the aid transparency agenda and for the management of China's aid'. Smith (ibid.: 3) also reports that in 2010 the UAE reported for the first time the whole of its government aid data to the OECD-DAC, and was the first NDD to disaggregate it fully according to the OECD Creditors Reporting System (CRS). The DAC is working with the Arab Coordination Group secretariat to discuss greater transparency; and with Mexico, which recently launched a 'Reporting System for International Development Cooperation' (SIMEXCID). South Africa and India are also improving their aid reporting and management.

Transparency and accountability was high on the agenda of the 2008 Accra meeting, and strongly expressed in the formal Accra Agenda for

Action (OECD-DAC 2008). Following the Forum, the International Aid Transparency Initiative (IATI) was launched, with the aim of building a new standard for publishing aid information that would be acceptable to all donors, DAC and non-DAC – and indeed, to multilaterals, philanthropic foundations and civil society organizations.[13] Hubbard and Sinha (2011) argue that the IATI should be able to reflect and respect the differences between 'traditional' foreign aid and 'South–South Development Cooperation' (SSDC). They suggest that out of the thirty-three reporting categories set up in the IATI database, twenty-seven are compatible with SSDC. This is an important claim, given the widespread perceptions of considerable technical and political barriers to greater aid transparency. However, the issue of reporting on and including export credits and other OOF flows continues to act as a hurdle. Hubbard and Sinha (ibid.) suggest that:

> the lack of consensus between DAC and non-DAC donors of what constitutes 'official development assistance' should not be the limiting factor to disclose information. Whether lines of credit are classified as aid or not is less important than whether they are transparent. And the same holds true for opening up of officially supported export credit data of DAC donors which is hidden.[14]

However, although its membership is growing slowly, many important DAC and non-DAC donors remain uncommitted, including Japan, China and Brazil. The issue of whether or not to extend understandings of 'aid' to include export credits and other flows from both DAC and non-DAC donors is likely to be a central debate in questions about transparency and accountability, as discussed in later chapters.

Conclusions

This chapter has shown that understanding the contested, complex and varied definitions of 'foreign aid' and 'development cooperation' is a vital foundation to making informed judgements about the legitimacy of different approaches to development, and the ways in which different norms and expectations of foreign aid – social, political and moral – are shaped and contested. The following description of the main Arab donors exemplifies a construction of 'development assistance' that goes far beyond DAC boundaries of ODA, as well as the dynamism of development cooperation:

> The initial strategic imperative of Gulf financial assistance agencies was to finance infrastructure projects, but more recently corporate

strategies have emphasized poverty reduction, social sector development, private sector development (including investment support), trade expansion and coordination (through the Arab Trade Financing Program [ATFP], for example), introduction of Islamic financing instruments, and regional cooperation. As Arab aid agencies have matured and expanded, corporate strategies have introduced new business processes, partnership modes, and assistance instruments, and launched a number of special initiatives to focus assistance on disaster reconstruction, development in sub-Saharan Africa, and reaching the poorest of the poor. (World Bank 2010: 19)

Although it is evident that the (re-)emerging development partners are highly varied – in their aid/development cooperation definitions, volumes and institutions – what this chapter suggests is that common to them all is a sense of dynamism. Most appear to be increasing their aid or development cooperation volumes (albeit some from very low levels); launching or rearticulating their development organizations and systems; and extending their numbers and geographical reach with partner countries. There is a sense of change and opportunity, but also challenges and costs, as the (re-)emerging actors raise their commitments to foreign aid and development cooperation. However, it may be that the speed and dynamism of these relationships in a new era of development cooperation are outstripping the institutional capacities of both 'donors' and 'recipients' in many contexts. This can give the (re-)emerging donors a pace and flexibility that many of the 'traditional' donors often lack, but it can also result in weak monitoring and oversight (by all stakeholders), leading in some cases to inefficiencies, ineffectiveness and corruption. Sato et al. (2010) argue that the uniqueness of the aid provided by emerging donors inheres in the speed of decision-making and implementation; the flexibility in aid provision; the reasonableness of project costs; but also weak attitudes towards harmonization with other donors working in the same country. We examine these strengths and weaknesses in the next chapter, which turns to the modalities of development cooperation – the substance of these relationships.

4 | Modalities and practices: the substance of (re-)emerging development partnerships

This chapter starts by looking at the beneficiaries of different non-DAC partners, and the different rationales expressed or evident in the choices that are made. It then turns to the substance of (re-)emerging development cooperation and foreign aid – its different modalities or elements. Here we start with a section on various financial flows and arrangements that fall within the broad category of foreign aid and development cooperation, and then turn to the rich field of technical assistance. The discursive positioning of diplomatic solidarity as part of South–South development cooperation is also noted.[1] The next section examines the sectoral preferences of the various non-DAC actors, choices that cross-cut the financial and technical assistance modes of aid and development cooperation. Many non-DAC development partners are engaged in health, education and other social programmes; some, like Brazil, are becoming leading innovators in these fields. But more emblematic of many non-DAC partners is the focus on infrastructure, energy provision and productive capacity aimed at enhancing growth, rather than poverty reduction directly. This is an issue of considerable debate, earning official and some public approval within many recipient countries, and very probably the growing emulation of the mainstream development community. But it also raises concerns that social welfare and poverty reduction may be relegated to a residual outcome of economic growth, at best. At worst it could accelerate deeply spatially and socially uneven growth, and do little to combat poverty while widening inequality and dispossessing poorer people of resources, land and livelihoods. The chapter concludes with two discussions, the first on the blurring and blending of aid and commercial interests, and the second on conditionalities.

Recipients of non-DAC foreign aid and development cooperation

As for the DAC donors, the choice of recipients or partners for the (re-)emerging development actors appears to be driven primarily by strategic concerns. These include competition with rival states; commercial benefits; the strengthening of diplomatic allies and allegiances;

the promotion of soft power; and interventions in fragile or conflict-prone states where instability may create problems for the donor. All states confront a range of incentives regarding the choice of recipients, some of which may be in conflict with each other and some of which may align. Different interest groups within donor states may disagree on where strategic priorities lie – EXIM banks and ministries of commerce may want to focus on countries that can provide profitable economic returns or strategic resources; a ministry of foreign affairs may wish to deploy aid to help cultivate an important diplomatic relationship; while donor publics in non-DAC countries may wish to see highly visible contributions to humanitarian emergencies.

Of course, what is considered strategic can change over time. A recent trend in India's development assistance has been the relative decline of older ties with eastern and southern Africa that were fostered through colonial networks of indentured labourers and migrants, and later through the Commonwealth and India's diaspora (McCann 2011). These relationships remain important, but it is clear that India's growing demand for energy and raw materials is driving a more dynamic focus on Central and West African countries (Singh 2007; Vittorini and Harris 2011a). Reflecting new imperatives, the 'Techno-Economic Approach for Africa-India Movement' (TEAM-9) initiative was launched in 2004 by the government of India together with eight resource-rich West African countries: Burkina Faso, Chad, Côte d'Ivoire, Equatorial Guinea, Ghana, Guinea-Bissau, Mali and Senegal. It is indicative of the growing commercial and strategic direction of India's development cooperation that a large proportion of the country's rapidly growing lines of credit are directed at these TEAM-9 and other West and Central African countries (Chanana 2009). This differs from India's development cooperation profile with its South Asian neighbours, where a higher share is taken by technical assistance, grants and concessional loans, reflecting an agenda that is tilted more towards political and solidarity concerns (Singh 2007). Strategic considerations can also be event and time specific. Kondoh et al. (2010: 47) suggest that:

Thailand's eagerness to assume a leadership role in the South East Asian region was particularly evident during the Thaksin [Shinawatra] administration, which began in 2003. This may have been heightened by the candidacy of then Foreign Minister Surakiat Sathirathai for the position of UN Secretary General. This policy accelerated after March 2004 when Thailand committed to giving assistance to three African countries (Egypt, Morocco and South Africa) through South–South

Cooperation agreements. In 2005, Thailand became the first non-OECD member to draft an MDG report emphasising the importance of South–South Cooperation.

The Arab donors are particularly concentrated in terms of their regional focus – the greater part of their development assistance is directed to countries within the Middle East, notably Palestine, Yemen, Morocco, Tunisia, Syria and Lebanon. However, some Arab aid is directed more widely. Villanger (2007) reports that the OPEC Fund prioritizes sub-Saharan Africa (SSA) and non-Arab Asian countries, and only 17 per cent of its funds went to Arab countries. The World Bank (2008) reported that 28 per cent of Saudi Arabia's loans went to SSA in 2009, although it appears that this tends to be spread very thinly. Conflicts within the Middle East have strongly shaped the choice of recipients in this region, and demonstrate the politicization of aid. Much Arab aid to Egypt, historically one of the largest regional recipients, was suspended for about a decade after it signed the Camp David peace accords in 1978 and recognized Israel in 1979. Villanger (2007) notes that there was an openly stated policy among the major Arab donors to financially reward those states that supported the invasion of Iraq in the 1990 Gulf War. These politically contingent events can amplify the volatility of Arab aid. Religious motivations for giving also play a part, less controversially when following Islamic precepts on giving to the poor and vulnerable; more controversially when aid is used to proselytize and spread Wahhabi Islam in sub-Saharan Africa, or support Muslims elsewhere in conflict with other faith groups (Grimm et al. 2009).

Concentrating on neighbouring countries and regions is common across all of the (re-)emerging development partners (Davies 2010). There are evident incentives to build relations with proximate countries in order to maximize the value of development assistance (notably in terms of trade and security), and demonstrate to one's own domestic constituencies the mutual benefits of development cooperation (Chandy and Kharas 2011). Kondoh et al. (2010: 61) note that many emerging donors have economically weak and politically unstable countries on their borders, unlike most Western donors.

China borders Laos, Myanmar and Vietnam; South Korea borders North Korea; Thailand borders Cambodia, Laos and Myanmar; and India borders Bhutan, Myanmar and Nepal. These geopolitical and geoeconomic circumstances both promote and constrain the aid activities of the emerging donors; for example, they often allocate relatively large amounts of aid to economic sectors such as road construction. Through their assistance to economic sectors, the emerging donors strategically intend the stabilisation of their borders, the prevention of illegal immigration, an increase in their influence over their neighbours, and improved active cross-border trade. This strategic geopolitical and geoeconomic environment is unique to them.

New EU donors debate whether they should be directing their assistance primarily to the South or more strongly eastwards, to countries like Moldova, Belarus, Ukraine, and regions like the Caucasus and the Balkans (Drazkiewicz 2007; Lightfoot 2008). While their regional neighbours are not as absolutely poor as many low-income countries in the South, it is these more proximate countries with which many CEE states have stronger commercial and diplomatic interests, from trade to concerns with political stability, crime and migration flows (Kuuisk 2006; Rehbichler 2006). Some advocates of stronger 'East–East' relations make the case that while this regional focus does indeed reflect political rather than developmental choices, the CEE states bring specific advantages to working regionally, including closer language and cultural insights, and the experience of economic and political transition from socialism to capitalism (Bucar et al. 2007), something analysed in more detail in the next couple of chapters. By the same token, some of the CEE states, such as the Baltic countries, have very little historical interaction with or current knowledge of Africa. Dominant EU norms that prioritize Africa may not in fact be very appropriate to the CEE states, but rather reflect the interests of the group of former colonial powers such as France, Belgium and the UK (Horky 2006; Lightfoot 2010). Historic ties and affiliations also shape recipient choices – much of Russia's ODA is directed towards countries of the Commonwealth of Independent States, which were formerly part of the Soviet Union.

China and India are in something of a different category to most of the other non-DAC donors and development partners. While both are strongly engaged with regional development cooperation strategies and relations, they also have development cooperation relations that historically have spanned the world; relatively substantial economic resources; and, just as importantly, ambitious geopolitical visions which encourage and enable a far wider spectrum of activity. Countries receiving substantial aid from India, for example, include Senegal, Tajikistan, Ethiopia, Vietnam and Cambodia (Bijoy 2009); while Oglesby (2011) notes that between 2000 and 2011, India provided humanitarian assistance to no fewer than seventy-one countries. As Chanana (2009: 13) suggests, India's 'near-abroad, as illustrated by its aid periphery, has expanded substantially'.

Challenging the 'traditional' geographies of aid, Southern development assistance is sometimes directed 'North' towards the industrialized countries, usually in the context of natural disasters and crises. For example, India sent naval assistance and 10,000 woollen blankets to Japan following the 2011 tsunami – the Indian foreign secretary tweeted news of this gift to her followers. After Hurricane Katrina devastated New Orleans in 2006, Sri Lanka was one of many poorer countries that sent assistance to the city. The symbolism of these gestures is discussed in more detail in Chapter 5, but as well as political expediency, the satisfying reversal of roles is clearly part of the rationale.

A controversial example of South-to-North development assistance is Venezuela's provision of subsidized heating oil for poorer and Native American communities in the USA. When George W. Bush proposed cuts in funding for heating assistance to low-income families in 2005, Venezuela's national oil company stepped in to offer discounted heating oil to about 200,000 households in twenty-three US states. By 2008 it had been expanded to include 220 Native American communities in Alaska. The acerbic challenge of this South–North aid programme is that America's poor are also victims of an exploitative capitalist economy and imperialist polity. However, like other Venezuelan aid programmes, it has also attracted domestic dissent. The main opposition candidate to Hugo Chávez in the 2006 election, Manuel Rosales, stated, '[n]o more dollars to any foreign country as long as there are slums in Venezuela, as long as there is unemployment and hunger' (cited in O'Keefe 2006; see also Americas Forum for Freedom and Prosperity 2011). Critics clearly resent what is seen as politically motivated spending abroad in the context of considerable need within Venezuela. Supporters argue that poor Venezuelans are benefiting from its ambitious foreign aid programmes through the exchange of goods and services (such as doctors), but also through the creation of more policy independence within South America which can favour progressive politics and economies, in contrast to the neoliberal regime heavily promoted by the USA and its allies.

One of the most vociferously debated issues concerning the choice of NDD recipients is the willingness of some to cooperate with 'odious regimes'. China is the main target of criticism here: its relationships with Sudan and Zimbabwe, for example, call down trenchant criticism that it is helping prop up authoritarian and even genocidal governments. China has provided financing, engaged in trade, refused to condemn such regimes within the UN, and supplied them with weapons and other military equipment. These are genuine concerns, and should be taken seriously: financial and diplomatic support, especially from China given its place on the UN Security Council, can give 'pariah' regimes material resources and a degree of international protection that may allow them to maintain and extend their brutality. However, we should note three complicating issues.

First, many Western countries continue to prop up extremely dubious regimes, including through foreign aid (Dosch 2007). The realpolitik of energy security, trade and geopolitical concerns means that various Western powers retain close and even convivial ties with, for example, authoritarian monarchies in the Middle East; deeply corrupt and sometimes brutal West African oil regimes; and Central Asian republics, some of which, such as Uzbekistan, have atrocious records of human rights violations. Moreover, Western companies are actively doing business in all of the countries with which China is criticized for engaging, often with tacit official support. Leung (2010) reports that in Zimbabwe, for example, in 2008, Anglo-American had a $400 million chromium investment; a South African mining company loaned it $100 million for platinum development; while the French government provided a substantial bank loan to access nickel. There is a distinct stink of hypocrisy when China's support for odious regimes is criticized.

Second, individual bilateral relations are often rather more complicated than the simple assertion that China or other 'rogue donors' support pariah regimes with no questions asked. In the complex politics of the Sudan, for example, China's role has both changed over time and been rather more nuanced than many commentators imply (Large 2008; Lee et al. 2010). It is not in China's interests to do business in a war zone or a failed state, and notwithstanding its own claims of non-interference, China has played a more active role in brokering deals than is often acknowledged.

Third, while China draws a lot of the flak, there is far less moral outrage directed at other countries doing similar business in similar contexts. The Malaysian and Indian governments and state and private oil firms, for example, are also players in Sudanese oil deals (Patey 2011), and India has had increasingly close ties with Burma (which preceded the recent détente between Burma and many Western governments), some of which are massaged through development cooperation activities (Bijoy 2009), but it is yet to be charged as a 'rogue donor'.

These observations are not intended to dismiss the problems surrounding support for odious regimes, but the debate should be conducted with an appreciation of the wider complicity of many different Western and non-Western states and firms with highly problematic states; and with an awareness of the resentment that many countries and commentators feel when the USA and other traditional powers start criticizing unethical foreign policy. In recent years the invasion of Iraq and Afghanistan, the establishment of Guantánamo Bay and injustices at Abu Ghraib, and the use of 'extraordinary rendition', for example, have had a disastrous impact on the global image and reputation of the USA and its allies. This should not be used to shrug away difficult moral questions and critical positions on the (re-)emerging development actors, but to recognize that the debate is often conducted through a heavily biased and partial lens in the media, although perhaps less so in the last couple of years within the aid community.

We conclude this section with two points. First, just as with DAC donors, the geopolitical and commercial interests driving non-DAC assistance may cause concern or conflict among governments and particular interest groups within recipient countries. While much non-DAC assistance is welcomed and appreciated, there are also concerns that it can serve the pursuit of regional hegemony, or has other motives. Following flooding in 1988, for example, Bangladesh rejected helicopters offered by India for fear that they would be used for ulterior purposes (Price 2005). Some commentators on South African politics view its development cooperation activities as one part of its wider projection of economic and political power in the continent, aspects of which have detrimental outcomes for its southern African 'partners' (Daniel et al. 2003; Schoeman 2003; Alden 2005a).

Finally, there are also broader underlying trends shaping recipient/partner choices for all donors, such as the growing prominence of Africa over the last decade (Kraxberger 2005; Kornegay and Landsberg 2009). China's accelerating relationships with different African countries have been the subject of intense debate, speculation and analysis in recent years, but it is far from alone. Western, Arab and other Southern states have all re-evaluated Africa's importance to them, owing to oil discoveries, rising prices for primary commodities, biofuel and food demands, and security concerns (Davies 2010). African governments, firms and citizens are negotiating not just the growing role of the rising powers as traders, investors and development partners, but also the growing interest and attention of its 'traditional' European and American partners (Cornelissen 2009; Carmody 2011).

Modalities of NDD foreign aid and development assistance

Financial tools and elements Over the last decade there has been a substantive change in the world of development financing. Until relatively recently, many low- and even middle-income countries had to rely completely or in large part on multilateral development banks and bilateral foreign aid in order to borrow, giving traditional donors considerable power over their debtors. However, global shifts in wealth have meant new channels of financing have opened up, including foreign direct investment from Southern and Gulf state and private firms, and sovereign wealth funds (Chahoud 2008). Moreover, the improving economies of a number of Asian, African, Pacific and South American countries have allowed them greater access to commercial loans on the open market (Davies 2011). The array of grants, loans, credits and debt relief provided by (re-)emerging development cooperation partners contributes to this changing landscape of development finance through the provision of more resources, and just as importantly through the creation of more channels and actors. The traditional donors are losing their monopoly power over development financing, and therefore some degree of monopoly leverage.

Non-DAC donors and partners provide funding to regional and multilateral development banks and UN programmes, such as the African Development Bank, the World Bank and the World Food Programme (discussed in Chapter 3). As part of their bilateral programmes, some (re-)emerging development partners provide grants – straight transfers of funds as well as goods in kind, notably food aid. China and India, for example, have been significant donors of food aid, including substantial contributions to North Korea and Afghanistan. Food aid also accounts for a high proportion of the assistance provided by Poland and Slovenia: in 2004 it came to 61 per cent and 100 per cent respectively of their total humanitarian assistance (Harmer and Cotterrell 2005: 22). Most technical cooperation, which is discussed in the section below, also comes in grant form.

More commonly, the NDDs offer various forms of concessional loans, and it is here that the conceptual and operational differences between the mainstream donor community and many of the (re-)emerging development actors are most visible. That said, as we shall see, very often these are differences of degree rather than kind, and the debate is one that tends to be problematically coloured by insufficiently acknowledged normative assumptions about the 'proper' nature and conduct of aid and development assistance. Key issues include alternative constructions of foreign aid and/or development assistance discussed in the previous chapter; the practice of tying aid to the purchase of donor goods and services; and the use of export credits.

Some (re-)emerging development partners offer loans which are understood as part of their 'foreign aid' portfolio, although they may not conform exactly to DAC definitions or approaches. For example, as well as grants, China's foreign aid includes the face value of zero-interest loans administered by the Ministry of Commerce (MOFCOM), and the interest rate subsidy given to the concessional loans administered by China EXIM Bank (but not the face value), expenses for health teams and training programmes, but not scholarships (Bräutigam 2011).

In other cases, loans may be considered to constitute 'development investment' – they are not entirely commercial in terms or intent, but are considered part of the development cooperation relationship. Loan concessionality can be achieved through low or even zero interest rates, and through extended repayment periods. Villanger (2007) notes that most Arab loans tend to have a rather low grant element but that interest rates are used to vary the concessionality index, with poorer countries being offered lower interest rates, and better-off countries being charged more. Loans can also be made more attractive for poorer countries through agreeing partial or full repayment in goods and resources, or the use of resources to act as security for a loan (Potter 2008; Chanana 2009: Kiala 2010).

The 'Angola model' is China's resource-backed provision of concessional loans to African countries, particularly for infrastructure, social and industrial projects. The low-interest loans are secured with commodities as collateral. A typical example is a US$ 4.5bn concessional loan for infrastructure allocated by the China EXIM Bank to Angola for over 17 years, secured by the delivery of 10,000 barrels of oil a day. (Chahoud 2008: 2)

This arrangement has been subject to some scrutiny and criticism, but Bräutigam (2009) argues that in contexts where a country may have substantial resources but low levels of foreign exchange, resource-backed loans constitute an achievable form of repayment or securitization. Japan has deployed this approach in the past, including in its lending to China during the 1980s. It is interesting to note that as the recipient in this case, the Chinese government felt that this modality was beneficial – it brought in much-needed investment, it enabled a foreign-currency-strapped China to repay Japan in coal, for example, while the accompanying technical assistance also promoted learning and capacity development (Bräutigam 2010; Nissanke and Söderberg 2011). This is, moreover, a modality deployed by many Western investors and banks. Bräutigam reports that Angola had no fewer than forty-eight resource-backed loans with 'respectable' EU and US banks, but when China set one up it caused a furious debate and much criticism within many policy and media circles.

As we have seen in the previous chapter, China has extensive export credit programmes, but it does not refer to these as foreign aid nor report them as such. Export credits can support state and private companies in the 'donor' countries in the conduct of business in recipient countries: firms borrow from these funds on concessional terms, stimulating investment in business and trade. Their concessional nature can in this case help offset some of the costs and risks of expansion into new sectors and locations. Export credits can also be offered to overseas financial institutions, regional development banks, governments and businesses in the recipient country to stimulate productivity and trade (buyers' credits), enabling them to pay for goods or services from the donor country on concessional terms.

India abjures the language of foreign aid almost completely. It prefers the term 'development cooperation' for its grants, technical assistance and various forms of concessional financing, but also its growing export credit portfolio (which it terms lines of credit, LoCs). These are managed by the EXIM Bank and the Ministry of Commerce with oversight by the Ministry of External Affairs. In 2007/08, approved lines of credit through the India EXIM Bank of $704 million brought its total outstanding commitments to US$2.96 billion by March 2008 (Bijoy 2009). Sinha (2010) reports that 136 LoCs covering 94 countries were available by 2010, and that the total operative portfolio of the EXIM Bank was US$4.5 billion. Sinha (ibid.) also reports on new initiatives to double India's LoCs to sub-Saharan Africa to US$5.4 billion over the next five years. In some cases, these LoCs may in fact be sufficiently concessional to meet DAC guidelines, but Sinha (ibid.) argues that intentionality should also be taken into account. The DAC excludes lending by export credit agencies with the pure purpose of export promotion rather than 'economic development and welfare' (something discussed in more detail below), and Sinha suggests that the main objective of LoCs is to stimulate trade and exports, and therefore:

A line of credit is not a foreign aid instrument, but rather an instrument for promoting international trade. It is used as a tool not only to enhance market diversification but also as an effective market entry mechanism for small and medium Indian enterprises. Indian LOCs are tied to the 'project exports' to the tune of 85% of goods and services to be procured from Indian firms. In order to participate in the promotion of economic growth of these developing countries, Indian companies tend to participate in the execution of many projects such as railways, information technology, power generation and transmission, buses, sugar mills and agricultural projects.

However, it bears repeating that the ODA/OOF distinction is founded upon norms that have evolved within the DAC. This divide arguably does not reflect a more complex contemporary reality of the development financing architecture, or the alternative conceptualizations of development cooperation. Although development cooperation overlaps (sometimes heavily) with commercial interests, a credible distinction can be made with pure, profit-oriented business arrangements. For the donors and recipients such financing arrangements and avenues are recognized to be part of officially supported efforts to promote mutually beneficial economic growth, which is projected as the foundation for 'development', generally understood in this context as enhancing economic growth. This is often framed as part of the strengthening of the 'developing' world, and while certainly blended with commercial intents and practices, is conceived of as more than simple trade and investment. These financial flows are often packaged up with other elements – grants, loans and technical cooperation may all be mobilized in support of a joint venture, for example, with each element complementing the others. For example, a mixed credit package may include credit for the buyers (the borrowing country), for the sellers (domestic producers and exporters) and concessional loans, which may then be combined with technical assistance. These difficult questions about the various ways in which aid, trade and investment are blurred and blended through the notion of 'development cooperation', and through practices such as tied aid and integrated approaches, are discussed more fully at the end of this chapter.

Another financial form of development cooperation is debt relief. Various (re-)emerging development partners have cancelled the debt of poorer countries, or softened the terms of their repayment rates and/or schedules. Coming from less wealthy nations, these decisions appear striking and often generous. Russia has recently written off considerable African debts that had accrued as a result of Soviet investment in Africa during the Cold War, in part responding to obligations to contribute to debt relief as a G8 member (Jordan 2010). As is often the case in development cooperation agreements, debt relief may be one part of a wider package. For example, in 2007 China cancelled US$20 million of Mozambican debt, at the same time setting an agreement establishing that the number of goods that Mozambique exported to China on a tariff-free basis would rise from 192 to 442 (Piçarra 2011). However, debt varies in its origins and nature. Deborah Bräutigam[2] makes the following observation about China's debt cancellation:

> Between 2000 and 2009, the Chinese government has cancelled an accumulated [US$2.8 billion] of debt for 35 African countries. This is interesting to me, as it shows a *slowdown* in debt cancellations over time. It reinforces my conclusion that the debt cancellations were only (as announced by the Chinese) about the old, overdue, zero-interest foreign aid loans, and not the new concessional and/or market-rate loans provided by the China Eximbank. As far as I've seen *none* of those loans has been cancelled.

This supports an argument that Bräutigam (2009) makes more broadly, which is that some official development cooperation funding is intended as a temporary measure to assist public and private Chinese companies to 'Go Out'. As they gain a more secure foothold in overseas markets, state-run banks move towards more commercial terms and agreements (see also Nissanke and Söderberg 2011). As we shall see later, this is an evolving strategy that mirrors the earlier path of many industrialized countries.

One concern expressed by Manning (2006) among many others is that the growing availability of loans and financing may lead poorer states to become remired in debt, leading to excessive financial and resource repayments. In response, the Chinese government argues that it is closely concerned with 'development sustainability', and thus with ensuring that its partners do not take on unmanageable loans (Bräutigam 2009). This is an issue that will need ongoing scrutiny (see Davies 2010), but a study by Reisen and Ndoye (2008) found that the emerging lenders (and particularly China in the case of sub-Saharan Africa) did not appear to be 'free-riding' on international debt relief efforts (by taking advantage of the ability of HIPC and other countries to take on more loans), and that they did not appear to be guilty of 'imprudent lending'. Indeed, by stimulating exports and growth, their overall impact appeared to be to lower debt ratios.

Technical cooperation Technical cooperation (TC), also known as technical assistance, has a long history for both DAC and non-DAC donors and development partners, although, as we shall see in this chapter and the next, there can be important differences in its conduct, cost and nature. TC is aimed at strengthening individual and organizational capacity by providing expertise, training, learning opportunities and equipment. It can support specific development cooperation projects, such as dam design and construction, an agricultural research station or the implementation of social protection programmes; or it can be part of an exchange of goods, finances and services – such as the supply of Cuban medical staff to Venezuela in return for oil. TC can also be a stand-alone element of development assistance, such as the provision of places on training programmes within the 'donor' country. It may include consultancies, the supply of technicians and expert advice; equipment and tools; scholarships, educational support, study tours and research collaborations; shorter-term training in managerial, professional and technical skills, and so on. The scope can range widely – in 2007 India sent archaeological teams to Indonesia to assist in rebuilding a temple complex damaged by earthquakes under its technical assistance programme; while Brazil has hosted study visits for Russian health officials to demonstrate how they are tackling AIDS/HIV.

Under the new millennial aid paradigm, in line with the agenda of improving recipient country ownership, there has been a renewed focus on TC for capacity development within the mainstream development community (Hosono et al. 2011). However, a number of concerns are often raised about Western TC. The first centres on value for money – consultancy rates and salaries are frequently very high compared to those for local peers. Bilal and Rampa (2011: 12) quote an African official who observed that an EU engineer on a one-year project costs the donor US$150,000, whereas an equivalent Chinese engineer costs US$19,000. Second, Western personnel may have technical skills, but some may have a poor grasp of local sociocultural, institutional and political contexts, and an unquestioned belief in the superiority of their own systems and cultures. Few have appropriate or sufficient language skills, for example. Third, TC is not apolitical or dissociated from other economic interests, although it is often couched as such. Different knowledges, skill sets, capacities, expertise and even equipment are all embedded in particular political assumptions and interests. They also have economic consequences, potentially locking in firms and governments to certain technologies, export markets and so on. Of course, as discussed in more detail below, non-DAC development partners are equally open to some of these charges (Bijoy 2009), but in some cases there are distinctive differences. These are particularly evident in the case of the Southern development partners, and the following discussion focuses on them, although not exclusively so.

Rhee (2011) argues that while only the large Southern and Gulf partners like China, Saudi Arabia and Venezuela can provide substantial grants and loans, even the poorest countries can offer an exchange of ideas. Rhee suggests that this breadth of actors democratizes participation in development cooperation, and that it should be understood as the emblematic modality of South–South cooperation. An ECOSOC report (2008: 15) notes that '[m]any of the smaller Southern contributors (for example Argentina, Chile, Egypt, Singapore and Tunisia) have focused on technical co-operation programmes, some of which have been in existence for more than 35 years' (cited in Grimm et al. 2009). Kondoh et al. (2010) report that Singapore, which initiated development cooperation in 1992, engages only in technical cooperation. This includes bilateral programmes, third-country training programmes, support for the Initiative for ASEAN Integration (IAI), study visits, and various scholarship schemes that mainly assist its ASEAN neighbours. Training programmes include English language, IT, Tourism to Trade, urban management and public administration.

A key assertion made by supporters of South–South technical co-operation is that it differs significantly from the North–South model, in which knowledge is conceived as moving vertically, from the West to countries assumed to be deficient in skills, abilities and technology (Hobart 1993). The knowledge provided by the North is often constructed as superior, and its transmission is effectively intended to allow poorer countries to 'mimic' the more industrialized countries (Narayanaswamy 2010). Thus the World Bank's 1998/99 *World Development Report* on 'Knowledge for Development' starts with the words:

> Knowledge is like light. Weightless and intangible, it can easily travel the world, enlightening the lives of people everywhere ... Poor countries differ from rich not only because they have less capital but because they have less knowledge about technology and about 'attributes'. (1998: 1)

This opening has deeply undesirable resonances with nineteenth-century ideas about bringing the light of civilization to the 'Dark Continent', while it conceives of knowledge as having no political, cultural or contextual aspects. It also acts to depoliticize the causes and the consequences of development – a lack of knowledge is a more palatable explanation to some development professionals than structural colonial and post-colonial inequalities and injustices. In contrast, Rhee

(2011: 264) argues, 'South–South exchange is a horizontal process of experience sharing and knowledge co-creation rather than a vertical transfer in traditional North–South relations'. This knowledge, he suggests, is more likely to be practical and experience-based. Southern countries may share certain conditions – in the case of agriculture this might include tropical weather regimes, lateritic soils, fragmented landholdings, the co-presence of pastoralists and agriculturalists, low capitalization, a substantial proportion of agricultural workers, and so on. In health it might mean experience in tackling HIV/AIDS within informal settlements, or vaccination programmes in widely dispersed rural communities with high degrees of illiteracy. Ideally, these shared experiences result in shared knowledge that is more appropriate and therefore more effective. Other similarities may include socio-political background and development capacities and challenges. For example:

> ... current local government reform in Lao PDR, a heavily centralized, ex-Soviet socialist country, has benefited from Vietnam's experiences, which proved to be more effective than those of Japan and other developed countries. Lao PDR and Vietnam share socialist traditions, a centralized governance system, and foremost, a single party political system, in which Japan or any western country could hardly have expertise. (Ibid.: 263)

Advocates of South–South development cooperation claim similar advantages in infrastructure projects (such as roads, bridges, energy production and transmission), science and research (for example, into biofuels or rice production) and information and communications technologies (ICTs) (e.g. providing broadband connections and ICT training and investment). India, for example, deftly claims that its technology innovations are 'Triple-A': affordable, available and adaptable. This competitive advantage extends beyond its commercial sector to become a 'unique selling point' for its development cooperation initiatives also. For example, in July 2002 the Indian cabinet approved an initial $100 million for the Pan-African e-Network, which was eventually launched in July 2007 in Addis Ababa. The scheme aims to provide facilities for tele-education, tele-medicine and network videoconferencing for heads of state in all fifty-three members of the African Union. The network will also connect fifty-three learning centres, ten super-speciality hospitals (three of which are in India), fifty-three other hospitals and five universities (two in India). In these endeavours, India asserts its expertise in creating 'knowledge economies' for sustainable development in the context of low-income societies (Mawdsley and McCann 2011).

Some of the specificities of South–South technical assistance can be explored in the context of the long-standing provision of doctors, nurses and other medical personnel. This flow of people tends to differ from most Western equivalents in a number of ways. First, the majority of such South–South flows of personnel and materials are supported through government funding as part of official development cooperation. Western volunteers are more likely to be organized privately through companies or NGOs (although these may in turn be assisted by foreign aid). Another distinction lies in the discourse, conduct and performance of 'volunteering'. There are some shared features – for example, in the motivations of young people and professionals in applying for these schemes, which might include a wish to do good, a sense of adventure, and a way of building one's professional experience and career opportunities. These mixed motivations are portrayed, for example, in a Hong Kong soap opera which includes a medical humanitarian mission in Kenya, in which a cast of Chinese and African doctors, nurses and patients play out the dramas of love, jealousy and the search for personal fulfilment – sounding remarkably familiar to, say, elements of the African storyline in the American TV series *ER* (Saavedra 2009).

But there are often significantly different constructions and practices of volunteering. One of the most striking is the insistence that Chinese development workers earn the same salary as their partner country counterparts, and live in similar circumstances and conditions. This contrasts very sharply with a section of the Western development sector. While some live very modestly, many NGO workers and development officials enjoy a rather lavish expat lifestyle, with cleaners, drivers and nannies. Chinese or Turkish equivalent personnel tend to live on a par with local counterparts. The distinction is one that is understandably emphasized by South–South partners. As we shall see in the next chapter, the discourses and performance of South–South cooperation, in official state discourse and in individual conduct, are rhetorically constructed as profoundly different from Western aid relations and motivations – although not without their own problematic occlusions and associations.

Official support for educational scholarships and shorter training programmes is again a long-standing form of development assistance (Chisholm and Steiner-Khamsi 2009; King 2011). Nordtveit reports that China is now the largest supplier of higher education scholarships for Cameroon (with forty places) followed by Morocco and Algeria – a good reminder that it is not just the big Southern players who are active in these forms of cooperation but smaller ones too. Funding scholarships has a number of attractions for all donors and development partners. They can help promote soft power and influence, as students who come to do undergraduate and postgraduate degrees will, ideally, look back on their days in the host country with affection and gratitude. It is expected that they will develop a greater understanding and awareness of their host countries, as well as language skills. On their return to their home countries (or indeed to third countries), it is hoped that in some measure they will act as interlocutors and ambassadors for their former hosts. Ideally, they will eventually become influential figures – parliamentarians, senior civil servants, diplomats, journalists and business people and so on – with good regard for their former hosts, and will continue to have ongoing networks and relationships with them. However, there can be negative repercussions when the experience in the host country has not been a happy one. For example, for all the official rhetoric of Afro-Asian solidarity, ordinary Chinese people can hold very negative perceptions of Africans. In the case of the Nanjing riots in 1988, African students were attacked by local Chinese residents of the city (Crane 1994), and there is still anxiety and rumour among young Africans considering studying in China about being isolated, ostracized or subject to outright racism (Sautman 1994; Nordtveit 2011). African students have also suffered vicious racist attacks in Russia (Jordan 2010).

Many non-DAC development partners appear to be investing in increased numbers of places and/or partner countries, and some are extending and deepening the relationship. For example, over the 1990s Chinese and African universities sought to develop joint research collaborations and programmes. Here again we can see a difference with Western donors, who have tended to focus more strongly on primary schooling. While understandable and desirable for many reasons, this has contributed to an African higher education sector that is woefully under-provided for, and once proud universities now struggle to provide high-quality teaching or research. Jordan (ibid.) notes that Russia also shares this preference for supporting higher education and training; as does Brazil, which has a strong and growing focus on joint research for development through its technical cooperation efforts. This is described in detail by Vaz and Inoue (2007: 15), who provide the following example:

> Two programs are illustrative of the kind of action Brazil is pursuing in research for development: PROSUL and PROAFRICA. These programs

are sponsored by the [National Council for Scientific and Technological Development] and focus on South America and Africa – priority regions of Brazilian foreign policy. PROSUL was originally proposed by Brazil in the context of the 2000 South America Summit as a means to create a regional strategy for science and technology development. It aims to enlarge science and technology cooperation by intensifying regional research initiatives. PROSUL supports initiatives and projects that generate regional networks, innovation, joint research, and science and technology events. During the past two years, the program has supported 102 projects in agriculture, biology, health, social and human sciences, the natural sciences, and engineering – 61 projects in the latter two areas alone.

As well as educational positions, many NDDs offer shorter training courses and professional development opportunities. By 2007, some six thousand people had been trained in Singapore, for example, mainly from China, Indonesia, Vietnam, Laos and Cambodia. China has trained over ten thousand African personnel in various fields under its African Human Resources Development Fund (Nordtveit 2011). India's ITEC programme also supports shorter-term training programmes, including accountancy, ICTs, management training, media training and so on. ITEC is demand-driven – each partner country has a quota of places, and the partner government selects the candidates, who are then put forward via the Indian embassy or high commission in that country. While this supports the claim that Southern development cooperation is based on genuine partner country need and agency, it can also lead to the capture of these programmes by local elites. In his analysis of Chinese educational aid to Cameroon, Nordtveit (ibid.) reports on frustration concerning the bias in selection of candidates. He quotes a Chinese official who said:

> … the Ministry send their family and friends to the training. Teachers and real people don't go: only administrators. It's really desperate, they go away [to China] and come back without [having learnt] anything … and they just have some pictures and souvenirs that they have bought. (Ibid.: 106)

This small vignette points to a much bigger debate around the non-DAC donors and development partners. While there is much to be welcomed and learnt from a stronger recipient role in the relationship (or 'ownership', as the Paris Agenda would have it), there is still a need for checks and balances. Complacent assertions about the virtue of South–South cooperation and non-interference do not confront the issue of corruption and elite capture of benefits. We return to this issue in the discussion of conditionalities later in this chapter.

Non-DAC technical cooperation is also open to a range of other critical readings. The first is that technical cooperation may be designed not around partner country interests or needs but around the commercial and strategic interests of the donor or development partner. The provision of equipment and training, for example, can act to promote technologies in which donors are commercially competitive. Brazil's strong backing for biofuel research, training and infrastructure in Africa is in part intended to build a market for its own biofuel industry, expanding the demand for goods and services in which it is a global leader. Technical cooperation can lead to contracts for service provision (e.g. ICTs), and have a demonstration effect for potential buyers and potential sellers. As noted above, many non-DAC donors actively seek to blend these economic interests with their development cooperation initiatives, which can lead to more integrated and effective projects and programmes. But it can also reflect donor interests to the detriment of partner priorities and needs.

The claim to superior, shared and appropriate development experience also needs to be problematized. For example, following the 'Arab Spring' of 2011, the Polish government sent Lech Walesa to Tunisia to advise social movements and the government on democratic transition, and particularly the role for civil society in securing change. Walesa had been the iconic leader of the Polish Solidarity movement, which in the 1980s played a major role in contesting Soviet rule, and he was independent Poland's first president. But while he may have had much to offer protesters in Tunisia, some observers felt that Poland's confidence that its own very specific experience of transition could be extended to profoundly different contexts was not sufficiently critical or reflexively questioned (Drazkiewicz, personal communication, 2011).

Technical cooperation is indeed a major non-DAC donor modality, and I would agree with Rhee (2010) that it is in many ways emblematic of these development partnerships. It claims to avoid the assumptions of superiority coded in dominant North–South relations; it is a more democratic and inclusive modality, allowing smaller and less wealthy states to contribute, benefit and position themselves as development partners; and it valorizes the development choices, paths, abilities and technologies of Southern, Arab and Eastern nations. Many commentators and analysts are enthusiastic about this modality, and understandably so. But there is a danger of essentializing 'Southern' affinities, identities and interests – mutual empathy and shared understandings don't necessarily flower between Brazilian and Mozambican individuals and institutions, for example; while the promoters of Indian intensive irrigation technology in Ethiopia may be just as imbued with a sense of superiority as their Western counterparts. The *cultures* and *politics* of development – understood as power differentials in ideas and knowledge, capacities and voice; and differences in identities and interests – are not confined to North–South binaries. Notwithstanding confident and assertive claims otherwise, such differences are also present in South–South and East–South/East relations. There is a pressing need to reorient critical scholarship, from international relations to ethnographies of the new 'Aidland', towards these new development partnerships and programmes. This is something taken up further in the next chapter.

Diplomatic shows, statements and solidarities As well as various forms of material assistance (financial flows, goods in kind and technical support), high-profile statements and enactments of international fraternity and solidarity can also be included as a meaningful element of development cooperation. The symbolic importance of such high-level meetings, state visits and ministerial summits is discussed in both Chapters 5 and 6, so here I simply flag this up. Assertions and practices of 'development cooperation' can play a substantial role in wider foreign policy agendas, building relationships with neighbours and potential allies; securing resources and markets; and as a competitive manoeuvre against rivals. For example, Tull (2008) records more than a hundred high-level meetings between Chinese and African envoys between 2003 and 2005 alone, efforts that were redoubled before the 2006 Forum on China–Africa Cooperation (FOCAC) summit: fifteen African countries received the president, the prime minister or the foreign minister of China. President Lula of Brazil also made an explicit commitment and concerted personal effort to publicize his foreign policy agenda of deepening relations with Africa (and especially Lusophone Africa). Lula made dozens of high-profile tours to different African countries and opened a large number of Brazilian embassies, locating development cooperation flows and initiatives (as well as commercial relations) within a strategy of high-visibility diplomacy. Vieira (2011) points out that Brazilian development cooperation is projected as an instrument of solidarity within wider foreign policy goals. This construction of development cooperation is something picked up in detail in the next chapter, but the South–South discourse of aid and development cooperation (if not always the politics or practices) is unquestionably one of the genuine differences with Western donors.

Sectoral preferences within NDD aid and development cooperation During the 1990s and into the new millennium many DAC donors and multilateral organizations started to place a growing emphasis on social programmes, decentralization efforts, empowerment objectives, and the nurturing of more participatory modes of democratic governance. The World Bank (2008) reports that of sector-allocable ODA to low-income countries, the share of social sectors rose from 29 per cent in the early 1990s to an average of 52 per cent between 2001 and 2004. At the same time, the combined share of ODA directed towards infrastructure and production dropped from 59 to 38 per cent. Japan continues to direct a larger share of its ODA towards physical infrastructure, including transport and storage, communications and energy, but this has tended to mark it out as something of an outlier

---

Box 4.1 Chinese support for agricultural productivity in Africa

China's agricultural development assistance is closely bound up with a host of agribusiness developments in Africa, including joint ventures, agro-technology demonstration centres, research facilities and training, agricultural elements of free trade zones and so on. Leung (2010) reports that since 1960 forty-four African countries have hosted Chinese-funded and -supported agricultural aid projects, and 20 per cent of all turnkey projects in Africa have involved agriculture. Between 2003 and 2008, over four thousand Africans took part in short agricultural training courses (three weeks to three months) in China, and recently President Hu has pledged to build ten agricultural demonstration centres, and to train 5,000 Africans every year in agricultural technologies and processes. China is also an active participant in the FAO's Special Program on Food Security in Africa. Leung (ibid.) observes that, at the same time, World Bank funding for African agriculture plummeted from 23 per cent of loans in the early 1980s to 5 per cent by 2000, while the USA switched from funding the agricultural sector to food aid.

in DAC, and during the 1990s Japan came under some pressure to adopt a more poverty-focused and 'soft wiring' focus (Castellano 2000). In some respects this shift in sectoral profile among DAC donors can be seen as a progressive one which responded to the criticism that growth did not always trickle down to improve the lives of the majority, or reduce poverty. However, there are concerns that the mainstream development community has come to neglect the underlying foundations of productivity and economic growth (Chang 2010).

In contrast, many of the non-DAC development partners have tended to focus on the more directly 'productive' sectors of the economy, often through specific project funding and technical cooperation (Foster et al. 2008). This includes the building of connective infrastructure such as road and rail networks; energy infrastructure, including dams, power plants, refineries and electricity transmission networks; and a focus

---

Box 4.2 Social policy: Brazil's newest export?

Brazil has achieved considerable social development successes in the domestic sphere through the consolidation of myriad social protection instruments started during the Cardoso presidency (1995–2003) into two national programmes: *Bolsa Família* (Family Grant), a comprehensive conditional cash transfer aimed at low-income families, and the *Fome Zero* (Zero Hunger) food and nutrition security policy. By 2008 Brazil had halved the proportion of people living on less than US$1/day, achieving the first Millennium Development Goal well ahead of the 2015 deadline. The consensus? It must be doing something right. Brazil's growing role in development cooperation can partly be attributed to these successes, as well as a desire by the global development community to diffuse policy learning on global public goods and replicate the '*Bolsa Família* effect'.

Brazil has been enjoying a honeymoon period over the last few years, seen as a preferred development partner by many of its new cooperation partners, particularly in Africa. The new kid on the block, it is trading on its *Bolsa Família* and *Fome Zero* image, and the significant economic growth and performance of the last few years. Brazil claims to promote 'technical cooperation which seeks to sow capacity for autonomous development' (ABC 2010) but it is not clear how far it has advanced in identifying and adapting its policies to local African (or other) contexts. Brazil is well known for developing context-specific social development solutions on the national level. And yet it appears to be exporting a 'one size fits all' product, which differs radically from its own experience.

While there is no concrete evidence of a new paradigm as yet, Brazil's burgeoning cooperation with South Africa, particularly in Social Protection for Health (specifically in the reform of the provision of decentralized primary healthcare and a focus on non-communicable diseases), seems to indicate a more systematic approach, motivated by the South African government's recognition of the political importance of managing social protection adequately. The Ministry for Social Development, responsible for social protection in Brazil, sees the drivers for exporting social policy 'models' as being rooted in a strong evidence base, supported by the prolific research, monitoring and evaluation done on a national level. However, Brazil's successful social protection programming is in fact underpinned by financial and political commitment gained through careful coalition and consensus-building. This does not currently translate to the majority of Brazil's cooperation interests abroad.

Brazil's brand of development cooperation is currently bolstered by its successes at home, by the dedication of many of its civil servants hosting and staffing technical cooperation visits and missions, and by the enthusiasm and optimism of prospective Southern partners. It is not as yet underpinned by a coherent and cohesive policy or set of policies, and is fragmented in its politics, as well as in its design and delivery. There is no systematic monitoring and evaluation, or a concerted attempt to systematize learning from the Brazilian experience that can then be exported and adapted abroad. If the Brazilian government decides to continue its role as a 'non-traditional' donor, be it as an instrument for soft power or based on principles of solidarity, it may have to start taking a more systematic and policy-based approach to its development cooperation if it is to preserve what Shankland calls the Brazil 'brand' (Constantine and Shankland 2011).

Authored by Jenny Constantine, based on Constantine (2011)

on agriculture (see Box 4.1). For example, Shushan and Marcoux (2011) trace a remarkable continuity from 1978 to 2007 in the sectoral priorities of the three main Arab bilateral donors. In each of the three decades, infrastructure has dominated the agenda, within which the top three areas have been transport and storage, energy generation and supply, and water supply and sanitation. Indeed, over this time the share of total aid that has gone towards these sectors has increased from 60 to 67.2 per cent. Shushan and Marcoux (ibid.) observe that this same sectoral preference also holds for Arab multilateral institutions.

There are a number of reasons for this strong emphasis on economic productivity. Development partners and donors are able to benefit more directly and immediately from infrastructure and economic investment. Domestic firms in the 'donor' country (private and state-owned) can be contracted to supply technical expertise, materials and even labour. Kondoh et al. (2010: 76) point out that for most emerging donors, the construction sector has a particularly high comparative advantage in cost performance, and suggest that 'it is thus logical that these donors regard infrastructure construction as their priority'. Beyond these direct benefits, as noted above, many (re-)emerging development partners have a strong interest in promoting regional integration and communication, partnerships, joint ventures and economic dynamism (World Bank 2010). Some of this is oriented towards promoting trade, investment, resource extraction and market penetration. In other cases, there are also security and stability motivations. Thailand, for example, has stated interests in mitigating the marked poverty of its close neighbours, which include Burma, Cambodia and Laos. By encouraging stronger economic growth in these countries, it hopes to lessen the risks of disease pandemics, political instability and large-scale migration. The focus on growth and productivity also reflects the needs and desires of many poorer countries and peoples, notably their elites and middle classes, but also many ordinary people.

Notwithstanding this notable focus on economic growth and productivity, a number of non-DAC development partners also run and fund social programmes, and in some cases – Brazil is the exemplar here (see Box 4.2) – there is a far wider commitment to various forms of social and welfare spending.

Other characteristics of NDD modalities Three other characteristics of much (re-)emerging foreign aid and development cooperation should be noted. The first is a widespread preference for project over programme financing, reflecting in part the emphasis on infrastructure and productivity. In some cases these can be very substantial – major road and transport initiatives, for example. Second is the speed of many of the Southern donors, especially in terms of project negotiation, agreement of contracts and building/undertaking the project. The reasons for this include in some cases the nature of the cooperation portfolio (fewer larger projects rather than more complex and varied smaller programmes), and very often the absence of policy-based conditionalities that often accompany DAC financing (see below). A final characteristic of some of the NDDs is their willingness to fund high-profile sports stadiums and buildings. India, for example, funded the new Afghan parliament building, while China has funded many official buildings and sports facilities, including providing $200 million for the new African Union conference centre (Glennie 2012). These can be criticized as 'white elephants' that don't reflect wider needs or priorities, and which are emblematic of gesture politics that don't reflect a mature commitment to meaningful development. There is some force to this, and in some cases it would be hard to disagree, but perhaps to some extent it is also too narrow a reading – these stadiums and buildings are often appreciated by poorer countries for the prestige they bring and indeed for the spectacle of modernity and international standing. This should be understood within the broader conceptualization of development cooperation, in which dignity, respect and solidarity are also recognized to be part of a country's desire.

Boundaries and conditionalities: two key debates

The chapter concludes by picking up on two issues in a little more detail. The first has surfaced at various points previously, and will also inform discussions in later chapters and the conclusions. This is the 'blurring' and 'blending' of aid, trade and investment. The second concerns the question of conditionalities.

Aid, trade and investment: blurring the boundaries and blending the instruments? One of the principal issues debated by analysts of the (re-)emerging development partners concerns the conceptual and practical overlaps between 'aid', trade and investment. This has two main elements: the first is 'blurring' the lines, notably through tied aid; and the second is the 'blending' of multiple instruments – bringing together development-oriented and commercial instruments to support a particular project or suite of public and private projects. These sit at odds – in theory – with mainstream aid norms and practices, but as the following discussion demonstrates, the issues are generally more complex and dynamic than any simple DAC/non-DAC narrative suggests.

Many of the grants and concessional loans provided by most of the (re-)emerging development partners are tied to the purchase of donor goods and services. For example, a donation from India of US$22.2 million to the government of Bangladesh following floods in 2004 was tied to the procurement of food grains, medical supplies and building materials from India (Oglesby 2011: 38). Infrastructure projects, such as road and rail construction, are often established in ways that ensure contracts for donor companies, whether state-owned or private. In the case of the Central and Eastern European states, Carbone (2007: 47) observes that 'all CEE states, with the exception of the Slovak Republic, still make giving aid conditional on the receiving countries buying goods and services from them'. As well as aid and aid-like activities, many other elements of development cooperation are similarly tied. Tan-Mullins et al. (2010) report that Chinese loans to Angola have been accompanied by the condition that 70 per cent of civil engineering contracts be awarded to Chinese firms, and at least 50 per cent of inputs be procured from China. This is regulated by the EXIM Bank, which states that:

> Chinese companies shall be selected as the project contractors. And for procurement projects, equipment supply shall come from a Chinese exporter in principle; priority shall be given to the equipment, materials, technology or services from China. In principle, no less than 50% of total procurement shall be made in China. (EXIM Bank 2009, cited in Park 2011: 43)

However, tied aid is not universal. The main Arab states, for example, tend not to tie the ODA component of their development cooperation programmes. With the exception of the Saudi Development Fund, none of the Arab funds is mandated to support home-country trade, but rather to foster economic and social development.

Tied benefits can also come in the form of employing one's own labour force. Again, it is China which appears to be most heavily engaged in this, and the practice is heavily criticized. Bringing in manual and semi-skilled labour from China significantly reduces the benefits of a particular project to the local people if their job opportunities are decreased. That said, Tan-Mullins et al. (2010) argue that the Chinese labour component is often exaggerated – they looked at an EXIM Bank-financed project to build the Bui Dam in Ghana and found that 700 jobs went to Chinese workers and 3,000 to Ghanaians. Bräutigam (2009) argues that Chinese firms must often import skilled and semi-skilled labour (which includes many construction workers): bridges, buildings and dams require expertise that may not be sufficiently supplied locally.

Tied aid appears to clash with the stated norms of the OECD-DAC, and other major allied development actors such as the European Union:

> The EU has a commitment to move towards removing [tied aid], in line with OECD recommendations. In addition, the Commission regards this conditionality as a breach of internal market rules on ODA and has threatened legal action, which is likely to be a major incentive to change practices in the new member states. (European Commission 2007a, cited in Lightfoot 2010)

The DAC has led an impressive fight against some of the worst forms of tied aid, and has made substantial progress in this regard. Supporters of this agenda argue that tying aid can undermine its developmental or humanitarian effectiveness. Goods and services may be unsuitable and overpriced, and they may represent an opportunity cost or, indeed, act as competition for struggling domestic producers and providers. In theory, then, tied aid diminishes aid effectiveness. However, as Richard Manning (2008) ruefully acknowledges in his end-of-tenure assessment of the DAC, with regard to tied aid many of the DAC donors still have a long way to go (the United States and Austria are two notable offenders); and in practice, most ODA contracts still go to the donor countries' own firms (Ellmers 2011; OECD-DAC 2011b). In any case, much of today's ODA falls outside the agreement, including technical cooperation, food aid and aid to middle-income countries. As with so many of the debates around the non-DAC donors, the issue here seems to be one of degree rather than kind, as well as subject to a rather partial assessment of the evidence.

But tied aid can also vary. Chandy and Kharas (2011), for example, suggest that Southern tied aid may be less detrimental to the interests of poorer recipient countries than, say, tied aid from the United States. This is because these goods and services are likely to be cheaper and, in some cases, more appropriate to the needs and conditions of poorer countries. Thus, the export of Brazilian agricultural technology may achieve more benefits for Mozambique than that from Germany, say. A large share of Indian lines of credit may have to be spent on goods from India, but a municipal government or private investor may be able to buy significantly more buses with that funding than they could from Italy. Although still undesirable in many regards, Southern tied aid is arguably not quite comparable to similar DAC practices.

Xu (2011) goes farther, and asks whether the mainstream community has allowed the issue of untying aid to become something of a religious principle – it sounds virtuous and may be well intentioned, but its underlying assumptions and real impacts still need to be scrutinized. Xu argues that the real reason for OECD-led efforts to untie aid (and separate out and reduce export credits) was to ensure an even playing field – in other words to prevent unfair competitive financing between the industrialized states – rather than primarily a concern for recipient interests. As developed country firms became more internationally competitive, some states such as the UK started to argue that there was less need for tied aid – companies could win contracts without it – although others, like the French, were more reluctant to give up this means of export promotion.[3] This suggests that the impetus to untie aid has as much if not more to do with the market principles and interests of the industrialized economies of the OECD as it does with recipient benefits. These arguments disrupt the 'self-evident' argument that DAC donors are virtuous and don't tie aid; while the (re-) emerging donors (usually pictured as the Southern actors rather than the CEE ones) demonstrate their inferior aid ethics and self-interested agendas by tying aid. This is not to dismiss the problems of tied aid, but to urge a more nuanced approach, and analysis of specific donors, recipients and practices.

Tied aid blurs the aid/commerce boundaries, while the more 'integrated' approach adopted by many (re-)emerging development actors tends to blend development, trade and investment. Park (2011: 47) describes many developmental cooperation policies of the new development actors as:

> ... based on a more holistic approach than classic ODA policies, in the sense that the provision of development assistance is not strictly separated from countries' trade and investment activities ... [NDDs] have a greater willingness to merge policy instruments in the pursuit of common objectives.

China, for example, 'links business and aid in innovative ways, using aid to subsidize Chinese companies' establishment of agro-technological demonstrations stations' (ibid.). For many Southern development partners, the integration is a natural one, which is considered to be more effective in leveraging growth and other developmental benefits. As ever, though, this is not universal – Brazil's Constitution of 1988 formally dissociates aid from trade or economic interests, but locates Brazilian aid within the realm of foreign affairs (Schläger 2007).

Mixing 'aid' and commercial instruments and interests has traditionally been criticized on two fronts. The first arises within the mainstream aid policy community, and suggests that promoting other commercial activities in parallel with foreign aid and development cooperation tends to undermine aid effectiveness. Commercial priorities may overtake the needs of poverty reduction and good governance. A different criticism comes from governments, business analysts and firms concerned that by subsidizing goods and services, or providing soft loans for national companies and investors, non-DAC donors and development partners are unfairly distorting the market and undermining fair competition between firms. Thus, if a large Southern or Arab public or private sector firm is bidding for a major infrastructure contract or an oil concession, 'development cooperation' funding for, say, building a hospital, or providing educational scholarships, may be used to provide incentives to the recipient government to award the contract to them. Development cooperation can also be used to minimize the risk to firms through the provision of export credit guarantees, allowing them to make a more competitive bid than they otherwise could. This is leading to significant competition within the financial services sector, and even with the traditional multilateral and regional development banks. Here the concern is not with the effects on the recipient country in question, but with the implications for market competition. 'Traditional powers' are feeling the pressure of the rising powers, and are quick to complain about unfair practices.

For these reasons, as outlined in Chapter 1, the mainstream aid and development community has aimed conceptually (if less so in practice) at separating aid out from commerce, sequestering it within a supposedly more virtuous realm. From 2000 to 2008, for example, on average the OECD countries collectively issued less than US$500 million annually in export credits to Africa (Saidi and Wolf 2011). Xu (2011) argues that even those elements that do formally link with commercial agendas, such as Aid for Trade, are constructed as not working in the donor's national interest, as if the only proper purpose of aid is charity (a normative construction I discuss in detail in the next chapter). However, as Langan and Scott (2011) demonstrate, the reality is that industrial country firms also benefit from considerable official support. To take just one example, they note that the European Investment Bank appears to subsidize the commercial operations of European mining firms in Africa. In other words, the situation is rather more complex than sometimes assumed. Moreover, when it comes to the really meaningful economic reforms – opening up currently protected

European and American markets to poorer countries, and reducing distorting subsidies – the situation is dire. Untying aid and monitoring export credits, while probably desirable, is the tip of the iceberg, and does little to counter the structural inequalities of the global economy (ibid.).

It is clear that 2011/12 will mark a sea-change in aid and development ideologies. Driven in part by the growing role and voice of the (re-) emerging donors, there is a strong set of debates emerging about the current aid effectiveness paradigm, contesting the premise that it should be (largely) separated out from commercial flows and activities. Kharas et al. (2011) capture this in their analysis of the major themes, issues and proposals for the Korean High Level Forum on Aid Effectiveness in December 2011. They suggest that 'aid' needs to be reconceptualized away from being a conceptually isolated flow that works on its own terms, and instead be deployed to 'catalyse' economic growth, poverty reduction and social welfare. They propose that aid should work to leverage benefits from wider processes, including banking, ICTs, mobile technologies, communications, mergers and acquisitions, joint ventures, research and development, and so on. The model provided by Japan (and now Korea: Kang et al. 2011), which has generally been criticized by the Western DAC donors, may in fact be the direction of movement within the mainstream. This shift from 'aid effectiveness' to 'development effectiveness' is taken up more fully in Chapter 6.

Conditionalities Conditionalities are one of the most contentious elements of mainstream foreign aid. For many critics they invoke the dogmatic imposition of free market policies under 'structural adjustment' policies that were rolled out across the developing world in the 1980s and 1990s, often with some success in achieving stable conditions for economic growth, but with frequently detrimental impacts on the poor, vulnerable and marginalized, and an almost universal record of increasing inequality (Mohan et al. 2000). While the 'post-Washington Consensus' era may have ameliorated the worst of these policies, Western aid is still tied in all sorts of ways to neoliberal policy change in recipient countries. In 2006, for example, Eurodad estimated that recipient countries were subject to an average of sixty-seven conditions per World Bank loan. Conditionality tends now to be more subtly massaged through the creation of apparently nationally designed and owned poverty reduction strategy plans and the like, or through the use of *ex ante* indicators on corruption, the business environment, and investment in health and education and so on (Mold 2009). Mainstream donors argue that without such accompanying agreements, aid is too easily captured by elites or in other ways wasted and distorted. Donors often treat these as 'technical' matters, but they are of course deeply political choices (Gould 2005; Mold 2009).

A defining characteristic of many Southern and Arab donors appears to be a lack of insistence on policy conditions in exchange for foreign aid or development assistance. Recipients are not required or expected to make changes in domestic laws or practices in order to qualify for grants, loans or technical assistance (e.g. Kiala 2010). Many commentators reasonably express concerns that this will undermine efforts to reduce corruption and achieve poverty reduction (e.g. Manning 2006), and in some cases it is taken as evidence that the donors in question have little or no commitment to 'development' as such, but are more interested in the pursuit of their own interests – securing investment opportunities, opening access to markets, capturing resource flows, and soaping diplomatic solidarities with political elites (Naím 2007). China is often the key target of such criticisms. Its riposte, like that of others, is located within its historic commitment to foreign policy principles that were first articulated between India and China in 1954, and then enshrined in declarations at the Bandung Conference of 1955. Against the backdrop of colonial rule and post-colonial Cold War interference in the government of many newly independent countries, the NAM insisted on the primacy of state sovereignty. Western aid conditionalities have repeatedly breached that sovereignty – insisting that states adjust their currency rates, drop their tariff barriers, change economic priorities and policies, rewrite their tax codes and so on. China and most other Southern donors have been highly critical of this interference in the past, and the assertion that they respect the sovereignty of their partner countries is claimed to be a central principle of their development cooperation politics and conduct. Of course, while this provides an attractive implicit and explicit critique of the many example of Western interference in developing countries, it is also a position consistent with China's insistence that other states have no right to interfere in its domestic matters, including its dealings with the Falun Gong, Tibetan resistance and political dissidents.

Are DAC conditionalities essential to ensure aid effectiveness, better governance and environmental protection, or do they continue to undermine sovereign states, with (thus far) patchy evidence that they achieve the desired change? Are the Southern development partners right to assert respect for sovereignty, or is the lack of conditionality reflective of their willingness to secure resources and markets with no concern for wider development impacts? There can be no singular response to this, but two issues disrupt the simplistic binaries that are sometimes offered by supporters and critics on both sides of the debate. The first is that policy and media critiques are often levied at inappropriate targets. As we have seen, soft commercial loans and export credits are often labelled 'aid' and then disparaged for not conforming to 'international standards' of ODA. This mistargeting is a serious and widespread weakness in a surprisingly large number of commentaries. Just as Western firms would not be expected to demand policy conditionalities, neither should Indian or Brazilian commercial actors. Public and private sector firms may be required or desired to conform to international agreements and standards or corporate social responsibility principles, but their realm is not policy conditionality.

Second, the Southern donors do in fact set 'conditions' for most of their financial dealings, but these are overwhelmingly concerned with repayment schedules and ensuring that projects are financially viable. In order to be sure that repayment is possible, the commercial plausibility of projects is checked and scrutinized. Nordtveit (2011) quotes Cameroonian government officials who are very clear that while there may not be explicit policy conditionalities relating to Chinese aid, this does not mean that it is 'no strings attached': they want something back for their aid. Nonetheless, according to Nordtveit's respondents, this approach is preferred to that of most Northern donors because the dialogue is felt to be a mutual one. Famously, of course, China also specifically requires that recipients of its development cooperation flows state their support for the One China policy, and offer formal and exclusive diplomatic recognition of the PRC and not the ROC (e.g. FOCAC 2009: 4).

Villanger (2007) notes that Arab countries do not engage with good governance or democracy conditionalities, which are held to be a matter for sovereign states. For example, the Abu Dhabi Fund's 1982 Annual Report states that Arab aid is given to help developing countries 'set up policies for their economic and social development of their own free will outside of political and economic pressures' (Van den Boorgaerde 1991, cited in Villanger 2007: 22). Of course, most of the Arab donors would have no interest in speaking for democratic representation (or legitimacy to do so). However, Villanger notes that the main Arab donors are tackling issues of corruption (for example, in the Palestinian Authority), efficiency and a sound tendering process, and making some efforts to ensure robust financial procedures to ensure that the money is spent as it should be.

Foreign aid also works within and across other international guidelines and initiatives on corruption, environmental and social standards, and human rights. These include agreements like the Extractive Industries Transparency Initiative (EITI), the Equator Principles, the Kimberley Process, and various codes of conduct regulating timber, fisheries, resettlement for displaced peoples, health and safety, environmental impact assessments and so on. Given multiple and very diverse development actors, and the spectrum of different codes, agreements and initiatives, it is impossible to make any blanket statement about the extent to which they are observed by the non-DAC development partners. A very general conclusion would be that there is a lower level of formal agreement or de facto compliance among most of the rising powers, and many have a poor record on environmental sustainability, social welfare and labour laws (Fues 2012).

However, we should also note that these codes and initiatives are heavily Western designed and led, and may need to reach out more imaginatively and flexibly to incorporate firms and agencies with very different working cultures and practices. Moreover, for the most part these international codes and standards tend to be weak and somewhat toothless. Bräutigam (2010) reports on a Transparency International report of 2009 which observes that only four out of the thirty-eight countries signed up to the 1997 OECD Convention on Combating Bribery of Foreign Public Officials in International Business Transactions are actively enforcing it (and the Convention itself has many loopholes and omissions). Although this is principally an issue for the commercial arena, the blurring of aid, trade and investment means that these are relevant issues in thinking through the developmental impacts and implications of all donors, development partners, traders, business partners and investors.

Conclusions

As this chapter demonstrates, the (re-)emerging development partners are engaged in an enormous range of activities and relationships, encompassing modalities as diverse as Brazilian agricultural research stations in Mozambique, Cuban doctors working in Pakistan, Polish support for democracy initiatives among its eastern neighbours, and Indian loans to support energy infrastructure in Burma. Many of these activities are similar to those of the DAC donors, often different more in degree than in kind from 'mainstream' bilateral relationships, such as the greater attention paid by many NDDs to infrastructure and productivity. The explicit bundling up of 'aid' and 'aid-like' activities with a wider set of semi-commercial and commercial flows and relations is more distinctive – although in practice many DAC donors are far from making a full separation of ODA from OOF and other investment and business interests. A more distinctive difference concerns the rejection of policy conditionalities among some non-DAC donors – although this should not be mistaken for a complete absence of agreements and negotiations, or indeed for a lack of concern with issues of probity and governance. In the next chapter we examine claims to similarity and distinctiveness in a different set of registers, namely the symbolic, discursive and performative.

5 | Discourse, imagery and performance: constructing non-DAC development assistance

Introduction

The fields of aid and development cooperation are suffused with imagery and symbolism, expressed and enacted through documents, meetings and practices. Constructivist theory suggests that states intentionally and unintentionally project particular identities through their development cooperation discourses and policies. These both reflect and produce material and discursive power within this multi-scaled arena, from the prestigious ministerial meetings in plush conference halls in New York and Busan, to the day-to-day practices of development management and project implementation in recipient settings. Foreign aid and development cooperation activities can act to express social identities of prestige, solidarity and power, to domestic, partner and international audiences (Kondoh et al. 2010). Of course, the performance of aid relations and the imagery and language deployed can be aimed at obscuring unequal power relations or undesirable agendas; while development partners can also reveal unintended identities – no actor can determine how images, language and symbols are interpreted by respective audiences. This chapter draws upon the very rich set of insights and analyses offered by ethnographers of traditional 'Aidland' (Mosse 2011) to think about the ethnographies and perfomative regimes of non-DAC development partners.

The chapter starts by outlining briefly existing work on Western foreign aid. It then sets out three case studies of non-DAC symbolic politics. The first concerns the discourse of South–South development cooperation, which is constructed as a set of horizontal peer relations built on respect for sovereignty, solidarity between (formerly) marginalized states, and the notion of mutual benefit, or 'win-win' relations. This section focuses on China and India especially, but takes in many of the Southern development partners. It uses anthropological and sociological theories of reciprocity to argue that the explicit language of return benefits for the Southern development partners should not be viewed as implying 'inferior' charity, but as constituting a different moral geography based on the virtue of projecting more equal social relations between states.[1]

The second example looks at the relationship between foreign aid and national identity. With reference to the work of Drazkiewicz (2007, 2011), we examine the contention that Poland's return to donor activities is symbolically deployed to bolster the sense of it being modern, European and Western. Poland's political boundary with its non-EU neighbours to the east is cognitively augmented by the symbolic boundary of donor to recipients. However, Poland is also striving to assert a specific identity within the changing world of foreign aid. The country's transition from socialism to capitalism, and from authoritarianism to democracy, is foregrounded in its discourses and imagery as a donor that is able to bring particular skills and insights to other nations. The third case study examines Venezuela's pursuit of political capital. Under Hugo Chávez, Venezuelan development cooperation has been discursively constructed as a tool of the 'Bolivarian Revolution' in Latin America. This openly oppositional foreign policy makes Venezuelan oil diplomacy welcomed by some and excoriated by others.

In different ways these three examples demonstrate the discursive and performative 'work' of foreign aid and development cooperation. They also emphasize the importance of historical and contemporary specificity – different states draw on some shared histories and principles, and may articulate rather similar discourses in some cases and contexts. But each country also mobilizes distinctive languages, experiences and identities – Poland is different to Hungary, India to China, Vietnam to Thailand. Before elucidating the three case studies, the next section outlines some of the relevant theoretical debates and interventions.

Theorizing the symbolic and discursive in Western foreign aid

A substantial and rich literature exists on the discursive construction and symbolic values and politics of Western (rather than DAC) aid. Some authors focus on macro-critiques of the global geographies of aid, including Hattori (2001, 2003), Kapoor (2008) and Silk (2004). All draw on gift theory, which is outlined below, as a way of examining the role of foreign aid in producing moral orderings of superior and inferior, donor and recipient. These and other authors also contribute to more micro-scale ethnographies of aid by examining local and trans-local practices in and across particular sites, relationships and contexts (e.g. Stirrat and Henkel 1997; Crewe and Harrison 1998; Mosse 2004; Eyben 2006b; Korf 2007; Korf et al. 2010; Gray 2011; Amar 2012). They examine different bilateral and multilateral donors, as well as NGOs and non-state actors, working in the context of humanitarian disasters and longer-term development. They analyse how the languages and practices of aid are culturally produced in ways that shape policies, relationships and outcomes. These literatures draw on and contribute to theorizing Orientalism (Said 1978), power and knowledge (Ferguson 1994), anthropological analyses of gift exchange (Mauss 1990), and long-standing intellectual and philosophical debates on virtue and ethics (e.g. Corbridge 1993, 1998; Silk 2004; Smith 2000; Chatterjee 2004; Lee and Smith 2004; Massey 2004; Barnett and Land 2007; Lawson 2007). This section briefly outlines some of the theoretical contributions towards understanding the symbolic value and discursive construc-tions of foreign aid.

The essence of Marcel Mauss's (1990) landmark essay, written in 1923, on 'the gift' is that the act of giving creates a social bond between giver and receiver. According to Mauss, there are three elements to this: giving (which establishes the social bond); receiving (because to refuse would not just be to renounce the gift, but also the social relationship); and reciprocating (to demonstrate in return one's own honour, wealth and standing). Critically, there is ambivalence in the performance of the gift – it must be offered as voluntary, disinterested and free, even as it sets an obligation at some future point to recipro-cate. If you give a friend a present you do not ask that person to pay you for it, or enquire as to when they intend to buy you something in return. However, you would both understand that in a social relation-ship between equals that reciprocity is expected, even though it is not stated: gifts are not 'free'. The gift economy therefore has a social function – the creation and tending of social relationships. Mauss distinguishes the gift from two other forms of resource allocation, although noting the relationships between them: economic exchange (commercial transactions) and redistribution (social or political en-titlements transferred from the ruler/state to subjects/populations). Among other examples, Mauss drew upon the cultures of the indig-enous peoples of the American Pacific Northwest coast, and especially the potlatch – festivals in which the central ritual was the provision of feasts that expressed and symbolized the redistribution of wealth. Leaders and clans demonstrated their status not by amassing wealth but by the extent to which they shared it, gave it away or even, in some spectacular cases, destroyed it. For Claude Lévi-Strauss (1987), Mauss's work represented a landmark for the discipline, launching anthropological understandings of reciprocity. Gift theory has since been extensively examined, applied and critiqued in a wide range of fields (e.g. Sahlins 1972; Bourdieu 1977, 1990; Parry 1986; Derrida 1992; Titmuss 1992; Godelier 1999; O'Neill 1999; Laidlaw 2000; Osteen 2002).

A number of authors have drawn explicitly upon these anthropological theories of reciprocity in analyses of official foreign aid from the North to the South, notably Tomohisa Hattori (2001, 2003). He observes that international relations theory generally provides three answers for what aid 'does'. Political realists see it as a tool of foreign policy; liberal internationalists see it as a means of promoting development in recipient countries within a networked international regime; and world systems theorists see it as a means of securing ongoing uneven capitalist accumulation. Hattori suggests that we also need to ask how aid is socially constituted: what it reveals about social relations between states. To make this case, Hattori follows Wendt and Duvall (1989) in proposing that 'the state' has an ontological reality – that it is not merely the sum of individual actions, and nor is it simply the product of a deeper structural logic that commits it to pure security or profit maximization. The interplay of states, Hattori argues, can be legitimately subjected to concepts that derive from anthropology and sociology, which are concerned with social relations.[2] States seek to project certain identities, and not just interests, within the field of international relations.

Hattori argues that the grant element of official foreign aid should be categorized as gift rather than economic exchange or redistribution.[3] But unlike gifts between equals – gifts exchanged as part of a reciprocal relationship – the gift of (Western) aid is one that is supposedly unreturned: foreign aid is exempt (or rather, appears to be exempt) from the obligation to reciprocate with something to the giver. Here Hattori turns to Marshall Sahlins (1972), who finesses Mauss's arguments with a greater attentiveness to power. One of his categories is 'un-reciprocated' or 'negative giving', which acts to *affirm* social hierarchy over time. Where the norms of reciprocity are indefinitely suspended, gift giving signals the creation and maintenance of relations of superiority and inferiority rather than the relative equality of gift *exchange*. Hattori argues that official foreign aid clearly exhibits the features of Sahlins's negative giving: it arises from a condition of significant material inequality between donor and receiver; it makes a (supposed) virtue of unreciprocated giving; and it can be understood, therefore, as a practice that both signals and euphemizes symbolic domination. This is important in thinking about Western public understandings of foreign aid, which is dominantly understood as 'charity' to the less fortunate (Saidi and Wolf 2011). It is important to reiterate here that the reality is very different, and indeed, that Western foreign aid is also justified with recourse to national self-interest. But the 'charitable' framework remains a hegemonic meta-narrative with powerful public and even professional purchase (see below).

Bourdieu (1977, 1990) amplifies gift theory by exploring the acquiescence of the recipient in their symbolic domination, proposing in some cases active complicity in maintaining an unequal social order. Persistent unreciprocated receiving allows social inequality to be naturalized as the 'normal order of things', in relation to gender, for example, and thus perpetuated. In the case of foreign aid, we can see this expressed materially and psychologically as aid dependency. This is a problem identified by commentators across the ideological spectrum (e.g. Sogge 2002; Easterly 2007; Glennie 2008; Tandon 2008; Moyo 2009). Recipient individuals, institutions and economic and political systems may come to rely on aid rather than other resources (salaries, taxation revenues, economic growth, etc.), as their compliance with the demands of the international aid regime is rewarded and/or as their attempts to assert more autonomy and independence are enervated or undermined. They then have an interest in maintaining the flow of aid, observing donor conditionalities, but also producing the performance expected of a needy and grateful recipient.

Hattori's analysis of post-1945 foreign aid through the lens of gift theory includes some discussion of the Soviet Union, but his focus is otherwise on the dominant Western donors. Interestingly he notes, although does not elaborate on the fact, that China and India are exceptional among the recipient countries in also being donors; to which in his 2003 paper he adds South Korea, Taiwan and oil-exporting Arab countries as countries that have also transitioned from recipients to donors. They still, however, remain outside of his analysis.

Ilan Kapoor (2008) also draws on gift theory together with post-colonial theories of nationalism and Lacanian psychoanalysis in his powerful critique of foreign aid. He demonstrates the disjuncture between Western constructions of foreign aid as free and generous, and the multiple ways in which it actually serves Western interests while extracting a price from its recipients, including through tied aid, loan repayments, conditionalities that assist overseas investors, military aid, and the support of foreign policy objectives. Kapoor also explores the ways in which Western aid works to produce a unified and virile sense of the generous nation. Foreign aid, he suggests, allows the visible display of apparent generosity (for example, through the creation of heroic figures like relief camp workers, the politicians visiting poor countries, the branded sacks of grain being dispensed, and so on), while negative impacts, self-interest and payback are obscured. Interestingly, Kapoor similarly observes the growing presence of a range of non-Western donors, including China, India, Egypt and Brazil, and spends some time analysing the way in which they are excluded from the 'clan-like' DAC. He argues that DAC's donor classification is 'selective and insular, effectively discriminating against non-Western and southern donors' (ibid.: 89). But although Kapoor draws attention to these non-Western donors, his focus is only on Occidentalist nationalism and foreign aid: the role of aid in constructing a moral ordering of the superior West and the inferior Southern recipients of its largesse. It is not clear where the Southern and indeed Eastern donors (rather than recipients) fit into this schema.

Other commentators have used gift theory to analyse foreign aid in more ethnographic ways, paying attention to the etiquettes and rituals of 'gifting' aid. For example, Da Silva (2008) describes the aid regime in East Timor as a 'total social fact' to capture the extraordinary penetration of (multiple) donor rules and values in all spheres of the Timorese financial, political and judicial systems. Da Silva (ibid.: 2) examines the ritual performances around donor gift giving, uncovering the ways in which different actors construct and enact identities and relations of 'honor, alliance and precedence'. Observing the annual Donor Partners meeting in East Timor, for example, she elucidates the remarkably stable ritualized etiquette through which each bilateral or multilateral in turn competes to stress its praise for 'the government' (in fact an edifice largely of their own creation), their identification of shortcomings, their generosity to date (echoing Stirrat's formulation of 'competitive humanitarianism': 2006), and their commitments to future donations. This 'donor potlatch' represents the 'condensed and expressive manifestations of this universe's symbolic repertoire and modes of functioning' (Da Silva 2008: 1). Congruent with Hattori's reading of Bourdieu, Da Silva (ibid.: 1) goes on to argue that: 'East Timor's biggest counter-gift to the international community has been to function as an instrument through which the values cherished by aid donors, expressed in Western myths of good society, can once again be cultivated in the process of building a new national state.' Its compliant recipient status allows the donors to pursue their material and geopolitical interests (for example, securing access to East Timorese land-based and marine resources), but to veil this under a symbolic regime of generosity and altruism. Da Silva also mentions a number of non-Western donors (Brazil, China, Malaysia and Thailand) operating as donors to East Timor, but does not comment on any similarities or differences with the mainstream DAC donors.

Theories concerning the symbolic power of foreign aid therefore provide rich and vital insights into the social relations constructed between official and private donors on the one hand, and poorer recipients on the other, whether states, communities or individuals (for the latter, see Korf 2007). But whether in terms of the macro-scale or more ethnographic analyses, commentators to date have focused overwhelmingly on the so-called 'traditional' donors – the DAC bilaterals, UN agencies, large NGOs and foundations, and the publics of richer, industrialized countries (Amar 2012 is an exception). During the 1990s, and especially with the advent of the Paris Agenda, the aid community increasingly used the language of 'partnership'. But Western public imaginaries remain heavily tied to the notion of aid as ethical, charitable giving (whether or not they agree with it: Darnton 2007; Xu 2011). In fact, as Rowlands (2008: 8) observes, even among Western aid professionals this 'moral' framing of official aid appears to be able to withstand a great deal of evidence to the contrary: 'Despite the consistent evidence that [Western] aid allocation tends to be dominated by ... political and strategic interests ... there remains within the development community as a whole a sense that the true objective and motivation of development is the moral one of assisting the less fortunate.'

In the next section we extend these ideas out to the Southern development actors by deconstructing the discursive claims of South–South development cooperation. Many of the Southern development actors are both explicit and adamant that they do not inhabit or replicate the hierarchical mindsets that characterize the dominant post-1945 official foreign aid regime, and that their relations are those of development partners rather than 'donors' towards 'recipients'. This claim to post-colonial solidarity with the 'South' and difference from the 'North' in the motivations and conduct of foreign aid is an issue of debate within the more usual realms of political economy and international relations (e.g. Grimm and Harmer 2005; Manning 2006; Kragelund 2008), but here we explore it from the standpoint of cultural analyses of foreign aid as gift.

The virtue of reciprocity: South–South development cooperation

As we have seen in previous chapters, just like the diverse members of the Western aid community, the Southern actors vary in their past and present development cooperation relations with different partners; the absolute and relative size of their contributions; their development cooperation institutions and modalities; their cultural repertoires and discourses of development assistance; their economic and political positioning within international and regional regimes; and in their histories and experiences of being aid recipients. Furthermore, Southern development actors are not unitary, but contingent and sometimes contradictory assemblages of different actors, institutions and interests, engaged in dynamic and differentiated relationships with their different partners (Mohan and Power 2008). Nonetheless, it is possible to identify some common aspects to their discursive positioning and performative embodiment of development cooperation. These are:

1 The assertion of a shared experience of colonial exploitation or suppression, post-colonial inequality and present vulnerability to uneven neoliberal globalization, and thus a shared identity as 'developing' nations.

2 Based on this shared identity, experience, historical ties, developing status and in some cases geographical and socio-economic commonalities, a specific expertise in appropriate development approaches and technologies.

3 An explicit rejection of hierarchical relations and a strong articulation of the principles of respect, sovereignty and non-interference.

4 An insistence on win-win outcomes of South–South development cooperation and mutual opportunity.

Gift theory opens up a productive means of examining the discursive claims of Southern development cooperation partners through its analytical concern with the symbolic politics and social relations constructed through reciprocity. Explicit in the characteristics outlined above is a view of the recipient country being an equal partner, able to offer counter-gifts in return. Leaders and politicians talk in terms of 'win-win' relations, with both countries benefiting from stronger trade, improved training, capacities and skills, improved infrastructure, diplomatic solidarity in international forums and so on. This symbolic regime is propagated through statements, speeches and declarations, and in the ritualized performances of respect and equality in various high-level meetings and forums. In contrast to the Western donors, for whom (apparent) charity constitutes the dominant symbolic and performative regime, in South–South development cooperation, recipient countries are constructed as sites of promise and opportunity. Table 5.1 outlines some of the contrasts in these symbolic regimes – although as the binary construction suggests, it must be understood as a heuristic device that sets out a highly generalized and simplified depiction of 'Western' and 'Southern' actors. For example, Japan has historically referred to its foreign aid as being managed for 'win-win' outcomes; while Arab donors could be argued to have a stronger 'charity' model (Saidi and Wolf 2011).

TABLE 5.1 The symbolic claims of Western donors and Southern development cooperation partners

Western donors	Southern development cooperation partners
Charity	Opportunity
Moral obligation to the unfortunate	Solidarity with other Third World countries
Expertise based on superior knowledge, institutions, science and technology	Expertise based on direct experience of pursuing development in poor-country circumstances
Sympathy for different and distant others	Empathy based on a shared identity and experience
The virtue of suspended obligation, a lack of reciprocation	The virtue of mutual benefit and recognition of reciprocity

How do the Southern development partners discursively assert and enact this symbolic regime? To start with, as we have seen, most resist the terminology of 'donor/recipient' and even that of 'foreign aid', contaminated as they are by dominant Western/DAC associations (Woods 2008). The Brazilian government talks in terms of 'horizontal cooperation' (Cabral and Weinstock 2010), while South Africa articulates its role as 'contributing to the African Renaissance', locating itself as an organic part of the greater whole to which it gives, but from which in turn it can expect benefits. Mutual opportunity and reciprocity are the themes that openly emerge in this language. China and India, for example, couch their development cooperation in terms of the benefits it brings to themselves as well as their recipients – drawing attention not just to what they give, but what they get in return. Senegal, Zambia, Ghana and others are not just the objects of charity or humanitarian compassion, but places that can redeem their honour and status by providing resources, investment opportunities and markets for China and India in return (Xu 2011).

Gift theory suggests that the social bond created through reciprocated relations is not that of inferiority that is naturalized over time by the endless cycles of (supposedly) 'free' aid, but that of equals. Many Western actors fail to comprehend the positive value attached to discourses of reciprocity. There is much evidence to suggest that countries that have for decades been humiliated by colonial exploitation and then by demeaning post-colonial foreign aid relations are appreciative of the social relationship this helps construct. Nel's (2010) analysis of 'what the emerging powers want' nicely complements the arguments made here. In a powerful paper, Nel suggests that as well as the long-standing demand for a more just redistribution of global wealth and decision-making power, the emerging powers also seek recognition – what Nel (ibid.: 1) calls 'the unfinished struggle against disrespect and humiliation'. His analysis endorses the value of being treated with respect and dignity within the international community of states – something, I suggest, that the language and performance of South–South development cooperation tends to foreground. To take just one example, Paulo and Reisen (2010: 539) quote the prime minister of Botswana: 'I find that the Chinese treat us as equals. The West treats us as former subjects.'

The language of South–South development cooperation is heavily inflected by the language and principles of the Non-Aligned Movement (NAM). Of course, the rhetoric of mutual self-respect can be easily dismissed as idealistic and naive, or simply mendacious, now as then. But it is noteworthy that this language has stood the test of time, even as the membership and functioning of the NAM, not to mention the geopolitical and economic contexts within which it has evolved, have changed enormously over the last sixty years. In any case, as Strauss (2009) reminds us, what matters here is not the distance between foreign policy rhetorics and foreign policy realities (the NAM countries or the G77 are hardly unique exemplars of this gap), but how such rhetorics serve as legitimizing devices, and in doing so, what they intend to signal and create.

China has perhaps done more than any other non-Western donor to set its development cooperation within a formally articulated set of foreign policy principles that insistently envision an alternative set of social relations between states. In 1963/64, Chinese premier Zhou En-lai made a significant tour of Africa. He announced eight principles of Chinese development cooperation (see Box 5.1). These have remained remarkably durable as stated principles of foreign policy engagement (Kondoh et al. 2010), and continue to infuse official Chinese statements, declarations and documents, including the historic release of the country's first White Paper on Foreign Aid in 2011. Regardless of actual underlying motivations and agendas or actions (and there are unquestionably discrepancies), what is key here is China's articulation of an alternative set of relations between sovereign states to those associated with colonial and post-colonial hegemonies and hierarchies between North and South. Specifically, the discourse of development cooperation is framed by claims to mutual benefit and solidarity rather than charity and 'aid'.

In her analysis of the legitimizing languages and practices deployed by China in its official relations with Africa, Julia Strauss (2009) exemplifies the arguments made here. Strauss observes the way in which a particular suite of historical events and relations (or, rather, sanitized and heroicized versions of them) have been elevated into a stable narrative that is repeatedly invoked in the opening rituals and ceremonies of official meetings. Intriguingly, this narrative includes idealized accounts of China's engagement with Africa during the Maoist era: what is striking, says Strauss (ibid.: 228), is the fact that within China itself the Maoist period is a subject to be avoided.

Box 5.1 Eight principles of Chinese development assistance

- China always bases itself on the principle of equality and mutual benefit in providing aid to other nations.
- China never attaches any conditions or asks for any privileges.
- China helps lighten the burden of recipient countries as much as possible.
- China aims at helping recipient countries to gradually achieve self-reliance and independent development.
- China strives to develop aid projects that require less investment but yield quicker results.
- China provides the best-quality equipment and materials of its own manufacture.
- In providing technical assistance, China shall see to it that the personnel of the recipient country fully master required techniques.
- The Chinese experts are not allowed to make any special demands or enjoy any special amenities.

In contrast, China's current official and semi-official statements and representations of China–Africa relations self-consciously and deliberately situate current Africa policies and initiatives in a distinguished lineage of principled relations, even when the actual links are at best tenuous and the substantive content radically transformed ... The PRC continues to trumpet its past 50-odd years of involvement in Africa as positive, progressive and grounded in the eternal and principled truths of non-interference, mutual benefit, unconditionality, and special friendship and understanding towards Africa.

Interestingly, then, although these claims to sturdy 'all-weather friendship', shared exploitation and ongoing unfairness consciously stand in contrast to the West's dominant rhetorical motifs (of an adult, superior West disciplining and leading the childlike Africa towards development and civilizational virtues), they share a certain projection of morality. Gallagher (2009) explores at length the way in which former British prime minister Tony Blair constructed 'Africa' as an apolitical space where good could conquer evil if 'we' cared enough to bring it about. Strauss's findings suggest that the Chinese also project on to Africa a certain purity of involvement, if with very different sets of cultural signifiers and constructions of virtue in their development cooperation activities.

India too repeatedly mobilizes a set of sanitized historical referents in its official pronouncements on development cooperation. In relation to Africa, for example, ministerial speeches will unswervingly start with the ancient trade ties of the Indian Ocean, move to shared colonial oppression, recall Gandhi's initiation into political and social activism in South Africa, and invoke Nehru's commitment to African independence and autonomy. In a visit to Mauritius in 2009, India's urbane UN representative, Sashi Tharoor, exemplified the content and tone of dozens of official speeches:

The India–Africa partnership has deep roots in history. Linked across the Indian Ocean, we have been neighbours and partners for thousands of years ... The advent of the Europeans and the colonial period disturbed these interactions but could not disrupt them. Later, both India and Africa shared the pain of subjugation and the joys of freedom and liberation. Satyagraha [truth force], non-violence and active opposition to injustice and discrimination were first used by Mahatma Gandhi on the continent of Africa ... Nehru was also a firm believer and practitioner of the principle of Afro-Asian solidarity.[4]

While all of this does indeed describe a part of Indo-African relations, more complex and contested histories (such as the role of South Asians as lower-level officials in the imperial machinery; Gandhi's sometimes problematic views of black Africans; Idi Amin's expulsion of Asians in 1973; and ongoing racial tensions and divides) are excised from these warm accounts of naturalized solidarity and shared identity. The performative work of these declarations is to symbolize difference from the West, respect for Southern partners, and the shared benefits of greater interaction, while obscuring more troublesome realities. Such rhetorics of friendship and equality are given expression in the ritualized performances that surround events like the India–Africa Summit (launched in 2008), as well as high-level meetings and delegations. The red carpet is literally rolled out, and every effort made to enact and convey respect, while underlining the dignity and sovereign presence of the partner nations.

China too makes good use of high-level events, notably the Forum on China–Africa Cooperation (FOCAC), which first met in 2000, and ministerial tours and meetings to promote images of respect, equality and honour. At the micro-scale too, its development assistance is conducted in ways that are often strikingly different from much Western aid work. As noted earlier, China's doctors, nurses, teachers, engineers and professionals generally live in the same circumstances and on the same salary levels as their partner country colleagues. The contrast with many Western development workers is captured in fiction by Somalian author Nurrudin Farah, in his novel entitled *Gifts*, discussed by Woods (2003). Ingrid, the Danish aid worker, is patronizing, arrogant and culturally ignorant. However, describing China's donation of the Benaadir Maternity Hospital to Somalia, Farah writes:

> The modesty of the Chinese as a donor government was truly exemplary. No pomp, no garlands of see-how-great-we-are … And you would meet the Chinese doctors, who came as part of the gift, as they did their rounds, soft of voice, short of breath when they spoke Somali, humble of gesture. Unlike the Italian and Dutch doctors on secondment from their governments as an overpriced package from the European Community, the Chinese did not own cars.

Finally, as we have seen in Chapter 4, the Southern development partners foreground claims to expertise based not on inherent culturally superior knowledge and institutions, but on their own domestic challenges and experiences, something that invokes long-standing discourses of 'mutual learning'. Brazil, for example, asserts its know-how in combating urban violence and youth gangs, literacy programmes, agricultural technologies, and HIV/AIDs awareness and prevention initiatives in slums (John de Sousa 2010). By making these assertions of subaltern expertise, and grounding development assistance in shared experiences and challenges, the Southern donors construct a position for themselves in the foreign aid arena distinct from those of the North.

The rhetoric and performance of South–South 'gift' giving in development cooperation flows is obviously meant to symbolize a particular set of social relationships: equal partners pursuing mutually beneficial interactions based on shared affinities, identities and experiences.[5] But if this is what the Southern development partners might be trying to signal, what then might such symbolic repertoires seek to obscure? I suggest there are three issues to explore here. First, as with all states, elite projections of national self-interest drive much of the decision-making about the provision of Southern development cooperation, including the choice of recipients and its nature and conduct. This is not necessarily a problem – indeed, it can easily be construed as a strength of South–South development relations. As Six (2009: 1109) argues:

> Precisely because China, India and other Southern donors act in an interest-oriented manner and, for historical reasons, cannot apply the same pseudo-emancipatory rhetoric as the Western development paradigm does, we should consider their rise as a unique chance for real progress towards serious partnership.

I agree with Six here, but while win-win relations are perfectly feasible under this dispensation, such mutually beneficial outcomes are not always the case. Southern development actors have prioritized their own interests and will continue to do so, even if these might conflict with those of their 'partner' countries. Whereas the West deploys a symbolic regime of charity and benevolence to obscure this truism, the Southern donors invoke the rhetoric of solidarity, mutual benefit and shared identities.

Moreover, assertions of win-win outcomes are founded on a simplistic construction of the 'national interest' of both partners, which obscures the contested and dislocating nature of 'development'. Building roads, developing raw materials and 'modernizing' agriculture will bring benefits to many, but they will also bring costs, particularly to indigenous peoples, small farmers, forest-reliant people and the poorest. For India and China especially, but also Brazil and South Africa, the vision of development is unabashedly modernist – economic growth equates with development. The uneven social and economic consequences of such modernization and economic growth are glossed over beneath a symbolic regime of striving nations seeking to contest inequalities and injustices within the international hierarchy of states (Nel 2010). The contested sub-national politics of development are concealed in this account of win-win relations and Third World solidarity (Prashad 2008). When China talks about 'respect for sovereignty', there is no acknowledgement that sovereign power may be contested from below, and that it by no means necessarily translates into an empowering relationship between a nation-state and its citizens. At the Seventh India–Africa Confederation of Indian Industries Conclave in Delhi in 2011, which was organized jointly with the EXIM Bank, I heard a number of plenary speakers declare that India had 'solved its own food security problems and could help African partners do the same'. There was no acknowledgement that while India's agricultural productivity ought to mean that no one goes hungry, the political economy of food is such in India that malnourishment and hunger remain widespread. Indeed, Sen (2011) points out that at over 40 per cent, India has the highest percentage of malnourished children of any country in the world. The *politics* of economic growth, poverty reduction and development – within and between Southern partners – are obscured within some of these confident South–South forums.

Second, the repetitive invocation of solidarity that arises from a shared colonial/post-colonial identity and common experience acts to diminish acknowledgement of the ever-widening differences within the global South. The emerging powers of the South have complex relationships with the poorer and smaller countries of the rest of the G77. As Kaplinsky and Messner (2008) document in the case of the Asian Drivers, the direct and indirect impacts of China and India's growing economic and political clout, as well as their changing industrial profiles, can be complementary to some sectors and interests in the rest of the global South. Their economic growth is raising the price of many resources and raw materials; they are providing more affordable goods and services for consumers; and their political clout is helping them to stand up to the traditional powers in various global forums. However, as we saw in Chapter 1, their interests can also clash. The major emerging powers do not and cannot automatically be assumed to represent the interests of the world's poorest countries.

Third, the Southern development actors are not immune to the aura that donor status confers. Among a complex mix of motivations and incentives it seems clear that like their Western counterparts (Kapoor

2008), Southern donors seek to augment a sense of 'national virility' through the gift elements of their development cooperation. In some cases this can be deployed in attempts to 'rebalance' the gift, to reciprocate in a way that restores national honour:

> After Hurricane Katrina ... Sri Lanka offered aid to the US. Even though it was only a small amount of money, this symbolic act was important for Sri Lanka to regain dignity and to escape from the status of a 'pure' recipient country, as a victim country. Now Sri Lanka had become a donor country. It also showed how Sri Lanka could feel compassionate to Westerners, being generous, within their capabilities, to the distant needy, but also able to rebalance the asymmetric relations that had developed after the tsunami, where Westerners were always donors and generous, and Asians were always recipients and forced to be grateful. (Korf 2007: 370–1)

However, in other cases, South–South development cooperation reinforces the social hierarchies that it purports to reject. For example, a number of commentators have noted India's susceptibility to locating its growing role as a development partner, and its decision in 2003 to ask most of its own donors to exit the country, in a sometimes aggrandizing narrative of increasing global status. While many welcome the adjustment that Western powers will have to make in response to the emergence of a more multilateral world, smaller nations may be less enthused about the rise of regional hegemons. Nepal, which has received aid from India since the early 1950s, has often experienced it as an overbearing and interfering neighbour. Development cooperation personnel are quite as capable as any Westerner of assuming and constructing Nepalese inferiority (Mihaly 1965; Paudel, personal communication, 2012). Kondoh et al. (2010: 36) argue that:

> Official Indian sources confirm that these South–South Cooperation principles continue to guide Indian aid. However this cannot be accepted unreservedly as a comprehensive description of India's aid characteristics. Firstly, a quite different aid policy, rather like an Indian version of the Monroe Doctrine, is pursued by India where neighbouring countries of strategic importance – for example, Bhutan and Nepal – are concerned. Here, India both overtly and covertly flexes its economic and military muscle to intervene in domestic affairs, and massive aid has been given over long periods in blatant pursuit of India's national interests.

DN (2003) argues that India needs to be aware that it is opening itself up to the same criticisms it has often directed at its own major donors in the past. Although the rhetoric may appear to avoid the inequalities and humiliations that accompany the unreciprocated gift, the Southern donors may not always avoid the association of aid-giving with superiority. Chanana (2009: 13) notes the symbolic value of India's donor activities, as well as the material interests that can be pursued through development cooperation: '[i]f anything is new [in India's development cooperation profile] it is the hope that through aid India can gain recognition as a world power and advance certain strategic interests'. With the same caveats about the highly generalized nature of these binary categories, Table 5.2 presents a simplified picture of what 'Western' and 'Southern' actors seek to mask in their symbolic and performative narratives.

TABLE 5.2 What the symbolic regimes of Western donors and Southern development cooperation obscure

Western donors	Southern development cooperation partners
Commercial and geopolitical self-interest	Commercial and geopolitical self-interest
Sectoral and class interests within and across domestic and international realms; alternative and competing notions of 'development' (as goal and process)	Sectoral and class interests within and across domestic and international realms; alternative and competing notions of 'development' (as goal and process)
National virility and superiority; cultural and racial hierarchies	National virility and superiority; cultural and racial hierarchies
Differences and divisions between dominant bilaterals; non-compliance with DAC guidelines	Differences and divisions within the G77

The danger with these binaries is of course that they overly homogenize and separate Western donors and Southern development cooperation partners, whereas throughout this book I have suggested that these divides are often artificial ones. Western donors also talk about 'partners' rather than recipients (increasingly so); and many Western politicians and policy-makers seek to legitimize foreign aid to their citizens and parliamentarians by reference to the economic, political and security benefits it brings to them as donors (e.g. the 2002 United States National Security Strategy). Moreover, the precise cultural, historical and socio-political contexts for all donors vary, and with them, the symbolic registers and resources upon which they draw, or which they seek to project. Nordtveit's (2011) analysis of Chinese educational aid to Cameroon both endorses the argument made here and helps nuance it. He reports that many Cameroonian officials felt that the relationship with China was more honest as it was quite clear that they wanted something back in return for their development cooperation. Nordtveit quotes a senior adviser to the PM, showing, in this case, some ambivalence about the Chinese expectations, while distinguishing between two different Western donors.

> Norway let us steer towards the areas of intervention that we felt were appropriate and needed in Cameroon. France would never have let us steer the process. ... China, on the other hand, is more calculating. China would like to give you something, but they would like something in return. The Norwegian cooperation is generous. Psychologically the difference between the two styles is very important. China has good intentions, but wants something in return. France would like to be generous, but there's a background of a debt to repay, of a re-compensation for something. The relation is like an adult towards a child. (Ibid.: 106)

Although there are many contradictions and tensions within these discourses, they can provide a meta-narrative around national identity that is genuinely meaningful to citizens and officials. Just as Rowlands (2008) observes that the notion of the morality and charitable nature of aid runs deep within the Western psyche, I would suggest that the discursive construction of Southern development assistance as being based on solidarity and mutual respect has a genuine and meaningful hold on Southern imaginaries. In some recent research into domestic perceptions of India's development cooperation, for example, I found a powerful construction of India as a virtuous actor in global politics, which is contrasted not just to the West, but to negative constructions of China in particular (Mawdsley 2011). Susan Bayly also notes the ways in which the historical ties and projected virtues of the socialist ecumene are being rearticulated in contemporary globalizing Vietnam:

> I have been struck by the adoption of an idiom of socialist neo-tradition in official representations of Vietnam's present-day pursuit of overseas trade and investment opportunities. What has been said since the early 2000s in official media accounts of these initiatives is that Vietnam's quest for export markets in a host of 'liberalising' African economies is not a pursuit of narrow economic gain or 'interest'

(*loi ich*). On the contrary, say the ministries' media spokesmen, these efforts are wholly consistent with the country's heritage as a socialist provider and maker of 'traditional friendships' (*quan he huu nghi truyen thong*) through the imparting of aid and tutelage to the continent's 'needy' postcolonies. (Bayly 2007: 226–7: see also Bayly 2009)

In large part the dominant international relations and popular analysis of the motivations, impacts and outcomes of Southern aid and development cooperation tend to quickly dismiss the language of equality, seeing in it only a strategic or even hypocritical gloss over the material realities at play. The analysis set out here suggests that the symbolic regime around SSDC is a great deal more important than it is sometimes given credit for. The disjuncture between rhetorics and rituals on the one hand, and the complex and messy realities of engagement on the other, is evident. But gift theory suggests that the discourses and performance of mutual development cooperation are constitutive of meaningful social relations between states. While ambiguous, contested and contradictory, they help create and maintain a particular set of social identities in South–South relations. They ease some of the contradictions, point to aspirations, and reveal the extent to which some Southern donors and recipients seek to reject the humiliations and impositions of Western aid. Interestingly, as we shall see in the next section, the theoretical challenges to the construction of Orientalist hierarchies can also be deployed in more critical accounts of East–West geographies.

Being Western, looking east and south: Poland

During the socialist period, Poland was one of the CEE countries that provided development assistance to socialist and friendly regimes throughout the world, mainly in the form of technical assistance, commercial credits and educational scholarships. Grimm and Harmer (2005) observe that this was managed by the state government in accordance with the Cold War priorities of the Soviet Union. Like those of other socialist countries, the Polish government declared its solidarity with Third World countries, and supported efforts like the NIEO, which in theory aimed at a more just world order (Lawson 1980; Baginski 2007). Socialist Poland also supported the calls for increases in development aid, but emphasized that the primary responsibility for Third World poverty lay with the former colonial powers. However, with the fall of the Soviet Union in 1991 and the sharp economic contraction that followed as Russia and the CEE states were exposed to IMF-imposed 'shock therapy' (Stiglitz 2002), Polish development cooperation evaporated. Indeed, during the 1990s, Russia and the CEE states found themselves the objects of the Western development gaze, and the recipients of official foreign aid and private assistance (Wedel 2001). Like other CEE states, Poland received significant financial and technical assistance in pursuit of transition – between 1990 and 1996 foreign aid flows to Poland constituted on average 1.5 per cent of GDP annually (Drodz 2007). However, by the late 1990s and the new millennium Poland had started to re-engage with foreign aid as a donor.

The return to aid donorship was driven by several factors, including the need to comply with the EU *acquis* and related global development accords and agreements described in Chapter 2. But as Baginski (2007) and others suggest, this was not merely an instrumental decision intended to help advance Poland's candidacy for EU membership. Two other rationales also played a role. The first was strategic and commercial interests of the sort that have been discussed elsewhere in this book. The 'Strategy for Polish development cooperation' released in 2003 stated:

> Development co-operation ... serves to achieve the basic goals of Polish foreign policy ... The security of Poland will be served by prevention of potential conflict-prone tensions between North and South, its economic interests will benefit from greater involvement of developing countries and those undergoing transformations in the world economy, including trade and investment co-operation with our country ... Dissemination of positive knowledge about Poland will indirectly facilitate various forms of cultural, scientific and technological cooperation, as well as increased exchange of people. (Ministry of Foreign Affairs 2003: 5–6)

The second rationale can be understood as primarily symbolic, and here we draw on Drazkiewicz (2007, 2011), who offers an extended anthropological analysis of Poland's re-engagement with development and foreign aid. Drazkiewicz examines the relationship between constructed geographies of territory, modernity and the hierarchy of nations. Poland is a classic borderland, which throughout its modern history has been cognitively and politically situated in liminal spaces. In some cases this status is proudly asserted, such as Poland's role as the historic defender of Christian Europe in the seventeenth century, securing it against the expansion of Islam and Asia. More recently, of course, Poland was positioned in the western zone of the Soviet sphere of influence, and it now marks part of the eastern boundary of the European Union. Drazkiewicz argues that since 1991 Poland has sought assiduously to bolster its 'natural' identity as a Western state, and suggests that engaging in official development constitutes a particularly powerful means of expressing this rightful place within the 'core'. She draws on theorists like Escobar (1995, 2004), Comaroff and Comaroff (1993) and Ferguson (1994), who deconstruct the colonial and post-colonial ordering of the world through the hierarchies of development and modernity. Like Kapoor (2008), Drazkiewicz suggests that there are few tropes more powerful than the notion of 'who does development to whom', and where that situates states within the global or regional hierarchy of nations. Within hegemonic Eurocentric development theories, 'proper' modernity is that achieved by the West, and imitated (inevitably imperfectly) by the Rest. In the case of Poland, internal anxieties, tensions and feelings of failure to become properly modern and Western are, she suggests, assuaged through the symbolic identity provided by being a donor of foreign aid – of bringing modernity to others. Drazkiewicz argues that we need to understand Poland's internal psychological longings and its territorial imagination in order to reflect on its projection as a donor. The desire to be recognized as an advanced, cosmopolitan and globalized country and culture is openly articulated in the 2003 strategy document:

> The provision of aid will have the important effect of promoting Poland among the opinion-makers of recipient countries as a state open to co-operation, dynamic economically, politically stable, culturally interesting and possessing rich human resources. (Ministry of Foreign Affairs 2003: 5)

Drazkiewicz suggests that the harnessing of a donor identity to the claim to modernity also explains why there is such strong support among the Polish leadership and public for directing their development cooperation east rather than south. Materialist explanations (trade, regional integration, security and so on) are only one part of the answer for this orientation. Drazkiewicz argues that the spatial categories of 'eastern', 'Central' and 'Western Europe' carry social meaning and power that have significant influence in Polish imaginaries of its place within a global hierarchy of value. Poland's development cooperation 'thickens' the boundary to the east, with the territorial edge of the European Union also marking the disjuncture between donor and recipient. The sense of Poland's natural place with other Western nations is enhanced.

In a classic manoeuvre of constructing Self and Other, Poland has further sought to claim its place as a 'Western' (modern, civilized) country, by projecting an Orientalist imagery of Russia as primitive, still mired in socialist attitudes, dangerous, aggressive, drunken and barbaric (although see Gray 2011, discussed below). It becomes Poland's responsibility to assist its eastern neighbours to assert their independence from Russia by promoting democratization and the growth of civil society in Ukraine, Belarus, Moldova, and even the Central Asian republics. These qualities are particularly meaningful for Poland, given the central role played by Solidarity in winning freedom from the Soviet Union, and the Western focus on creating and encouraging Polish civil society in the 1990s.

Drazkiewicz suggests that this geographical imaginary is supported by an interrupted history in which Polish development accounts and discourses actively redact its socialist era development relations, ideologies and identity. The 1990s were a period of 'shock therapy' during which Poland, encouraged by the West generally and the EU in particular, aimed at drawing a thick line under an aberrant socialist past. The aim was complete transformation, assisted by Western aid and modernization programmes, and subordinated to (internalized) Western ideas, plans, policies, knowledge and practices (Wedel 2001). Drazkiewicz talks about Poland's pursuit of a 'modernity project' entailing the rejection and suppression of the recent past: 'history from zero', as she puts it. She interviewed many academics, policy-makers and NGO personnel working in development, and found that all of them asserted a complete detachment from socialist experiences of development cooperation: it was as if it had never existed. For this reason, she suggests, Polish aid has been positioned as entirely new, and, unlike the Southern donors discussed above, Poland does not invoke its socialist genealogies. However, Drazkiewicz (personal communication, 2012) does suggest that Poland's involvement to the east is backed by 'nationalistic nostalgias, and Polish memories of the pre-war Polish state which included western parts of Ukraine and Belarus. Contemporary interest in this region in a way is linked to the Polish past as a colonizer of this region, and is a way of exercising the dream of the great (lost or perhaps future) Poland.'

A different example, but one that shares some features of the arguments made here, is provided by Russia. Gray (2011) sets out a fascinating and rich analysis of Russia's formal return as a foreign aid donor in 2007. Like Drazkiewicz, she examines how foreign aid is deployed as a cultural claim to developed status, here particularly pegged to Russia's membership of the G8, arguing that the symbolic identity of a donor is at least as important as any material or strategic benefits that would be the focus of realist international relations theorists. She too looks at the geographical imaginaries of North and South, East and West, and the ways in which embracing a donor identity can transgress, restructure and consolidate these problematic binaries. Interestingly, given the observations made in the previous section on China's projection of virtue on to its engagement with Africa, Gray (ibid.: 8) observes a similar process in Russia, and suggests that:

> It appears that for all states aspiring to be leaders in the world and wishing to join an elite peer group of donors ... Africa is the arena where they can demonstrate their power and privilege by rendering aid to those presumed to be perpetually powerless and underprivileged. Donors need recipients in order to be donors – in order to get to give – and Africa remains the world's most iconic perpetual recipient.

Russia sits at an interesting historical and contemporary confluence of geography and identity. Collins (personal communication, 2012) observed that at the Fourth High Level Forum on Aid Effectiveness in 2011, Russia actively distanced itself from the other BRICs, downplaying this identity in favour of identification with the traditional Western donors in its emerging aid activities. That said, in a salutary reminder of the gap between rhetorics and realities, Jordan (2010) suggests that Russia failed to push the G8 to keep its development commitments to Africa during its period as chair in 2006. Russia also provided arms to the Sudanese government despite sanctions, and has supported other authoritarian regimes, such as Syria. Russia's aid discourses and claims sit somewhat at odds with other foreign policy positions and alliances – a disjuncture that is not unusual or unexpected for any donor, but which reveals competing agendas and identities within and between different ministries, as well as within the political establishment (Gray, personal communication, 2012).

Contesting hegemony: Venezuela

In this last section we will look at Venezuela, a controversial development partner that has a particularly strong interest in making political capital out of development cooperation. Venezuela is the only major non-DAC donor to articulate an explicit critique of the West's promotion of neoliberal globalization, and specifically the economic and political interference of the United States in Latin America. Under Hugo Chávez aid has become a significant plank in Venezuela's foreign policy in Latin America and beyond, and is symbolically and materially positioned quite transparently as a means by which Venezuela wishes to assist other countries to reject US hegemony. This has caused fury within many circles in the USA and elsewhere, and the country was listed as a prime 'rogue donor' in Naím's (2007) provocative article (see also Collins 2007).[6] Corrales (2008: 3) provides a critical assessment in a report to the US House Committee on Foreign Affairs, but one that recognizes the way in which political capital is being created through foreign aid:

> The real challenge that Venezuela poses to the United States has less to do with aggressive actions that Venezuela could take against the United States, but rather, something else in Venezuela's arsenal: the use of generous handouts in its foreign policy, peppered with a pro-poor, distributionist discourse. Let's call this weapon: 'social power'. In the United States we are used to discussing the requirements of 'hard power' (military and economic might), even 'soft power' (the spread of appealing ideas and values), but less time discussing the requirements of social power – either as something to project or contain ... As a foreign policy tool, social power is a spectacularly effective way for world leaders to earn allies, even admirers abroad ... The result could be the meaner rogue states masquerading as international humanitarians.

The enabling factor behind Venezuela's aid programmes is its vast natural resource wealth, and most importantly its oil reserves. Venezuela is a founding member of OPEC, and like a number of the Arab OPEC countries, first became an official aid donor in the early 1970s. According to a 1990 Country Study for the US Library of Congress,[7] between 1974 and 1981 it contributed a reported $7.3 billion to international development, 64 per cent of which went to multilateral organizations, including the United Nations Special Fund, the Andean Reserve Fund, the OPEC Fund, the Central American Bank for Integration and the Caribbean Development Bank. Like other OPEC donors at the time, Venezuela was also generous in relative income terms, averaging 1.88 per cent of GNI, a figure well above that of Western nations at the time. However, over the 1980s and 1990s economic contraction in Latin America and falling oil prices led to a decline in the desire or ability to allocate resources to foreign aid. Indeed, in this period Venezuela had to seek funds from the IMF and the World Bank, which were accompanied by the demands of structural adjustment.

In 1999 the populist leader Hugo Chávez was elected president, receiving the vast bulk of his support from the poor, indigenous, coloured and the otherwise marginalized. Historically, Venezuela has been a deeply divided society, with discrimination persisting well beyond the formal end of colonial rule. For many commentators, marginal gains that were made in equality and justice in the 1950s and 1960s were reversed during the 1980s and 1990s. From 1970 to 1998 per capita income fell by 35 per cent (a fall unevenly distributed between poor and rich), an economic decline that was even worse than that experienced by many African countries in this period. Chávez promised a radical new agenda of progressive growth, which he termed a 'Bolivarian revolution'. Policies have included the renationalization of oil production, higher taxes for the rich, and much greater social spending on the poor. These measures have strong support among the poor majority, but are loathed by Venezuela's elite and many observers in Washington. However, even sympathetic commentators express reservations about other elements of Chávez's leadership, notably his authoritarian inclinations.

Under Chávez, the Venezuelan government reinstated foreign aid on a very substantial scale. Based on a review of public pledges, Pearson (2006) estimates that over eighteen months during 2005/06, Venezuela promised some $1.1 billion in loans, donations and financial aid, while the US State Department estimated $3.3 billion in financial and development aid. Chahoud (2008) suggests that Venezuelan assistance amounts to 0.7 per cent of GNI – putting it at the top end of the generosity index. As always, though, we should be wary of the definitions used here, and the blurred line between aid and various forms of concessional finance and private sector investment. Nonetheless, Venezuela has supported hospitals, airport runways, studentships, oil and energy infrastructure, housing, road building, social programmes and much more.

Three features of Venezuela's development cooperation are particularly relevant to this discussion. First, as noted above, is the sheer scale of resources disbursed in aid, other concessional loans and investment. For example, Venezuela offered $2.5 billion to Argentina in 2005 when Argentina decided to pay off its remaining $9.8 billion debt to the IMF (no less than 5.4 per cent of its GDP). Kirchner, the Argentinian president, was clear about the reasons for throwing off the IMF, which he said 'acted towards our country as a promoter and vehicle of policies that caused poverty and pain among the Argentinean people' (quoted in Weisbrot 2006). The second significant feature is Chávez's direct challenge to the USA and to the Western-dominated instruments of global organization, notably the IMF and the World Bank. In 2006, Venezuela campaigned for one of the rotating seats

Box 5.2 The San José Accord

In 1980, Venezuela and Mexico, the two largest oil producers in Latin America, signed the San José Accord. Described as a joint foreign aid programme, it constitutes a commitment to supply affordable oil to some of the region's poorest states: Barbados, Belize, Costa Rica, Cuba, the Dominican Republic, El Salvador, Guatemala, Haiti, Honduras, Jamaica, Nicaragua and Peru. In the past it was claimed that this was an entirely apolitical programme, and indeed, even when Cuban–Mexican relations were under severe strain in 2004 (to the extent that ambassadors were recalled), the San José Accord was honoured. However, in 2009 Mexican officials were reported to be highly annoyed by Chávez's positioning of the programme as a part of the ideological campaign against the USA. The Mexican officials insisted that the San José Accord should be seen as a non-political form of assistance for the poorer countries of the region. Hugo Chávez was explicitly enrolling the San José Accord in his wider agenda of regional autonomy and the promotion of the 'Bolivarian revolution'. Chávez is reported to have said in a radio broadcast, 'We must use oil as a weapon to fight American imperialism ... it can help finance socialism for us and our neighbours' (quoted in Nevaer 2007). The Mexican government appears to be increasingly concerned by the anti-American political agenda that is being attached to this long-standing programme, especially given the very biased reporting on Cuba and Venezuela that is characteristic of certain popular sections of the US media (Shah 2006).

on the UN Security Council, leading to frantic US efforts to prevent this. In the run-up to voting on the Security Council membership, the Dominican Republic's foreign minister is quoted as acknowledging that Venezuelan aid 'cannot go unnoticed' as a factor in the decision to support Venezuela's candidacy (Pearson 2006). Venezuela was supported by China, Russia and a number of Latin American and other countries, and made no bones about the fact that if elected it would be a voice for Third World solidarity and justice (in the end, US-supported Costa Rica took the position). Together with China and Saudi Arabia,

Venezuela is the only non-DAC donor that has the scale of resources to potentially allow an 'exit option' from Western-led conditionalities and governance demands. But unlike the Chinese leadership, which is mostly at pains to smooth over or minimize the perception of a 'revisionist' challenge, Chávez takes evident pleasure in goading the US leadership. He has even attempted to redefine the long-standing San José Accord in an anti-US light (see Box 5.2).

The third salient feature of Venezuelan foreign aid is the clear intent to deploy such aid to influence the domestic politics of other nations, leading to sharp criticism from opponents and detractors, but even from some more sympathetically inclined. This interference stretches back to before Chávez – the Venezuelan government supported the Sandinista National Liberation Front against the Somoza dictatorship in Nicaragua in the late 1970s, for example, and helped fund the (successful) opposition Nicaraguan party in the 1990 elections. One of the characteristic claims of South–South development cooperation is non-interference. However, Chávez's commitment to forging a Latin American Bolivarian revolution means a different stance for Venezuela's foreign aid.

Conclusion

Foreign aid is usually theorized and critiqued from a materialist standpoint within international relations, development studies, political science and geography. This chapter has attempted to draw on constructivist IR theory and ethnographies of foreign aid to examine the alternative norms, rhetorics and rituals of non-DAC identities and relations. It argues that these discourses and performances should not be seen as simply masking or supporting the 'real' geopolitical and commercial strategies that motivate them as donors, but are essential to understanding the social relations they seek to create and those they seek to obscure in their constructions of themselves and their partners. Some non-DAC development partners also seek to project and enact 'moral' stances and engagements, if with different constructions of what might comprise 'virtue'. This is not to suggest that any non-DAC development partner is more or less altruistic or virtuous than any DAC partner – that would be too simplistic. A complex array of rhetorics, realpolitiks and intended and unintended outcomes is characteristic of all donor/recipient/partner relations. Extending aid ethnographies and constructivist understandings of norm creation to the non-DAC partners provides rich insights into the multiple scales, sites and meanings of foreign aid and development cooperation.

6 | Institutional overtures, challenges and changes: changing development governance

Introduction

Global governance regimes aim to regulate nuclear safety, intellectual property rights, trade, the law of the sea, air communications conventions and many other areas of multilateral cooperation, including foreign aid. Global governance regimes are multi-sited and multi-scaled; they enrol state and non-state actors; they are historically shaped in ways that tend to reflect past rather than present power structures; and they are invariably subject to ongoing negotiation and contest. They are also subject to different forms of monitoring and policing. At the 'harder' end are international laws and courts (which may or may not be recognized by particular states), but more frequently 'soft law' works primarily through institutional membership, agreements and conventions that rely on social pressures to encourage states to conform to 'global' expectations. Liberal internationalists see a vital role for global governance. As Boughton and Bradford (2007: 11) put it:

> The ideal of global governance is a process of cooperative leadership that brings together national governments, multilateral public agencies, and civil society, to achieve commonly accepted goals. It provides strategic direction and then marshals collective energies to address global challenges.

However, this is very much an ideal, and Boughton and Bradford (ibid.) go on to argue that the global architecture of the twentieth century is dangerously inadequate given current challenges. Leipziger (2011: 27) suggests that:

> [A] reasonable assessment of the multilateral situation is that we are experiencing a surfeit of negative externalities and a paucity of global solutions. New problems are becoming more severe and older institutions are not adapting sufficiently to cope with them. Hence, we are entering a period of major new challenges to globalization.

Different elements of the global governance system work with varying degrees of effectiveness, consensus and consent, but one systemic feature is the dominance of the industrialized nations. The institutions and normative regimes that shape global governance emerged largely in the context of colonial and post-colonial Western hegemony, and reflect these inequalities in the distribution of economic, political and military power. To take just one example, the permanent membership of the UN Security Council – an especially powerful and prestigious UN body – hasn't changed for six decades. It continues to reflect a dispensation of power that held in the 1940s rather than that of the new millennium (Reisen 2010). Global governance regimes and structures also tend to project 'Western' values and agendas, such as human rights conventions and democracy, as 'universal'.[1]

The more powerful nations exert hard and soft power over formal and informal agenda-setting, dominant norms, and the uneven implementation of global governance regimes; while the majority low- and middle-income countries have historically had far less influence in shaping the (so-called) 'international community'. That said, Alden et al. (2010) persuasively argue that the global South has not been powerless within international relations, uncovering the ways in which such states have been able to shape global norms and conventions over the last fifty or so years. Third World agency within international relations is therefore not entirely novel, but the new millennium is starting to reflect a qualitative shift in the growing voice and influence of the poorer and middle-income nations, led by Southern emerging powers. Other regions and states are also pushing particular agendas and interests into 'mainstream' institutions. The CEE states, for example, are individually and together promoting some shifts in EU norms and priorities (Lightfoot 2010). Although highly differentiated in power and interests, the growing economic weight and prowess of the emerging powers are underpinning a new assertiveness in many global forums and institutions, including in relation to trade, climate change negotiations and so on.

In this chapter we examine foreign aid and development cooperation governance. The arena is a messy one, with multiple actors and agendas, interactions and outcomes. We start by charting in a little more detail the nature of contemporary global development governance, highlighting concerns about credibility, legitimacy and incentives. The chapter then outlines the arguments for greater cooperation that are being articulated by many within the mainstream development community. Drawing partly on Woods (2011), we parse out the spectrum of potential relationships, from isolation to coordination to cooperation to co-option. This provides the foundation for the next section of the chapter, which addresses four institutional assemblages that comprise key sites of contestation and change in relation to global development governance (Killen and Rogerson 2010). These are the IMF and the World Bank; the OECD-DAC; the Working Party on Aid Effectiveness; and the UN Development Cooperation Forum (DCF). This section also engages with the emergence of the G20, and briefly raises the roles of regional institutions and banks, and two newly emerging alliances or platforms for dialogue and cooperation between key emerging powers, IBSA (India, Brazil, South Africa) and the BRIC Forum (Brazil, Russia, India, China).

The penultimate section examines trilateral development cooperation (TDC), a relatively new form of development partnership between 'traditional' and 'emerging' donors. TDC is one response to the rise of the (re-)emerging development partners, and it offers some insight into the changing development arena, and the new relationships, discourses and geographies of development that are being forged in the new millennium. The final section shifts scale to examine what institutional changes and shifts might be happening within recipient countries. How are the donor networks and institutions within specific countries responding to the rise of the non-DAC development partners? The example of the Kenya Joint Assistance Strategy (KJAS) offers a glimpse into how and in what ways the international initiatives and changes with regard to the non-DAC development partners do or don't 'trickle down'.

The nature and purpose of global development governance

The actors that make up the institutional nodes of global development governance are extraordinarily numerous and diverse. As well as the very major players – the World Bank, the OECD-DAC, the EU and so on – there are dozens of regional and international multilateral organizations, bilateral development agencies and major non-state actors that are big enough to bring significant lobbying pressure to bear on official systems. A wide array of other development actors aim at projecting their presence and leadership in the international arena, vying for funding, roles and voices within the system. While some constitute key nodes of power within the system, none is hegemonic, and the global development governance system has no apex body.

As Paulo and Reisen (2010) demonstrate, within this complex institutional assemblage there are actually very few hard laws or even formalized regulations. The vast majority of mainstream development is governed by tacit agreements and acquiescence to informal codes and working practices based on a normative framework designed by richer, industrialized countries (see also Bräutigam 2010). Some more simplistic analyses appear to assume a clear and coherent set of 'mainstream' rules and practices, towards which different non-DAC development actors are supportive, indifferent or undermining. The reality is more nuanced: the mainstream is characterized by soft laws, institutional complexity and diversity (and considerable non-compliance), making for a 'fuzzy arena' against which to compare the positioning of different (re-)emerging development partners. Moreover, they are not singular actors, of course – India is a member of donor coordination groups in Afghanistan and Nepal, whereas in most African countries it does not engage with other donors, and in some cases actively asserts its rejection of dominant ideologies and practices. Paulo and Reisen (2010) suggest that the Western construction of aid and development norms and rules, and ongoing domination of the global institutions, means that many non-DAC development partners are deterred from (or actively critical of) greater coordination and cooperation efforts. However, they also observe that these soft laws may be amenable to shifts which help synthesize 'traditional' and 'new' approaches, and therefore to the negotiated emergence of shared minimum standards and agreement over the nature of co-responsibility between otherwise rather different donors.

Three aspects of global development governance are central to this discussion: credibility, legitimacy and incentive. The credibility deficit proceeds from the failures of mainstream foreign aid, evident in enduring poverty and weak economic growth in many parts of the world. Despite billions of foreign aid dollars, vast numbers of people live in dire need of the basic elements of a dignified life. The reforms of the last decade or so have attempted to address developmental and aid deficiencies, but as discussed in earlier chapters the evidence suggests the new paradigm has achieved only partial success. The (re-)emerging development partners may reasonably ask why they should join forces with what appears to be a rather ineffective set of institutions and practices if they want to contribute to global poverty reduction and economic growth (Bräutigam 2010; Chandy and Kharas 2011).

The second issue is legitimacy: who speaks for whom in international development? The OECD-DAC is made up of industrialized countries, which with the exception of Japan and only very recently South Korea are all Western. Perhaps as important as its geographical parochialism is the fact that it is made up only of donors – and yet the ideologies and policies of its members have their greatest impacts in recipient countries. The various United Nations agencies are in theory more democratic, being subject to the oversight and management of all members. However, in practice they are often dominated by the rich nations that can afford to fund them, and which then have greater power over priorities, practices and ideologies. The personnel of multilateral institutions like the World Bank may be drawn from all around the world, but many elite non-Westerners have been educated in Western universities or employed in 'global' companies, and bring with them hegemonic orthodoxies and understandings (Wade 1996). Institutions tend to change slowly and reluctantly – even with a greater non-DAC presence the foreign aid architecture is likely to reflect dominant Western agendas and assumptions for a long time to come. As we will see later in this chapter, many global development governance actors are embarking upon much greater 'outreach' to the (re-)emerging development partners, including through dialogue in new forums, and by opening up previously monopolized spaces and conversations. Others are changing their voting systems and executive boards to reflect the inputs and demands for a stronger voice coming from the emerging powers. The 'traditional' states and institutions *must* now accommodate to the force of the rising powers, and often use a language of welcome, partnership and opportunity (Woods 2010; Mitchell 2011). But many non-DAC partners feel that for the most part these reforms still lag behind the realities of the changing balance of power (Davies 2008), and some may well feel that they will have greater voice and influence in new forums and institutions rather than the slowly reforming older ones.

Finally there is the question of incentives. What would induce a (re-)emerging development partner to move closer to the mainstream, for example by drawing closer to the DAC, agreeing to emerging transparency initiatives, or buying into the attempts to reforge a global aid architecture based on common but differentiated responsibilities and principles? The CEE states are clearly under specific conditions of pressure and reward – their membership of the EU is dependent upon their compliance with EU standards and practices, including mainstream foreign aid practices and principles (although there is still considerable room for manoeuvre and non-observance: Lightfoot 2010). Turkey and other potential accession states are also seeking to move closer to the EU in their foreign aid and development cooperation processes and practices to demonstrate their willingness and ability to meet the *acquis communautaire*. The current Turkish government is also keen to pursue a closer strategic relationship with the USA, incentivizing aid strategies that reflect this aim. Thailand is notable for a strategy of cooperation and engagement with the 'traditional' powers in its own transition from recipient to donor (Kondoh et al. 2010), while Fues (2011: 10) reports that:

> Indonesia, a G20 member country with growing ambitions as a global leader, has taken a positive stand on the Paris Declaration at the [Development Cooperation Forum] 2010. It has translated that document into a national programme called Jakarta Commitment on Aid Effectiveness and indicated that the country would abide by the Paris principles in its incipient programme of assistance to low-income countries.

For South Korea, membership of the DAC represents another marker of international status. It signals to its domestic population, neighbours and the community of states that it seeks to play a role in global governance and project itself on the global stage (Kim 2011). South Korea may well help lead a dialogue with other Asian and 'new' donors, and be a voice of change within the mainstream, but it is clearly positioned in broad alignment with the hegemonic powers (Lumsdaine et al. 2007; Chun et al. 2010). As a member of the G8, Russia too states its commitment to supporting mainstream development structures and goals (Jordan 2010).

Other states may not wish or be able to claim membership of the key institutions, or command much power within them, but they may still consider investing in the new forums that are opening up within the mainstream, and seek to influence their outcomes. For example, the government of Mexico co-hosted a meeting of the Task Team on South–South Cooperation in 2009 with the OECD-DAC; while the Colombian, Thai and Egyptian governments (among others) have also hosted important events aimed at promoting emerging development dialogues and relationships within a reforming foreign aid architecture. While not necessarily aligning entirely with the mainstream, they are willing to enter into dialogue with the 'traditional' powers, even as they seek to achieve change. Schulz (2010a) speculates whether, as development actors, the CIVETs (Colombia, Indonesia, Vietnam, Egypt and Turkey) and other 'second order' emerging powers may be more amenable to dialogue and cooperation with the traditional aid powers than the larger and more assertive BRICS. In many cases, while 'non-traditional' development partners may wish to retain some autonomy over their development cooperation practices, they also wish to maintain good relations with the more powerful nations, and promote more inclusive

Box 6.1 China and foreign aid governance in the Pacific

At a meeting following the Pacific Island Forum in New Zealand in September 2011, the Chinese Vice-Foreign Minister Cui Tianka stated that China would not be bound by the Cairns Compact, an agreement for better coordination and information sharing about aid programmes ... Cui emphasised initiatives to provide more support for tourism in the region, as well as support for the development of the energy and fishery sectors. China's assistance to the Pacific will include more high-level visits, more educational scholarships, more infrastructure projects, forums to facilitate closer business ties, debt write-offs and a US$ 400,000 contribution to the China–Pacific Island Forum Cooperation Fund to be used for agreed projects. Cui described China's aid to the Pacific as 'mutual assistance' between developing countries, as opposed to official development aid that is provided by the likes of Australia and New Zealand. 'For many years, China has been extending economic and technical assistance to Pacific Island countries and regional organisations, despite the fact it is not a rich country itself,' he says ... However, Cui also signalled that China is ready to learn from the experiences of other aid-giving countries and will begin to look at cooperative initiatives, as long as certain conditions are met. 'Under the principle of adopting a step-by-step approach and starting with easier issues, China is ready to discuss trilateral cooperation on aid with relevant countries and organisations, on the condition that the will of recipient countries is respected with no political strings.'

Source: pacific.scoop.co.nz/2011/09/china-plays-own-game-for-constructive-pacific-aid/

forums and norms which more strongly reflect their voices, agendas and interests. John de Sousa (2010) argues that while Brazil is reluctant to accept the Paris principles as a donor because they are perceived as rules being imposed by the 'traditional' powers, it still views itself as sharing values and ideas with European donors. Coordination and collaboration are welcomed, but on its own terms.

For other states, the incentives to cooperate and coordinate with the mainstream are much weaker while the disincentives are higher. At the most basic level, the considerable bureaucratic, legal and administrative costs of cooperation may act as a deterrent to some governments (re-)engaging in development cooperation. Greater coordination within the mainstream donor community might require implementing particular operating and accounting systems, measuring and monitoring specific indicators, and spending administrative and political time on attending meetings and forums. These can impose direct and indirect burdens on newer or smaller donors. Stuenkel (2011) notes that many non-DAC partners, including quite substantial actors, are relatively weak in terms of institutional capacity, and training, knowledge and experience in 'development' and development governance. He suggests that this can produce an insecurity and unwillingness to engage in regional and global development forums.

More fundamental disincentives are the product of competing national interests (economic and political), and alternative political and ideological understandings of foreign aid and development cooperation articulated by some non-DAC actors, especially in the global South. This rarely translates into complete isolation, particularly in the context of humanitarian emergencies, where various degrees and forms of cooperation between donors appear to be more acceptable to all. Rather, donors such as India, China and Brazil selectively engage with the 'mainstream', and do so on their own terms, without committing formally to more binding agreements and protocols. An excerpt from a report on recent discussions about Chinese development assistance in the Pacific captures some of the flavour of this (see Box 6.1). Although the Chinese minister refused to formally sign up to a donor-led compact he did signal willingness to engage in dialogue and cooperation with the dominant Western donors in the region. The excerpt also reflects themes discussed in previous chapters, namely China's projection of itself as a long-standing partner, a 'developing country', but one that is positioned differently to the 'traditional' colonial/post-colonial donors.

We turn now to the changing approaches to the (re-)emerging development partners within the mainstream, starting with a discussion of coordination and cooperation.

The debate over greater coordination and cooperation

In sharp contrast to the earlier neglect and parochialism of the dominant foreign aid community there is a now a widespread recognition that the DAC donors need to find ways of enhancing dialogue and cooperation with the non-DAC development partners (Davies 2008; Fues et al. 2012). A number of reasons are generally offered as to why this is desirable. In a widely cited article, Richard Manning (2006), then chair of the OECD-DAC, evaluated the implications of the rise of the non-DAC donors for poverty reduction and global development governance. It is a judicious piece, but revealing of the difficulties that the DAC confronts in acknowledging the politics of development. Manning raises concerns that those non-DAC donors which choose not to comply with the core norms and practices of the aid effectiveness orthodoxy will contribute to the forces that threaten to undermine and fragment the still rather fragile unity or consensus that is in the making. Furthermore, by their not agreeing to follow the principles laid out in the Paris Declaration and Accra Agenda as donors as well as recipients, Manning (ibid.) argues that (re-)emerging donors may have detrimental impacts on low-income recipient countries, namely:

1 Recipient/poorer countries may find it easier to borrow from the (re-)emerging donors on inappropriately non-concessional terms, leading to the return of unsustainable debt burdens.
2 Access to low-conditionality aid may mean that much-needed reforms are delayed or avoided.
3 If good practices in project appraisal are not observed, this aid could be deployed towards unproductive capital projects.

Manning's article sets out an effectively technical set of reasons to cooperate within an apparently apolitical realm of development – that is, to ensure system coherence in the interests of poverty reduction. But while these are certainly relevant and important issues, this approach does not acknowledge sufficiently the contested (and multiply defined) *politics* of development, in the sense that different actors may not agree that the Paris Agenda represents an appropriate route to development; that all donor governments have a range of factors and motivations shaping their development cooperation relations (not just poverty reduction in recipient states); and that the traditional powers are also looking to moderate and shape the impacts of the emerging powers within the development field but also beyond it. In other words, 'outreach' and dialogue are being driven by concerns for the impacts of the (re-)emerging powers not just on poor countries and people, or even on the stability of the international aid system, but on the power and interests of the dominant donors themselves.

Paulo and Reisen (2010) set out a more political understanding of the potential challenge raised by the non-DAC development partners, which recognizes that mainstream concerns about their development impacts blur with commercial and geopolitical anxieties. They sum up the concerns of the traditional aid community as follows:

1 Fragmentation of aid delivery
2 Violation of corporate and national governance standards
3 Free riding on debt relief
4 Unfair company competition
5 Scramble for extraction rights and resource curse outcomes for poorer countries.

The fact that some NDDs are willing to finance and in other ways prop up what are viewed by many Western states as undesirable regimes, such as those in Sudan and Zimbabwe, and that some NDDs are blending their aid contributions with trade and investment agendas, means that as well as development rationalities there are other strong incentives to engage with the non-DAC donors about their cooperation ideologies and practices. Here attitudes and approaches range widely. As we shall see in more detail below, many Western commentators talk about 'socializing' the (re-)emerging donors into the dominant institutions and systems – an imagery and agenda that assume that others must inculcate 'proper' Western norms and practices. This is both patronizing and ignores the failings and problems of mainstream foreign aid. Wissenbach (2010: 26) suggests that, as in many other policy areas, 'the West's reflex is not to engage with China as it is, but to ask China to become as we would like it to be. This has paralysed Western China policy and created unnecessary polarisation.' Xu (2011) argues that no coordination would result in crass competition, but the problem for many with uniform and universal coordination is that it would result in the development hegemony of the strongest.

It is also increasingly obviously untenable in the face of a growing number of vocal (re-)emerging development actors who are able to resist and reject efforts to co-opt them into hegemonic norms and practices. More critical commentators propose substantial reforms within the existing institutions and norms of foreign aid, and even new governance structures. They suggest that engagement between the increasingly diverse fields of official donors should be based on principles of mutual learning, common but differentiated responsibilities, and greater respect for alternative approaches and ideas. Over the last five years, an observable trend within many Western policy pronouncements about the emerging powers as development actors is a more respectful tone and language, even if the latter often still embodies assumptions about the superior lineages, ideologies and practices of Western foreign aid.

Ngaire Woods (2011) helpfully unpicks the notion of greater cooperation with the NDDs. She first examines the costs and consequences of the failure to communicate and coordinate. The humanitarian response to the 2010 Haiti earthquake, for example, was overwhelming but extremely problematic, with dozens if not hundreds of organizations and agencies coordinating very poorly with each other and barely at all with the Haitian government. The outcome was duplication, gaps, waste, amplified transaction costs and inefficiency in a context of desperate need. But as Woods points out, while the earthquake response provided a 'spectacular' example of poor coordination and its consequences, it was entirely in keeping with pre-earthquake patterns of assistance. In Haiti, as in so many recipient countries, the traditional donors stated their commitment to the principles of harmonization and alignment but failed to translate them into action. The costs of such disarray and the value of greater coordination and cooperation are obvious.

Clearly, despite all the reasons for greater cooperation, donors of all hues face disincentives to engage in it: cooperation can be costly, and is often cumbersome; donors want to retain policy space to ensure that they can pursue national interests; and different donors have different priorities and principles of development. These disincentives are amplified for many (re-)emerging development actors, which have on the whole less development capacity and funding, and often have stronger historical and ideological commitments to different foreign policy relationships. Woods (ibid.) asks whether it is realistic to expect these states to move into genuinely cooperative relationships when the dominant aid community can't manage to work cooperatively itself. She suggests that the mainstream aid community should pursue greater coordination rather than cooperation. Coordination would require information sharing, and commitment to a principle of not undermining the work of another donor through one's own policies and practices. Even this would be a substantial undertaking, and would not necessarily be agreed by some more autonomous development partners, but it is certainly a more achievable agenda than cooperation, which implies working together. Park (2011) suggests that the most realistic (if still optimistic) approach would be to agree a sequenced set of development agreements on principles and practices, although in a sober review of the issues Chandy and Kharas (2011) suggest that even this modest agenda confronts a whole range of very serious hurdles.

Dialogue and change within the dominant institutions of the international aid regime

This section outlines the ways in which some of the key players in international aid governance are responding to the challenges and the opportunities of the (re-)emerging development partners.[2] The first four (the World Bank and the IMF, the OECD-DAC, the Working Party on Aid Effectiveness, and the UN Development Cooperation Forum) are all directly engaged with official development assistance. However, to these we add the G20, and also mention briefly the BRICS Forum, the IBSA platform and other regional assemblages that are emerging in the context of the rising powers, in which development cooperation (diplomatic, financial, technical assistance and so on) are showcased and discussed.

a) The World Bank and the International Monetary Fund In their different but related capacities, the World Bank and the International Monetary Fund sit at the heart of global development governance. For decades critics have pointed to the discrepancy between the decision-making power historically wielded by the richer countries in both institutions (including effective veto power for the USA), and that of the poor and middle-income countries that are most affected by their policies and ideologies, but which have to date been almost voiceless in these institutions (Peet and Hartwick 2009). However, in the last few years both have been forced to confront and to some extent adjust to the increasingly assertive demands of the emerging powers as it has become more difficult for them to resist the long-standing critique of their representative bias. Within their respective arenas, both also face competition owing to the growing availability of alternative sources of concessional and commercial funding, including lines of credit, concessional loans through development cooperation partnerships and borrowing from commercial banks and sovereign wealth funds (Sagasti et al. 2005; Ketkar and Ratha 2009). At the same time, China and other development partners seem to offer lessons different to the neoliberal pathways imposed by the IMF and the World Bank to countries seeking to industrialize and develop (De Haan 2011).

In the case of the IMF, while representation has slowly broadened, Boughton and Bradford (2007: 11) argue that it is 'still lagging behind the evolution of the world economy, with the consequence that oversight of the international financial system has become less and less accepted as politically legitimate'. As well as a legitimacy gap, the IMF faces a particularly acute credibility gap, something that the mishandling of the 'Asian crisis' of 1997/98 turned into a chasm. Poorer countries have increasingly sought to avoid borrowing from the IMF and have looked elsewhere for funds (McCulloch and Sumner 2009). In some cases this has led to more or less direct competition with the larger of the non-DAC development partners. By the mid-2000s it seemed that the IMF's monopolistic hold over development finance for poorer countries was subject to serious challenge, and responding to a significant drop in demands for loans, the former chair of the IMF, Dominique Strauss-Kahn, instigated financial and governance reforms. These included increasing the quotas of the most under-represented countries (including China, India, Korea, Mexico, Singapore and Turkey), with implications for their representation within IMF bodies, their voting share and their access to the IMF's resources. Working together with the World Bank and the G20 in the context of the global economic crisis, the IMF has since undertaken more steps towards greater multilateralism. However, in a detailed analysis, Woods (2010) argues that these changes have been so incrementally small that they have failed to transform the relationship with the emerging economies. She suggests that, as yet, IMF reforms have not gone far enough to win the confidence of the emerging powers. Indeed, Brazil still has a smaller voting share than Belgium (McCulloch and Sumner 2009). Thus, while many would welcome a root-and-branch reform of this most undemocratic and ideologically dogmatic of institutions, it appears to have made very limited concessions to date (see also Agarwal 2010). The global financial crisis has perhaps 'saved' the IMF, and since 2008/09 it has very much been back in business, notably within Europe. Interestingly, this may well accelerate the influence of the emerging powers, some of which are increasingly important creditors to its accounts. In August 2011, for example, it was announced that India was helping to bail out Europe through its contributions to an IMF fund which is being used to try to stabilize the economies of southern Europe.

The World Bank is also confronting, resisting and embracing reform in multiple ways. It too faces new competition from other sources of financing for development, as well as challenges to its authority as the 'knowledge bank', given its leadership of neoliberal development ideologies. Responses to the growing visibility and presence of the (re-) emerging development partners are varied. They include shifts within governance structures and the balance of voting rights; soliciting new and enhanced credit flows from the emerging powers (such as Russia's increasing contributions to the IDA); hosting conferences and meetings with the (re-)emerging donors; and financing and managing joint projects and programmes with 'non-traditional' development actors. The World Bank is enrolled in bilateral and triangular initiatives (see below), and in the traditional and new forums of global development governance described in this chapter. For example, in 2008 it set up a World Bank Institute trust fund on South–South cooperation financed by Mexico, China, the UK, Denmark, Spain and the Netherlands. The World Bank is to some extent retuning itself, finding or asserting emerging opportunities for an ongoing role within a changing world. A fact sheet that accompanied the 2010 High Level Event on South–South Cooperation and Capacity Development stated that:

> As a global connector, the World Bank can play an important strategic role in South–South cooperation ... It can be a global knowledge broker across regions. It is also an opportunity for the Bank to help Low-Income Countries share knowledge – a powerful instrument of development, while continuing to engage with Middle-Income Countries as providers of knowledge.[3]

However, Woods (2010: 60) concludes that, as with the IMF, the World Bank is seeking new compromises with the emerging economies, but that 'to date [it has] not relinquished their command of the tiller of the main multilaterals ... even as it becomes clear that the future efficacy of these institutions requires them to do so'.

Although broadening representation, decision-making and dialogue is very welcome, we should not assume that a greater voice for the political and economic elites of the emerging powers within the Bretton Woods institutions will necessarily lead to policies and outcomes that favour other poorer nations, or poorer people within nations. Will a greater role for, say, India, Turkey, Korea and Mexico result in more just and developmentally effective policies being formulated and pursued for Malawi, Papua New Guinea or Haiti? For that matter, will it lead to policies that favour the interests of the lower- and middle-income majorities within India, Turkey, Korea, Mexico, Greece, Portugal or the UK? Just as in the UK and the USA, the elites of China, India, Brazil and Russia do not necessarily share the same concerns or interests as the poorer majorities of their countries. Trade and investment policies may favour the wealthy of these emerging economies through the active exploitation of the poor. We take up these debates in more detail in the conclusions to this book.

b) The OECD-DAC[4] The DAC is acutely aware of and strategically engaged with the question of the emerging powers, and its journey – over really quite a short space of time, from relative neglect to 'outreach' to enhanced engagement to the language of partnership – is one indication of the depth and rapidity of shift within global development governance. Interestingly, in some cases this is a revival of older relations rather than a complete reinvention. In 2009, for example, the DAC and the Arab Coordination Group Institutions (ACGI) renewed a high-level partnership dialogue that had languished for two decades. In a 2011 meeting they discussed partnership to support 'transition' in the Middle East following the Arab Spring, but also global development governance and preparations for the Busan High Level Forum in December 2011 (ACGI 2011). However, it is telling that while the ACGI briefing document makes supportive comments about the aid effectiveness agenda, it concludes with the striking statement that 'the world has changed since the days when the Paris Declaration was agreed. There are new actors, new forms of partnership, new ways of achieving results, and new geopolitical coalitions' (ibid.: 7).

DAC's current phase of awareness and outreach started in 2005, when it adopted an 'Outreach Strategy'. In 2006, under the auspices of the Russian presidency, the G8, OECD and World Bank held a conference on 'Emerging Donors in the Global Development Community'. Since then, events have moved rapidly, and in 2011 the DAC officially announced an 'open doors' policy,[5] welcoming the development cooperation efforts of the non-DAC providers and stressing their crucial role in meeting the MDGs (Saidi and Wolf 2011; Xu 2011). The DAC has pursued various tactics in its attempts to familiarize these donors with DAC norms and practices (and persuade them to adopt them), and to open more dialogue and possible partnership with them. In the case of non-DAC OECD countries and the non-OECD new European states, this has included assistance and guidance in bringing them closer to DAC norms and guidelines, and they have a standing invitation to participate in all DAC activities (Chandy and Kharas 2011). DAC statements and communiqués now make an effort to stress the DAC's willingness to learn from and cooperate with other development cooperation providers. For example, China was invited to act as an observer on OECD-DAC peer reviews, and a China–Africa Study Group was established in 2009.[6] Jerve (2007: 4) reports that from about 2005, contacts between China and the DAC started to become more constructive. Paulo and Reisen (2010) also discuss DAC's dialogue with China on data collection and transparency, including environmental reviews and standards.

The DAC is reorienting itself rapidly to a challenging new world for aid and development cooperation. However, Glennie (2011c) argues that the DAC's instinct is still to integrate the new powers into the Paris process but that this is not what they want, and more significantly, they are quite capable of resisting any such pressure. While many are prepared to cooperate to some degree with DAC around the new aid paradigm (by expressing their commitment to the Millennium Development Goals, joining the DAC-hosted Working Party on Aid Effectiveness, or signing up to the Paris Declaration as recipients), to date they have largely resisted being drawn closer to the DAC itself (Fues 2011).

The DAC remains a powerful actor, and an important one, but it is clear that its hegemony is now eroded to some degree, and that its place in the future aid architecture will shift. Two recent forums, with which DAC is closely engaged, are playing a role in this transition. These are the Working Party on Aid Effectiveness, and the UN's Development Cooperation Forum, to which we now turn.

c) The Working Party on Aid Effectiveness The Working Party on Aid Effectiveness (WP-EFF) started as a 'traditional' donor-only group in 2003, as a 'classic subsidiary body of the OECD-DAC' (Manning 2008: 7). However, in 2005 it moved to joint partnership with developing countries – a change that was indicative of the imperative to confront the growing legitimacy crisis of donor-only forums. Although it was described by Manning (ibid.) as a genuine multilateral enterprise, it was still hosted by the DAC, which was also a constituent member, a double relationship that has not been fully clarified (Killen and Rogerson 2010; Chandy and Kharas 2011). The establishment of the WP-EFF was also a response to the eighth Millennium Development Goal, which called for increased and improved global partnerships for development. In 2009 it expanded again, and in 2011 had over eighty members, including twenty-four recipient countries, eight countries which both provided and received aid, thirty-one donor countries, nine multilaterals, and six civil society and other organizations.[7] The WP-EFF's mandate ended in June 2012, but it played a key role in shaping the 'Global Partnership for Effective Development Cooperation', which is intended to replace it (OECD-DAC 2012a, 2012b). This is picked up more fully in Chapter 7.

The WP-EFF was essentially a problem-oriented forum that primarily sought to address the quality of aid, although it also encouraged an increased volume of aid. It was the key driver of the Paris Declaration and the Accra Agenda for Action, organized around the four High

Level Forums to date (Rome, Paris, Accra and Busan), and the various regional and sectoral meetings that have accompanied this process (Davies 2008). In addition, the WP-EFF had two Task Teams, one on Health as a Tracer Sector (in the attempt to better monitor change), and one on South–South Cooperation (TT-SSC). The latter, created in 2009, was a Southern-led platform which has a mandate 'to contribute to the understanding of the dynamics of South–South knowledge exchange by providing policy guidance and documenting good practices, as well as exploring how it complements North–South exchanges' (at the time of writing it is not clear whether this Task Team will continue after the end of the WP-EFF's mandate).[8] For some commentators, the WP-EFF represented the most inclusive and credible forum for promoting the principles embodied in the Paris processes (Park 2011). In a High Level Event on South–South Cooperation and Capacity Building in Colombia in March 2010, for example, the TT-SSC provided a platform for a strong assertion of Southern voices.

As noted in Chapter 1, the Paris process claims some successes, including improved recording of aid budgets, some improvement in existing country systems and thus the reduction of parallel implementation units, enhancing the predictability of aid, and fostering greater mutual accountability between donors and recipients. It has, moreover, clearly allowed a greater voice for low- and middle-income recipient countries within foreign aid debates. As well as targeting North–South aid, both the Paris Declaration and the Accra Agenda for Action explicitly state the value of South–South development cooperation, asserting the legitimate presence and role of the non-DAC donors, and emphasizing the particular knowledge, dispositions and resources they bring. However, Killen and Rogerson (2010), among others, point to various problems. They suggest that the WP-EFF's focus on aid quality limited it in taking on wider development inequalities, and the structural inequalities that produce them. Moreover, it faced very considerable barriers in terms of what it aimed to achieve, and made less satisfactory progress in encouraging donors to make more use of recipient countries' financial, management and procurement systems, in coordinating missions and studies by donors, in improving the quality of countries' national development plans, and in creating a monitoring framework to ensure results-based evidence.

For some, the WP-EFF (like the Development Cooperation Forum below) was a means by which the powerful states mobilized to secure their own hegemony, even as they appeared to open up and engage with new and more inclusive forums. It certainly seemed to be successfully encouraging 'buy in' from many recipient countries (Schulz 2009), which saw the chance for a new voice and influence in these democratizing spaces. Interestingly, this may have some of the more autonomously minded development partners worried. Fues et al. (2012) report that at the Colombia meeting of the TT-SSC in 2010, Brazil, China and India and other emerging powers successfully intervened to prevent the adoption of a final document by the whole conference. Fues et al. (ibid.) suggest that this reflects a concern on the part of the more powerful (re-)emerging donors that the WP-EFF was effectively an instrument designed to draw Southern countries into a global foreign aid regime that remains dominated by Western ideas and agendas, but which has sufficient wider legitimacy to make it harder for the more powerful non-DAC development partners to resist its more representatively legitimate decisions and declarations. As such, it (and its successor) may end up limiting the current policy space afforded by the more malleable concept of South–South cooperation.

The WP-EFF marked a real watershed in global aid and development governance. But it continued to reflect rich-country (and notably DAC) dominance, as they were the funders and authors of reports, and the dominant managers of processes and structures (Hammad and Morton 2009; ECDPM 2011). China, Brazil and the Arab countries were not seriously engaged with the WP-EFF, undermining claims to a genuinely multilateral forum. With the end of the WP-EFF mandate, intensive discussions are now under way as to what sort of international aid and development regime will emerge. One institution that is likely to play some role is a relatively new UN institution, the Development Cooperation Forum, to which we turn next.

d) The Development Cooperation Forum The Social and Economic Council of the United Nations (ECOSOC) has traditionally been viewed as the weakest of the UN organs. This is because its original Charter led to a confused mandate and division of responsibilities with the General Assembly, its weak internal coordination, the efforts by some Western powers to undermine and divide it, and because its terms of reference were overtaken by more powerful external institutions like the World Bank and the International Monetary Fund (Rosenthal 2005). In 2005 the UN initiated an effort to strengthen and reform its institutions in an attempt to make the UN more coherent (Boughton and Bradford 2007). One outcome was the agreement by the UN General Assembly in 2005 to establish a Development Cooperation Forum (DCF) under the auspices of ECOSOC.

The DCF was launched in Geneva in 2007 with the purpose of becoming the premier global forum for foreign aid donors and recipients, in which they could share experience, debate good practice and principles, review current trends in development policy and financing, and encourage peer learning, coherence and aid effectiveness (Ashoff 2008). As such, it is supposed to facilitate the evolution towards common or shared understandings on principles, definitions and norms in development cooperation as well as ensure universal transparency, although as Fues (2011) notes, formal intergovernmental decision-making is not part of its mandate. The final communiqué of its first meeting in 2008 declared that the DCF would play:

> [A] key role as an international mutual accountability mechanism that will draw together analysis of progress in national and global-level mutual accountability processes, and thereby contribute to holding donors and programme [recipient] countries to account. (UN 2008: 4)

The creation of a forum which includes recipients as full members distinguishes the DCF from the other major development forum, the DAC. The DCF also includes representatives from civil society organizations, the private sector, parliaments and local authorities, and from regional and multilateral organizations. As it is a UN body, all sovereign states are members, something that could be expected to confer upon it considerable legitimacy. Samir Amin has suggested that 'it began the construction of *authentic* partnerships within a polycentric global perspective' (Amin 2009: 68, emphasis added). Thus the DCF represents a potentially radical forum within which alternative definitions, norms and principles of development assistance can be articulated, negotiated and advanced: here the (re-)emerging development partners might become rule-makers rather than rule-takers.

The DCF is therefore dually located: first within the mainstream, as it supports and runs parallel to the Paris process (and is approved by them); but at the same time it is indicative of a challenge to the existing aid architecture, and in particular to the dominance of the DAC in constructing the rules and norms of foreign aid. This raises a number of questions about how the DCF will function, with what mandate and what financing; whose interests and what agendas it will represent; and how it will engage with other bilateral and multilateral donors and forums, including the DAC and (formerly and through the process of transition) the WP-EFF.

After some debate and scaling down of the original vision for the DCF, it now meets every two years. The first two meetings, in 2008 and

2010, were both held in UN headquarters in New York. In the run-up to the main biennial meetings, a series of regional and preparatory meetings were organized, including events in Austria, Egypt and Italy. The DAC's tactics appear to have been to keep close. It holds two seats on the twenty-six-person Advisory Council, and DAC representatives have played an active part in DCF meetings and events. Furthermore, other members of the Advisory Council are drawn from DAC member states, and there is a strong representation from friendly European bodies and Western-dominated institutions like the World Bank. The DAC's active role in the DCF can be read as a constructive engagement with the changing realities of global development politics – an accommodation to the reality of the rising influence of the non-DAC donors. But there is an inherent rivalry between the DCF and the DAC that cannot be glossed over. The greater legitimacy and (apparent) neutrality afforded the DCF by its UN status inevitably draws attention to the DAC's donor-only membership and its overwhelmingly Western make-up. An alternative interpretation of its close engagement is that it represents a strategic attempt to influence the DCF's infant development in ways that will head off potential challenges – to co-opt the DCF within an ongoing Western-led development ideology. DAC members are unlikely to wish to concede power to the DCF and lose their current dominance of the arena. Yash Tandon argues that 'OECD countries have effectively seized the DCF so that they can import their own agenda and perspectives into the forum' (Tandon 2009: 42). Fues notes that only one developing country, Egypt, was substantively involved in preparations for the first meeting of the DCF in 2008 by hosting a symposium, while, in contrast, 'nine industrialised countries provided material support, namely Austria, Denmark, Finland, France, Germany, Italy, Spain, Japan, Switzerland and the United Kingdom. The British consulting firm Development Finance International was contracted to manage the preparatory analytical work for both the 2008 and 2010 DCF meetings' (Fues 2011: 10). As many analysts of development 'knowledge' have demonstrated, this unequal ability to produce reports, data and analyses favours the (re)production of hegemonic ideas and ideologies (Narayanaswamy 2010).

How have Southern donors and recipients responded to the DCF? A number of countries have expressed their support. For example, the Chinese ambassador to the UN, Li Baodong, said at the launch ceremony in 2007:

> The creation of the DCF marks another important step forward in the

implementation of the decisions taken at the UN Summit and important progress in reforms of the economic and social field. This will help boost UN input in development, ensure resources for development, strengthen development agencies and provide an important platform for closer development cooperation in the international community ... Expectations are high on our new established Forum. It should follow the principles of gradual progress, consensus, and ensuring equal participation of developing countries. China is ready to take an active part in its work, and maintain coordination and consultation with parties concerned to ensure that the DCF move forward on the right track. (Government of China 2007)

The DCF has been seen as a forum within which the mass of lower- as well as middle-income countries can assert a more powerful role within ECOSOC and the General Assembly. The Pakistan government, for example, stated in 2010 that '[w]e view DCF as a unique and inclusive platform where all countries can voice their concerns to help shape the international cooperation framework' (Government of Pakistan 2010: 4, cited in Fues 2011: 8). Can the DCF therefore emerge as a credible forum within which a more just representation of interests and transparent processes would result in a genuine dialogue about development cooperation, and the identification of where there might be shared agreements on foreign aid? Most commentators express caution. First, the DCF remains institutionally weak – in part the outcome of uncertain political commitments to its future and functioning, and in part because of limited financing (Schulz 2008; Amin 2009). This compromises the Forum's ability to exert influence and have a meaningful impact, which can create a vicious circle as countries with scarce or limited financial and diplomatic resources may choose not to invest in it, further eroding its potential effectiveness. Allyón (2009: 5) suggests that as it 'lacks infrastructure and is highly dependent on the will of individual countries, the DCF still resembles a loosely structured process more than a functioning platform for enhanced dialogue' (see also Paulo and Reisen 2010). Another problem inherent to many UN bodies is the difficulties of effective dialogue and policy-making among such a large and diverse membership.

Other problems are more political in nature. Fues (2011) notes that in the initial discussions that led to the creation of the Forum, some representatives from the global South wanted its mandate to be the politically sensitive (and potentially transformative) issue of external structural and political factors that shape development outcomes.

This was unpalatable to the UN as it would have led to considerable overlap with existing institutions, and it is unlikely it would have been welcomed by richer states, so in the end the DCF took as its objective the narrower field of development assistance. Second, Kofi Annan has called for the DCF to promote a more transparent aid regime among all donors, DAC and non-DAC. Thus in a 2008 report the UN secretary-general stated:

> South–South development cooperation is subject to relatively little evaluation beyond scrutiny of the timeliness and completion of projects. This reduces missions and studies, lowering the transaction costs of the Governments of programme countries, yet it also means that there will be a reduced longer-term perspective on the sustainability or wider development impact of the project. This cooperation is also subject to much less evaluation with respect to environmental and social impact, particularly in the case of infrastructure projects. (UN 2008)

As we have seen, while some non-DAC donors are moving towards improved monitoring and tracking mechanisms, and releasing these data for external scrutiny, some non-DAC donors are unable to comply, while others are reluctant to do so. If the DCF were to gather power and momentum it would likely work to elaborate international aid norms, possibly in conjunction with changing DAC norms, possibly parallel to DAC, or perhaps in some form of tiered compromise between them. Whatever the case, those development actors who currently act purely bilaterally and without external scrutiny risk some loss of independence in their development assistance policies and programming if they become subject to DCF-led peer reviews, definitions, external benchmarks and so on. As we have seen in previous chapters, this autonomy has both ideological purchase and strategic value, which China, India and others are as yet unwilling to concede. Fues (2011) argues that some of the larger (re-)emerging development partners are not only concerned about the Western powers, but are also inhibited from taking up a more prominent role in the DCF because they worry that they will come under pressure from lower-income recipient countries to increase contributions, or work in ways that suit their interests better. If the DCF becomes able to leverage its greater legitimacy to evolve into a genuinely powerful forum it would become harder to paper over the differences within the G77 plus China.

The creation of the Development Cooperation Forum indicates the degree of change within the global geography of power. Notwithstanding the internal weaknesses and divisions that may hamper it, or which may even terminally undermine it, the DCF represents one sign that change is irresistible within global development governance.

e) The G20 The superseding of the G8 by the G20 as the 'premier forum' for international economic policy discussion is a development that Kloke-Lesch and Gleichmann (2010: 13) have suggested 'may turn out to be as significant as the collapse of the Berlin Wall in ushering in a new global epoch'. The G20 was originally convened as a forum for the finance ministers of the world's twenty largest economies and first met in 1999 in the wake of the Asian crisis. In the decade that followed, the extraordinary growth of the leading emerging powers led the G8 to increasingly 'reach out' to the so-called G5 (Brazil, China, India, Mexico and South Africa) as it became increasingly clear that global economic decision-making was no longer the preserve of the traditionally powerful industrial nations alone (Cooper and Antkiewicz 2008). A meeting between the G8 and the G5 in 2007 at the German town of Heiligendamm launched a more formal dialogue process, but this was rapidly outpaced when the global financial crisis broke in 2008, leading to the consolidation of the G20 as the apex body of global economic governance (Fues and Wolff 2010). At the London summit of early 2009 the G20 met as a forum for premiers and leaders, and in a meeting in Pittsburgh later that year, it was announced that the G20 would replace the G8.

For some commentators, the emergence of the G20 signals the breakdown of the long-standing North–South divide. Every continent is represented, and no fewer than eleven states come from the 'developing' nations. Its limited membership may mean that it is more effective in translating Southern agendas into action compared to the perennially politicized and fragmented United Nations bodies, and more legitimate compared to the still heavily Western-dominated Bretton Woods institutions. However, as Richard Jolly (2010) observes, the G20 excludes 172 countries, an exclusion that is felt keenly by some. Singapore, for instance, led a group of twenty-three smaller states to protest at the UN in 2010 against the usurpation of power by the G20, insisting on the premier role of the UN, and arguing that global economic decision-making should properly reside in the global institutions. In fact the G20 has rather weak ties with the UN, and much stronger ties with the World Bank and the International Monetary Fund, the directors of which are also invited to its meetings.

The emerging powers within the G20 face a situation of flux, although we should emphasize that their positioning and choices are varied and individual (e.g. De Freitas Barbosa and Mendes 2010). Will they renounce their 'developing country' identity and affirm their place among the world's powerful nations; or will they continue – to some extent – to make common cause with the world's formerly colonized, poorer and less powerful states? In part this may depend on their assessment of the G20, and whether they can meet their interests within it. Some critics (e.g. Zhang 2010) suggest that the creation of the G20 is in fact a way of deflecting and absorbing the potential challenge of the emerging powers, ensuring that they do not become leaders of a revitalized rival Southern grouping. Ghaus (2010: 93) suggests that the G20's main role is 'to safeguard the rights and interests of major economies as opposed to making decisions that seek to bridge the North–South divide'. Kloke-Lesch and Gleichmann (2010: 14–15) suggest that:

> For the emerging economies, G20 membership mainly challenges their previous understandings of their role as countries and representatives of the (poor) global South. Their economic and geopolitical interests which brought them into the G20 only converge with the [lower-income countries] to a limited extent. To prevent an ever-widening gap between roles and realities the emerging economies must face up to and attempt to shape this changed situation – not only in their role as recipients and donors of official development cooperation. ... The [South–South cooperation] paradigms ... are fifty years old and have never been particularly effective ... A genuinely new joint development agenda based on equality is therefore very unlikely to emerge within the G20 without more transparency in relation to these realities and without the demystification of SSC.

A different set of criticisms is less concerned with nation-states and more with the economic ideologies that the G20 appears to represent. Kumar (2010: 37), for example, asserts that the G20 'continues to operate ... like an inter-governmental "informal consultative workshop" for condoning the sins of predatory financial capital and erasing the struggles of the global poor for survival and dignity in a post-crisis world'. For Kumar and other critics, the G20 has responded to the financial crisis with bail-outs for the guilty (and unrepentant) institutions and stimulus packages that open opportunities for the rich, while the costs of collapse have been passed on to lower-income groups in both the North and South in higher prices, higher taxes for the majority (but not for the rich) and government austerity cuts.

Clearly the economic and policy choices made individually and collectively by the G20 will profoundly shape the arena within which middle- and low-income states, as well as individuals, families and communities across the world, are able to make choices and achieve their goals. But as well as these indirect impacts, the G20 has also started to make noises about a more direct development remit. The 2009 G20 London Summit Communiqué announced that '[w]e recognise that the current crisis has a disproportionate impact on the vulnerable in the poorest countries and recognise our collective responsibility to mitigate the social impact of the crisis to minimise long-lasting damage to global potential'.[9] Korea, the newest entrant to the DAC, has been a notable champion of a more explicit international development agenda for the G20 (Fues and Wolff 2010; Kim 2010; Fues 2012), and at the 2010 Toronto Summit the G20 decided to set up a Working Group on Development. A Multi-Year Development Action Plan now forms the programmatic basis for the 'Seoul Development Consensus', which outlines the G20's commitment to overcome poverty and inequality.

Chin (2010) suggests that, while the UN should remain the premier site for international development discussions, the G20 may lead a more comprehensive and effective development agenda than the G8's former 'moral hand-wringing' over Africa. However, Jolly (2010) argues that the focus is mostly oriented inwards, and that it lacks a meaningful or coherent global developmental agenda. Le Pere (2010) is also critical, viewing the G20's statements on development as mostly platitudinous and rhetorical repetitions of earlier development pledges and statements; while Fues et al. (2012) point to the unwillingness to confront structural imbalances in the world economy. Fues (2012) observes that the rising-power members of the G20 have repeatedly 'softened' the wording of its commitments to environmental standards, responsible investment and disclosure obligations for natural resource payments; while in the 2011 report of the Development Working Group to the Cannes Summit, the rising-power members blocked any reference to a common social protection floor, insisting instead on national standards and conditions (ibid.). The elite negotiators of these positions may well feel that they are defending the rights and interests of poorer states which cannot afford these aspirational policies, and which perhaps see in them an attempt to inhibit their growth; but there appears to be more limited concern for poorer peoples within their own borders and beyond.

However the G20's development agenda is formulated and realized, it is unquestionably an exceptionally important and influential context for negotiation and dialogue over the changing geographies of power, including within the formal development arena.

Regional institutions and other multilaterals

In the second and third tiers of international relations and global development governance are a host of other organizations and forums. Some are regionally important and influential (e.g. the New Partnership for Africa's Development, the Asian Development Bank, the Association of South-East Asian Nations and so on), and others may be multilateral or non-state organizations which are highly influential within particular development sectors (e.g. Global Fund to Fight AIDS, Tuberculosis and Malaria, the World Food Programme and so on). Some of these organizations are starting to engage with the (re-)emerging development actors. This section sketches out a couple of the main issues and provides examples to illustrate the principal debates.

Rhee (2011) suggests that at present regional organizations constitute a highly fragmented field, and there is little or no coordinated discussion about how they might work with the (re-)emerging donors. He notes that NEPAD, for example, is unusual in actively debating and pursuing such partnerships. In addition to these longer-standing regional organizations are various new agreements, networks, platforms and forums that are being set up by the emerging powers. These include the BRICS Forum, comprising Brazil, Russia, India and China, and since 2011 South Africa; IBSA, a platform for collective discussion and action between India, Brazil and South Africa (Alden 2005b; Nel and Stephen 2010); the Forum on China–Africa Cooperation (FOCAC), which held its first high-level inter-ministerial meeting in 2000; and the India–Africa Summit Forum, which started in 2008 and brings together India and fourteen African governments. These and other emerging organizations are concerned principally with diplomatic alliances and agreements, trade and investment, but they are also venues in which (closely related) development cooperation funding and activities are discussed, highlighted and announced. In 2011, for example, IBSA announced the creation of a Poverty and Hunger Alleviation Fund (Smith 2011).

Regional and bilateral trade agreements are also an indicator of increasing South–South economic dynamism and cooperation. Chahoud (2008) points out that in the early 1990s there were only fifty such agreements; now there are more than two hundred. Interestingly, Woods (2010) asks whether these emerging bilateral and regional mechanisms (she mentions the Chiang-Mai Initiative as just one example) are an outcome of the failure of the dominant 'global' institutions – such as the IMF and the World Bank – to undertake sufficient reforms in the face of the rising powers. Woods describes the growing role of various regional banks, such as the African Development Bank and the Inter-American Development Bank, which are now lending in situations that once would have firmly been the preserve of the World Bank. These tend to have stronger regional representation and interests than the World Bank. She quotes Jiang Zemin, the Chinese premier, at the opening ceremony of the Asian Development Bank Meeting in May 2009:

> Asian countries should step up their own efforts and work in closer regional cooperation with Asian characteristics ... It is gratifying to note that thanks to concerted efforts of Asian countries, regional cooperation in Asia has been growing ever stronger in recent years. With the preliminary establishment of such cooperation mechanisms as the Asian Pacific Economic Cooperation, East Asian Cooperation, Shanghai Cooperation Organization and others, an open, healthy and mutually beneficial cooperation pattern has taken shape ... we should base ourselves on the existing cooperative mechanisms and constantly explore new ways of cooperation, centring first and foremost on closer sub-regional cooperation and probing for, on such a basis, effective approaches to Asian cooperation. (Quoted in ibid.: 59)

These initiatives and agendas clearly have significant implications for the economic and political contexts within which development cooperation is being formulated and conducted. Alternative ideologies, funding streams, power centres, practices and cultures are eroding the former hegemony of the global development institutions and the 'traditional' bilateral donors. This somewhat neglected level of development institutions may well turn out to be one of the most interesting and important in changing development governance.

Triangular and trilateral development cooperation

Triangular and trilateral development cooperation are often used synonymously, but Rhee (2011) argues that there is an important distinction between them. He suggests that triangular development cooperation should be understood to refer to the long-standing and continuing support for South–South cooperation by the United Nations, and now increasingly from other Northern/traditional partners. Trilateral development cooperation (TDC), on the other hand, is a relatively new kind of formal development relationship. In TDC a DAC donor (such as DfID or CIDA) and/or a multilateral agency (such as UNDP) partners with a so-called pivotal, emerging or anchor country (such as Brazil, Poland or South Africa) to work with a third, recipient country (such as Haiti, Moldova or Rwanda). TDC is therefore a specific mode of official development partnership that adds a third approach to the two dominant forms: North–South aid and South–South development cooperation partnerships. Its significance has been recognized at numerous high-level meetings: an official statement of the G8/G20 (Heiligendamm Process 2009: 4), for example, suggests that TDC offers 'an opportunity for enhanced national and regional ownership as well as an increase in the support, harmonisation and coordination of peace, security and development efforts of the international community'.

TDC is predicated on the idea of different partners bringing different capacities and strengths. DAC partners and/or multilaterals provide financial resources and development experience. Decades of engagement have led to robust institutions, trained personnel, strong networks with non-state actors and multilateral institutions, extensive experience of undertaking projects and programmes, as well as familiarity with the norms and requirements of the international development community. For their part, it is expected that the pivotal states can provide goods, services and assistance more cheaply, and in ways that are more appropriate to the recipient country settings. Their own experiences of development transition, and often their shared geographies and cultural and linguistic ties, may allow for more efficient and effective delivery of development assistance. The geographies of TDC reflect these notions of regionally and culturally appropriate partnerships. Many TDC initiatives involve pivotal countries working with beneficiaries from within their own region, such as South Africa (Fordelone 2009). In other cases, strategic motivations follow more diffuse colonial and post-colonial geographies. Brazil, for example, has a strong presence in various TDC projects in Latin America and the Caribbean (including in Haiti, Uruguay and Bolivia), but it also partners with Japan, France and Germany, among others, to work in Lusophone countries farther afield, including Mozambique, Angola and East Timor. As well as offering these advantages, the pivotal states are also expected to benefit through capacity-building and learning from the Northern donors.

Finally, recipient countries may be able to assert more country ownership and negotiate better development outcomes given the involvement of other Southern partners. However, this often seems to be the weakest assertion within the policy literature, which often falls back on fairly feeble evidence and ongoing platitudes about recipient 'ownership' of development policies and programmes. It may be that development objectives in recipient countries (poverty reduction, economic growth, social stability and so on) are likely to benefit from

Box 6.2 Brazil and TDC

Brazil has been a particularly enthusiastic supporter of TDC, although it is not without its reservations. It was one of the first to experiment with the approach, and has a substantial range of partnerships with Northern and multilateral donors (including Japan, the UK, Sweden and the UNDP), and with third countries in Latin and Central America, the Caribbean and around the world. Brazil has also helped disseminate the idea of TDC more widely within the donor community. Japan is an important Northern partner, in part reflecting its own interest in TDC, and also perhaps the ties created by the presence of over 1.4 million Japanese immigrants and their descendants in Brazil. Abdenur (2007) provides examples of some of the projects under way, including a partnership between JICA and FIOCRUZ (Brazil's renowned public health foundation) to train East Timorese distance-learning tutors in public health education. Here we see the enrolment of non-state actors, an issue that is discussed in Chapter 3. In another case, Brazil partnered with the UK to bring an array of senior Russian health officials, civil society leaders, parliamentarians and others to meet their Brazilian counterparts to learn about Brazil's extensive and multifaceted AIDS/HIV policies.

In her insightful analysis, Adriana Abdenur (2007) explores the relationship between SSDC, TDC and Brazil's wider foreign policy goals. She examines how Brazil, which has a substantial poor population, justifies directing resources to other countries. These include its claim to considerable technical expertise in a variety of social, health and agricultural fields, among others; support for its claims to be an altruistic regional

a more coherent set of relations between different sorts of donors, including new arrangements between 'traditional' and (re-)emerging development partners. But whether TDC adds to policy coherence or to proliferation and fragmentation is still a question to be answered. It may also be the case that the pivotal states do not necessarily live up to the high ideals of South–South relations. As discussed previously in this book, they too may work in ways that are top-down and inattentive and global actor; strengthening cultural ties, especially within the Community of Portuguese Language Countries, which in turn helps underwrite trade agreements, technology transfers and diplomatic solidarities; the pursuit of regional leadership within Latin America; and the boost that SSDC and TDC gives to Brazil's wider global status, especially in terms of becoming a nodal point in IBSA, the BRICs and the G20. Abdenur asks: why TDC? Bilateral (South–South) relations can be much more easily managed in the national interest (whatever that is deemed to be, whether helping promote trade or polishing one's image as altruistic) than multilateral relations. TDC represents something of an intermediary form between bilateral and multilateral. Abdenur cautiously argues (in the absence of more detailed socio-political studies and network analysis) that in the case of Brazil, TDC 'constitutes a specific tactic for national self-promotion within a broader strategy of foreign relations' (ibid.: 12). Abdenur suggests that engagement in, and promotion of, TDC helps consolidate Brazil's place as a pivotal Southern country in the international arena. And unlike traditional multilateral channels (e.g. UN peacekeeping), TDC allows Brazil closer engagement and a more visible profile with Northern partners and with recipient countries. Because TDC represents something of a break from the 'autarkic rhetoric of leftist developing states in earlier decades' it reflects a new spirit of compromise and collaboration with the 'traditional' powers. In the complex interplay of international politics – at the UN, the WTO and other global forums – this could, arguably, help promote Brazil's global image and reputation with powerful industrialized countries, without sacrificing its Southern solidarities or sense of sovereignty.

to context or power. Their commercial and diplomatic foreign policy agendas may, just like those of the 'traditional' donors, clash with the interests of recipient countries, and marginalized groups within them.

TDC is enrolled within and aims to create a new geography of international aid in which the industrialized, emerging and low-income countries are adjusting to and shaping a world witnessing the rise of the emerging powers (McEwan and Mawdsley 2012). While TDC remains a small element within the overall aid sector, it does appear to be growing. To date, sixteen of the twenty-four DAC donors have participated in TDC projects: Germany, Japan and Spain have most activities, but Canada, Ireland and South Korea are also developing TDC projects (Schulz 2010b). Multilateral development banks, UN organizations and Southern providers of development cooperation are also increasingly using this modality. It was one of the key themes of the 2008 and 2010 DCF meetings, and was firmly on the agenda of the 2011 Busan High Level Forum on Aid Effectiveness. The 2010 Bogotá Statement (issued in the run-up to Busan) emphasizes that TDC is part of a 'Southern-led process' that should act as 'a bridge between South–South and North–South cooperation' (Bogotá Statement 2010: 1).

A number of problems have also been identified with TDC. These include a set of technical/managerial issues that confront very different partners seeking to work together. These can include differences in sectoral priorities, appropriate staff, procurement regulations, reporting criteria, management structures and so on. Further problems arise if there is an unclear division of responsibility and tasks. Even the fact of different professional cultures and styles of dialogue may mean that from agency headquarters to national offices to field sites there are slippages and tensions. There is an irony in the fact that the Paris Agenda appears in many cases to have added to transaction costs rather than streamlined them, as different partners try (with greater or lesser commitment) to coordinate their aid practices – something that demands more rounds of meetings, negotiations, new procedures and so on. In the case of TDC, the administrative burden is inevitably higher, given the presence of (at least) three partners, and also given the novelty of some of the relationships, and in some cases the challenges of working with an inexperienced, decentred and weakly embedded aid bureaucracy in the pivotal states (Ashoff 2010). While all partners may suffer from this, the pivotal and recipient countries are usually least able to absorb the higher costs.

A more problematic concern is that TDC may effectively replicate older patterns of Northern hegemony, with the DAC bilaterals and/or Northern-dominated multilaterals setting the agenda while pivotal states act as little more than cheap contractors. DAC members and multilaterals may fail to internalize TDC experiences in order to critically reflect on their own development ideologies and practices, or learn from the pivotal and recipient countries (AECID 2010). If we look at which pivotal states are engaging in TDC, we see some major absences, notably China, but also India. Those which are experimenting with TDC are cautious: according to Rowlands (2008: 16), Brazil and South Africa are more open to trilateral cooperation, but even here, '[t]hough less reticent [than China and India], Brazil remains wary of such arrangements, and takes care to ensure that it is not simply re-establishing older hierarchical relations wherein it plays a subordinate role to a traditional donor'. From a different perspective, recipient countries may be suspicious of the intents and impacts of newer Southern partners, especially those that are regional hegemons. Brazil and South Africa, for example, both have to confront a degree of reservation, or indeed active concern, about their weight and power within their respective regions. Their role as donors, whether in the South–South mode or through TDC, broadens their range of foreign policy tools. The policy literature also acknowledges that TDC may not result in greater recipient country ownership, owing to indifference, continued excessive transaction costs or these concerns about the commercial and geopolitical ambitions of the pivotal states (see Box 6.2).

Governance regimes within recipient countries

What do these shifts in the institutional centres of power and in High Level Meetings and Forums imply for the ways in which the 'traditional' donors and (re-)emerging development assistance partners interact within recipient countries? At this stage we do not have enough evidence to point to definitive trends, other than the broadest recognition that there is indeed a greater level of awareness and interaction among 'ground-level' personnel in development agencies and institutions. The non-DAC partner that has attracted the most attention is China, but even here empirical evidence based on field research is scarce. Cautiously, then, I will make three observations based on a research project on India's development cooperation relations with Kenya (Mawdsley 2010), but acknowledge that all require greater empirical investigation.

First, different recipient contexts lead to widely varying strategic imperatives for donors and development partners of all varieties at the country level. Approaches to donor cooperation and coordination vary by specific country context and sector – there is always some flexibility within foreign policy and development assistance positions and agendas, while the role of individuals can also be important. Overall, India tends to be reluctant to get involved in donor coordination or TDC in most contexts, preferring not to be hemmed in geopolitically or commercially by agreeing to shared donor agreements, and in order to maintain its ideological position of difference from the Western donors. However, in Afghanistan it is a member of the Donors Group. In part this willingness to coordinate with other development powers reflects the security situation and the fact that all bilateral partners must work within a (relatively) militarily coordinated context. It is also in deference to the United States, with which, over the last few years, India has actively pursued close and friendly relations (Raja Mohan 2004). Acting cooperatively in the development arena in a context where the USA appreciates a show of allies will win approval. Finally, the complex allegiances and rivalries between different elements of the Pakistani and Afghan political, military and insurgent factions means that India has a close and strong interest in observing and indeed influencing decisions made within and about Afghanistan (Usher 2009). By choosing to work with the other donors in Afghanistan it increases its chances of leverage. Thus far, however, such donor cooperation has tended not to follow in other countries, with the exception of Nepal, which, as noted earlier, is a result of India's initial primacy as a development partner; and in the aftermath of the 2004 tsunami, when India joined Australia, the United States and Japan to coordinate the humanitarian response (Oglesby 2011).

The second observation is that many of the representatives of the DAC donors and multilaterals within recipient countries are already overwhelmed by excessive bureaucracy and substantial transaction costs, and attempts to promote greater dialogue and cooperation with more non-DAC actors is challenging. The (uneven) efforts to implement the harmonization and alignment agendas associated with the Paris process have led to considerable pressures on national-level offices to work through arduous detail and difficult negotiations in order to make this work on the ground. The high-minded language and technical rationality that inform the pronouncements of the High Level Meetings, Declarations and Accords have to be translated into the complex realities of bringing together different donor positions, languages, agendas and interests at the operational level. Incorporating yet more actors into this process, and moreover ones that are usually even more diverse and poorly institutionalized than the already variegated DAC members, is a tremendous challenge – even assuming they are willing to comply. An example of this comes from the Kenya Joint Assistance Strategy (KJAS), which was launched in September 2007 following two years of negotiations. KJAS is an attempt by thirteen DAC donors and a number of multilateral donors (the European Commission, the African Development Bank, the UN and the World Bank Group) in Kenya to move towards greater harmonization of aid in accordance with the Paris Declaration. In doing so, KJAS is the most ambitious effort yet to achieve donor coordination in Kenya. Earlier efforts, which were only partially successful (see Brown 2007, 2009), had resulted in the formation of a Donor Consultative Group (DCG) in Kenya. The DCG is described as a vehicle to achieve coordination, harmonization and alignment, thereby reducing transaction costs and improving efficiency and effectiveness (KCG 2003). However, it is a forum for Kenya's donors alone – meetings with the Kenyan government on donor/aid issues are held separately, which is one reason why China refuses to participate, arguing that this is detrimental to the sovereign authority of Kenya. Interestingly, some senior Kenyan correspondents suggested that in part donor coordination efforts were driven by the new threat from China (Mawdsley 2010). This chimes with Brown's (2009: 10) observation that:

> Many donors feel that, while they have provided an annual total of between $767 million and $1.3 billion in development assistance (net, 2003–2007), their leverage is not as strong as it used to be, especially since the Kenyan government increasingly enjoys access to other sources of funds, notably financial markets and China.

Interviews with representatives from the bilateral and multilateral parties involved in KJAS suggested a range of problems and benefits with the process and outcomes, but from varying positions of commitment to the principle of harmonization, and with a rather different range of interests and incentives to support or frustrate the process (Mawdsley 2010). What was clear was the very considerable difficulties achieving meaningful coordination between long-standing members of DAC and allied multilaterals – something that militated against the wholesale invitation to all other donors in Kenya to join the process.

KJAS is also an example of the third observation I will make here about the institutional impacts of the emerging donors at 'ground level' within the recipient countries. In policy analyses and international forums a whole range of non-DAC donors are discussed, from Poland to Thailand, Saudi Arabia to South Africa. But in Kenya at least, and I suspect more widely, the mainstream development community had eyes only for China. All interviewees in the DAC bilaterals and multilateral organizations were asked whether they had ever considered approaching India as a potential member or even simply as an observer of KJAS. While India has only a very modest development cooperation relationship with Kenya, it is a long-standing partner and a major emerging power. The response was universal bemusement. Most stated that this thought had never crossed their minds. As one respondent in a sizeable and active bilateral said, '[u]ntil you pointed it out, I didn't realise that we never talk about India'.[10] This stood in sharp contrast to the position on China. Although there were different degrees of interest in trying to engage China, every single interviewee had quite a lot to say about the country. All were aware of the various efforts to persuade China to attend key meetings, and were knowledgeable about main lines of debate between the various Chinese, Kenyan and DAC actors involved. All were well informed about the Chinese position on the different donor and donor-government forums, and most interviewees were interested and willing to discuss China's growing role in Kenya, Africa and the world in some detail. In the case of India, it would seem that its macro-scale ambitions and growing assertiveness and presence in various global forums (including mainstream foreign aid debates) still did not overcome the fact of its weak country presence. In the case of Kenya at least, despite being an important donor hub, the DAC donors have not sought to pursue an outreach policy to NDDs other than China.

Conclusions

The themes and principles that underlie this book are further elucidated in this chapter. The ways in which different (re-)emerging development actors are engaging with a rapidly changing development architecture points to a range of strategic compulsions and shifting positions within wider state relations. Commentators are currently sifting the evidence as to whether different non-DAC donors and development partners will choose to draw closer to existing (or modestly amended) mainstream guidelines; whether they will develop their own cooperative but parallel governance systems; or whether they will refuse to engage with the dominant architecture or norms and maintain bilateral policy and decision-making. The assumption made by most mainstream liberal commentators is that the first scenario is the most desirable, leading as it might to a concerted effort to tackle poverty and promote growth and development. Recognizing the hurdles to complete integration, most commentators argue that the 'traditional' community has some things to learn from these 'new' entrants, that the (re-)emerging development partners require incentives to join the mainstream community, and that initially at least the introduction of a tiered set of commitments for different donors is a desirable compromise arrangement. They are probably right – the foreign aid system of past decades has been undermined by its excessive number of actors, channels and programmes; and delegitimized by its complicity in the strategic pursuit of bilateral geopolitical and commercial interests. The Paris process attempts to address both of these flaws.

But while the new millennium aid paradigm takes on important problems, and is making modest progress with some, it does not sufficiently or fundamentally address the structural defects of the neoliberal global economy within which global development governance is situated. The reforming liberal mainstream does not primarily contest unequal trade relations, unequal protectionism, the erosion of worker and citizen rights, or the damage of excessive privatization, commodification and unrestrained financialization. From this perspective, bringing 'in' the non-DAC donors may increase the number of blankets available to those who have lost their irrigation water to commercial flower farms, or give more NGOs the resources to educate girls for whom there is no universal state-supplied secondary schooling system. It does not advance a rights-based claim to even the minimum requirements of a dignified life, or confront the surging national and global experience of inequality. Even if one does not subscribe to this radical critique of mainstream aid and development agendas, it is possible to make a more pragmatic case for less coherence. The largest of the (re-)emerging development partners have effectively opened up a market for aid – they have provided the competition beloved of neoliberals (for excellent discussions, see Sato et al. 2010; Xu 2011). 'Traditional' donors have lost the monopoly they had grown used to during the 1990s, which in large part explains the attempts by the dominant institutions to engage with the NDDs. The call for greater dialogue, cooperation and collaboration can be viewed as an attempt to co-opt the NDDs into a 'universal' normative agenda. Chandy and Kharas (2011: 748) quote the US State Department reporting on the views of Kenya's ambassador to China, Julius Ole Sunkuli, as revealed by Wikileaks:

> Sunkuli claimed that Africa was better off thanks to China's practical, bilateral approach to development assistance and was concerned that this would be changed by western interference. He said he saw no concrete benefit for Africa in even minimal cooperation. Sunkuli said Africans were frustrated by western insistence on capacity building, which translated, in his eyes, into conferences and seminars. They instead preferred China's focus on infrastructure and tangible projects. He also worried that Africa would lose the benefit of having some leverage to negotiate with their donors if their development partners joined forces.

As Chandy and Kharas (ibid.) say, such cynicism may be 'too extreme', and there are certainly positive possibilities and avenues for engagement and cooperation within an emerging system of global aid governance; and legitimate concerns that without a workable global governance regime there will be a 'race to the bottom' in foreign aid and development cooperation. They suggest donor coordination is likely to be best leveraged to developmental outcomes when it is managed and driven by the recipient countries themselves – if they are able to decide upon and insist on aid strategies and management, and on their relationships with their donors and partners, individually and jointly.

The overall picture is one of flux. The dominant institutions and regimes of 'traditional' foreign aid *and* the non-DAC donors and development partners are in a state of change, as the outcomes of the Busan High Level Forum demonstrate. In the last chapter we draw these thoughts together to consider the impacts and outcomes of the changing development landscape.

7 | From aid to development effectiveness and New Global Partnerships

The rising numbers, voice and influence of the (re-)emerging development actors is a major reason why the complex landscape of foreign aid and development cooperation is currently in a state of significant flux – indeed, of paradigm shift. In the run-up to the Fourth High Level Forum of the Working Party on Aid Effectiveness (HLF4) in November 2011 there was a palpable sense of change in the air as commentators started talking about 'a post-aid world' (Schulz 2010a), while a phrase that began to circulate widely was 'from aid effectiveness to development effectiveness' (e.g. Rogerson 2011a). Kharas et al. (2011) predicted a new 'aid ecosystem', suggesting that a single 'aid architecture' is simply no longer viable. We should not overstate the case – there is unlikely to be a complete rupture with the notion of or commitment to aid effectiveness, and many of its themes and principles will remain firmly on the agenda, but as we will see, it may well be displaced as the central organizing principle, however aspirational, of a rapidly changing and diverse international development community.

This concluding chapter starts by charting out how different actors are talking about development effectiveness and critically assessing what they mean by it. The second section then looks at future scenarios for development cooperation and coordination across the spectrum of actors. It focuses on whether and how different (re-)emerging development partners will join, modify or reject the emerging aid architecture and global development governance regime.

From aid effectiveness to development effectiveness?

The term 'development effectiveness' (DE) emerged in the late 1990s and the early millennium as the development community sought to ensure the value and purpose of aid (e.g. UNDP 2001; Lockhart 2004; Quibria 2004; *Journal of Development Effectiveness, passim*). Early in the coalescence of the aid effectiveness paradigm the UNDP (2001: 11) described it thus:

Development effectiveness reflects the extent to which an institution or intervention has brought about targeted change in a country or the life of the individual beneficiary. Development effectiveness is influenced by various factors, beginning with the quality of project design and ending with the relevance and sustainability of desired results.

In this register DE is associated with the Paris Agenda principles of organizational effectiveness and coherence, recipient country capacity and ownership, and is closely linked to the demand for improved monitoring and evaluation of development projects and programmes to improve results-based management.

In the months preceding HLF4, it was noticeable that the term 'development effectiveness' started to circulate strongly around the foreign aid community in blogs, preparatory meetings, research articles, background papers and position statements, but in something of a new formulation. At the same time the 'aid effectiveness' agenda appeared to be losing momentum and backing from former champions (Eurodad 2011). In the meeting itself, DE became perhaps the key subject of conversation. Indeed, some participants were surprised to find that the sessions that had been scheduled to assess progress on the aid effectiveness agenda were more or less sidelined.[1] As the DAC monitoring process demonstrated, progress on many of the targets was poor, especially those agreed to by the donor countries (OECD-DAC 2008, 2011a; Wood et al. 2011). Yet this unfinished business and implementation deficit was largely set aside in discussions as most delegations focused their attention on the emerging DE debates (Better Aid 2011; Eurodad 2011). Interestingly, it was the partner (recipient) states which did the most to try to keep aid effectiveness on the table, suggesting that they could see a value in holding donors (of all hues) to account in the ways outlined in the Paris Declaration and particularly the Accra Agenda for Action. For all its faults, the Paris Agenda attempts to hold stakeholders to scrutiny and to defined targets, and has attempted to push aid in a number of sound directions, including greater predictability, alignment with country systems and mutual accountability (Rogerson 2011a).

The emerging notion of 'development effectiveness' (DE) in its newest register remains vague, certainly compared to the agreements and targets of the aid effectiveness agenda. A number of CSOs have attempted to interpret it as a new rights-based agenda. Better Aid (2011), for example, has argued that a new development cooperation system should be built upon 'a focus on human rights, recognizing the centrality of poverty reduction, gender equality, social justice, decent work and environmental sustainability'. Ssewakiryanga (2011), a Ugandan CSO activist, asserts that: '[f]or civil society, [development effectiveness] is a concept that goes beyond efficient disbursement procedures (which is what aid effectiveness is) to focus on ensuring that human rights are at the core of the way in which aid is delivered'. Interestingly, Ssewakiryanga (ibid.) recognizes that the non-DAC development partners may constitute a particular challenge to this vision. He goes on to say:

> This call for adopting a rights-based approach to aid delivery will certainly be a touchy issue, especially because the new emerging donors have little to show in terms of linking up their rapid economic development with the protection of human rights. Indeed, as we go forward, the place of human rights in the aid discourse remains contested.

Ssewakiryanga (ibid.) is correct to expect resistance, and this rights-based projection of DE represents a minority view that is likely to be overwhelmed by a more dominant construction of DE that appears to be emerging among many DAC and non-DAC states alike. As noted above, there is no agreed or approved definition, and this is necessarily a highly generalized outline, but the key elements seem to cohere around a number of themes, all of which are clearly open to considerable variation in interpretation and implementation. Most of the elements are not new, but the concept has arguably coalesced into a discourse of paradigmatic change because of a confluence of interests among a range of actors, at a moment of wider instability and change, and given the 'policy window' provided by the HLF4 and the end of the WP-EFF's mandate. I would suggest that these elements are:

1 There is a recognized and respected role for foreign aid, but less as a direct instrument of development in itself and more as a catalyst working to improve the developmental outcomes of trade, philanthropic activities, private sector investment, corporate standards and so on (Kharas et al. 2011; Rogerson 2011b). The current DAC-led mainstream paradigm broadly (although by no means entirely) tends to separate aid out conceptually, administratively and as a resource flow. There now appears to be a growing sense that aid should come out of its silo.

2 Economic growth is being firmly elevated as the central plank of development effectiveness. From a range of ideological viewpoints, and with different degrees of emphasis, many commentators argue that productivity and economic growth, while not entirely neglected,

have moved too far off centre stage, while the official mainstream aid community has focused too strongly perhaps on social sectors and 'soft-wiring'. China's remarkable success in tackling its own poverty levels provides a lesson here, and one that is now being actively discussed within the aid and development community, notably through the China–DAC Study Group, which was formed in 2009.[2] Moreover, growth and poverty reduction elsewhere in the world are also being attributed to the economic dynamism of China and the other rising powers. Smith (2005) argues that trade with China is more important to African prosperity than Western poverty-relief initiatives (referring specifically to those being proposed by Gordon Brown at the time); while Watts (2005) observes that, driven by China, in aggregate Africa's GDP rose by 5.8 per cent in 2004, the biggest increase in thirty years. Among other things, this view elevates the potential role of the private sector, which is increasingly being discussed as a key driver of development (Davies 2011; Nelson 2011). It also intersects with the recent policy coherence for development debate (Droeze 2008; Picciotto 2005; Manning 2008; Hudson and Jonsson 2009), and the arguments that, to be effective, development efforts must go 'beyond aid'. The larger picture is that of modernization redux – industrial-based growth is being recentred at the heart of 'development'.

3 Building on these arguments is a new openness to the concept of development financing. Severino and Ray (2009, 2010) suggest that we need to move away from the very circumscribed concept of ODA to a broader notion of global public financing, including financing for climate change, export credits and other forms of non-concessional public funds, and private sector loans and investment. It is notable that at the 2010 meeting of the UN Development Cooperation Forum, in which recipient states and (re-)emerging development partners had considerable voice, there was an attempt to recognize export credits on concessional terms as aid contributions, something that at that time would represent a clear departure from DAC standards, but which is now being actively considered by the DAC (Chandy and Kharas 2011).

4 Finally, the turn to 'development effectiveness' appears to reflect the emergence of a new global development governance regime, in which Western/DAC dominance is replaced by a more inclusive set of nodes, networks and norms. However, whether this is desirable (for all non-DAC partners) or possible, or indeed would be effective, are issues we discuss later in this chapter.

In this formulation DE goes far beyond its earlier iteration, which was essentially a way of describing the means and goals of the aid effectiveness agenda. The new 'development effectiveness' debate recalls earlier modernization theories and trickle-down economics as it recentres economic growth as an essential condition for poverty reduction. The rising powers as development cooperation partners and more broadly have been active and tacit drivers of this agenda, and it seems to be one towards which the 'traditional' donors are increasingly leaning. Leipziger (2011: 28) suggests that:

> The rise of the G20 provides a massive political opportunity for development cooperation. Because several G20 countries are recent aid recipients and new donors, the G20 has a broader view of what constitutes acceptable development assistance. The belief often espoused by the most generous aid donors that assistance should directly alleviate poverty, rather than contribute to broad-based economic growth, is no longer the dominant sentiment. Indeed, current World Bank Chief Economist Justin Lin ... advocates for a new structuralist approach that is perilously close to government-led growth and strong on supporting the real economy and developing comparative advantages.

The question is, of course, whether and how the lessons of the last forty years of efforts to broaden out the concept of development will be expressed and shaped within this emerging agenda, including environmental sustainability, gender rights, social well-being, human security, rights and the rule of law, and so on. To what extent will workers, women, the marginalized, citizens, regions and, indeed, future generations command an equitable share of the benefits of economic growth? At the same time, how will the costs of growth – environmentally, culturally and in terms of specific places and livelihoods – be ameliorated, compensated and shared? To what extent will broader and alternative conceptualizations of 'development' prosper – equality, happiness, diversity, leisure, solidarity, creativity, community and freedom – as the rising powers drive improved economic growth and productivity?

Rogerson (2011a) documents the contexts within which these development and foreign aid debates are taking place. Most salient are the emerging shifts in power and wealth. These are by no means confined to the larger rising powers, but include a host of other, smaller dynamic economies. In turn, this has implications for the distribution of global poverty – nearly three-quarters of the world's poor now live in countries formally designated as middle-income (Sumner 2010), which in turn has implications for how poverty is understood, experienced and addressed (Glennie 2011c). The (re-)emerging development partners are formulating their development cooperation policies and discourses in a context in which many are also addressing or experiencing substantial domestic poverty levels. Another major global change centres on the increasing channels and availability of development financing, including remittances, South–South foreign direct investment, regional development banks and commercial lending. Climate change, potential resource scarcity, rapid urbanization and ongoing population growth are just some of the other factors in thinking through contemporary development contexts.

With these wider issues in mind, we can identify a number of reasons for what appears to be a transition from 'aid effectiveness' to 'development effectiveness'. First, it is clear that many of the DAC and other mainstream donors are, for various reasons, failing to meet their Paris Agenda commitments. As we have seen, the explanations for this vary, but it seems likely that the 'traditional' donors underestimated the costs and technical challenges of the Agenda. More importantly, it seems that they also proved reluctant to cede genuine ownership to partner countries, or policy space and national objectives to other donors. By treating development as a realm of technical rationality and suppressing the political nature (including geostrategic and commercial implications) of foreign aid and development, the Paris Agenda was only ever likely to make partial progress.

A second context for changing attitudes to aid among the 'traditional' donors has been the 'global' (but more pointedly the European, Japanese and American) financial crisis and its reverberations. Aid budgets have come under threat across the DAC membership, and among the traditional donors many national aid agencies are being subject to budget cuts and the imposition of new policy directions that link them more tightly and openly to national interests. At the same time, the older industrialized nations are observing the economic dynamism of many other parts of the world, something that brings great opportunities for the North, but also real and perceived challenges and threats. Indeed, we are witnessing not just the rise of 'new donors' but, in some cases, significant reverse flows of aid and financing. In 2011, for example, China and Brazil proposed to channel money through the IMF to prop up the Eurozone economy, demanding favourable trade concessions and currency rates in exchange for their aid (Childress 2011; Amar 2012). In this context, the reality and perception that many of the rising powers are harnessing aid and development cooperation to their national economic and strategic interests are encouraging many within Western/DAC governments, policy circles, the private sector and the public to redefine their own foreign aid agendas.

The (re-)emerging development actors are major contributors to the changing aid paradigm in a variety of ways. First, the growing numbers and voice of the 'new' development/donor countries (including many that also continue to be recipients) is driving a deepening multipolarity within the aid and development arena. As Narlikar (2012) argues in relation to global governance regimes more broadly, international regimes and organizations *must* now adapt to the power transitions that are currently under way, and it is necessary and proper that they do so. As we can observe within the multilateral arenas of foreign aid and development, this is resulting in institutions, norms and policies that are, ideally, becoming more democratic, representative and fair. But as Narlikar (ibid.) observes, greater inclusivity tends to heighten the proclivity to deadlock (a concern about the UN Development Co-operation Forum, for example). The rising numbers of development actors has made an already difficult task of securing agreement and coordination around aid effectiveness much harder.

Importantly, of course, this is not due to numbers alone, but also reflects greater diversity of political economies, interests, cultures and norms among the rising powers. Many of the (re-)emerging development partners articulate and practise rather different approaches to development cooperation. China is often the focus of interest here, but as many commentators observe, this is not entirely a DAC/non-DAC divide – China shares many outlooks and practices with other Asian donors, including India, Japan and Korea. As well as their material expression and impacts, which are discussed below, (re-)emerging development partners situate their activities and agendas in ways that speak to alternative historic and contemporary identities and experiences. Over the last five years or so, the mainstream foreign aid community has had to take much greater cognizance of the power and attraction of these positions and discourses. Drawing on the insights of constructivist international relations theorists (e.g. Finnemore 1996; Hulme and Fukuda-Parr 2009), I would suggest international development norms are currently in a period of challenge, instability and re-creation.

This is closely related to the third impact of many of the (re-)emerging development partners, which is (in some cases) their success in promoting economic growth and/or poverty reduction. As we have seen, the Southern partners especially tend to have a much wider concept of development financing, a stronger focus on productivity and growth, and a more holistic approach to blurring and blending aid flows with wider trade, investment and diplomatic activities. (Re-)emerging development partners are also leading innovators of social programmes, research for development, and technology that is affordable, available and adaptable. Recognizing these skills and comparative advantages, South–South and trilateral/triangular development cooperation are now strongly endorsed by the global development community. The (re-) emerging development partners, and especially China, have in many respects demonstrated successful and effective approaches to poverty reduction and development cooperation (Chandy and Kharas 2011). Xu (2011) argues that this has unintentionally but unquestionably led to shifts within mainstream ideas, organizations and regimes. While elements of these approaches have been the subject of significant criticism (e.g. Naím 2007) or, more commonly, measured concerns (e.g. Manning 2006), over the last few years it would appear that the mainstream aid community has been starting to re-evaluate these policies and principles. In some cases, for example, the non-DAC development partners have shown how bundling aid and commerce can work very effectively to enhance growth; while the enthusiasm with which many of the NDDs have been greeted by recipient countries, even if it has not been without reservation, has been a salutary experience for the 'traditional' donors.

The current 'development effectiveness' debate is at an early stage, and there are major uncertainties about whether and how it might consolidate in terms of agreed norms and institutional oversight. These questions are exceptionally important. Without meaningful agreements and safeguards the development effectiveness agenda may ultimately descend into a commercial and geopolitical race to the bottom. Profit-making and security rationales may rapidly overtake a 'development' agenda that has been absorbed back into an economic growth model (Grimm et al. 2009). Without social, environmental, gendered and labour rights, which tend not to be strongly supported by the more powerful of the rising powers (Fues 2012), or the restraints and commitments of the aid effectiveness agenda, the drive to improve economic growth and productivity may have little wider developmental benefit, especially if located within an expanded but unreconstructed commitment to neoliberal globalization (Taylor 2009).

The future of cooperation?

Summer 2012 marked the end of the extended mandate of the Working Party on Aid Effectiveness, which had to date been the most effective and inclusive global development forum. Although the nascent UN Development Cooperation Forum is more representative (and may well become a key node of global development governance in the future), it was the WP-EFF that, for all of its manifold shortcomings, attempted to systematically translate the principles of aid effectiveness into actual targets and commitments and monitor their progress. It achieved a rapidly widening membership and buy-in from a range of recipients, donor/recipients and non-state actors, and by HLF3 in 2008 was acting as a forum in which developing countries as recipients and donors were clearly exercising a more assertive voice, as evident in the Accra Agenda for Action. However, for all of these achievements, progress was at best partial, donor political will appeared to some extent to have faded, and its DAC origins, management and dominance put a brake on the extent to which some non-DAC development actors – and notably the large rising powers – wished to engage with it.

The Busan Partnership Document (BPD), the outcome of HLF4 in 2011, was the product of intense political negotiation and compromise, and beneath the rhetoric of progress and agreement we must recognize the ongoing differences of power and opinion that it represents. As widely expected, the BPD has attempted to enrol the full range of (re-) emerging development partners as founding partners within a new global development cooperation partnership. Recognizing different positions, needs and potential contributions, it sets up a picture of 'shared principles, common goals and differential commitments for effective international development'. The document is suffused with claims to a unity of purpose and essential principles, but at every turn is keen to stress the diversity of actors, and the necessity of recognizing and respecting alternative modalities and approaches to achieve development cooperation, as well as voluntary agreement and tiered commitments.

A Post-Busan Interim Group (PBIG), which is made up of representatives from a wide range of states and non-state actors, was tasked with the very considerable remit of formulating a new Global Partnership for Effective Development Cooperation, to be launched in June 2012, although the deadlines may shift. The Organisation for Economic Co-operation and Development and the United Nations Development Programme were invited to 'support the effective functioning of the Global Partnership, building on their collaboration to date and their respective mandates and areas of comparative advantage'. This book is being finished as these negotiations, consultations and proposals are under way (e.g. OECD-DAC/WP-EFF 2012a, 2012b), but by the time it is published the Global Partnership should be a reality. Its form, membership, authority and mandate will be revealing of the complicated and dynamic interplay of credibility, legitimacy and incentives for different donors and development partners.

The arguments in this book demonstrate the tremendous opportunities and challenges that the diverse array of (re-)emerging development partners have brought to this potential new era of development cooperation. I have sought to stress the diversity of the non-DAC donors, and the importance of seeing beyond China – critical though China's role is and will be. I have also stressed the importance of the historical lineages of non-DAC development cooperation: even in a rapidly changing world, their past experiences and identities have meaningful purchase on their current development cooperation ideologies, practices and relationships, and are essential to understanding their views, aspirations and concerns. While I agree with the vast majority of commentators who urge the importance of greater development cooperation and coordination, I have concerns about the claim that all development actors share 'common principles', even when these are very modestly couched (as in the BPD) within an emphatic recognition of legitimate differences. The dangers are that this will again produce a technical and depoliticized understanding of development, both as an outcome and as a process. In fact, as I have argued throughout, the nature and pursuit of development are profoundly political, in that what constitutes 'development' and how to achieve it are contested concepts, ideologically founded, and suffused with power differentials. These do not, of course, exist only between states – as the elites of both DAC and non-DAC states sometimes seem to imply – but are increasingly evident within them. The widening inequalities of the neoliberal era are not contested within the Busan Partnership document, and it seems unlikely that they will be foregrounded in the Global Partnership.

The rising powers are increasingly important drivers of development theory and practice. It is evident, and not before time, that the mainstream aid and development community around the world – political, practitioner and academic – is moving rapidly to understand, engage with and learn from these actors, in contrast to the parochial nature of much of the earlier (Western) focus, theorizing and analysis. It is likely that the rising powers will also come under increased scrutiny and interest from their own publics and civil society actors, as they will from different groups and interests in recipient/partner countries. This book helps understand how this complex and multidimensional set of actors and issues has evolved, and what sort of roles they might play in a new era of development cooperation.

Notes

Introduction

1 All of these categories intersect of course – China is also a socialist state, while some would argue that Brazil is a regional rather than a global power.

2 Glennie (2012) points to the film *When China Met Africa*, which follows three Chinese and Zambian individuals, as showing the 'human face of the relationship': whenchinametafrica.com/, accessed 15 February 2012.

3 O'Neill (2012) suggests that it is out of date and insulting to refer to the BRICs as 'emerging' economies, given they are now the dominant drivers of global economic growth.

4 As we shall see in later chapters, the geographical boundary and imaginative cartography of giving and receiving are also bound up in equally artificial constructions of 'West' and 'East' (Drazkiewicz 2007; Gray 2011).

5 The G6 was created in 1975 and was made up of the major industrial economies (France, Germany, Italy, Japan, the UK and the USA). Canada joined in 1976. It became the G8 in 1997 when Russia joined. The G20 consists of the G8 plus Argentina, Australia, Brazil, China, India, Indonesia, Mexico, Saudi Arabia, South Africa, South Korea, Turkey and the European Union.

1 Contexts

1 Jim O'Neill, who originally coined the term BRICs, on the other hand, argues that Russia is in fact an economic powerhouse, and while many Western commentators have all sorts of reservations about its economic and political management, it should most certainly be considered a BRIC economy (O'Neill 2012).

2 The full text of the speech can be found at: english. people.com.cn/english/200010/10/ eng20001010_52238.html, accessed 29 August 2011.

3 Rist (2003), however, argues that the NIEO was essentially an elitist project that would, even if it had been successful, not have resulted in democratic developmental benefits for wider populations. This is an argument that resonates with some concerns about the impacts of the contemporary (re-)emerging development partners, which are discussed later in this book.

4 The CEE states are something of an outlier in this discussion. They are among the original 'emerging markets', but they would not conventionally be described as 'emerging powers'. They vary widely, of course – Poland is significantly more influential than Lithuania, and is engaged within the EU and beyond its borders in very different ways. As we shall see in the next chapter, they are (re-)emerging foreign aid donors for distinctive reasons.

5 This is necessarily an extremely brief introduction to a vast field, and is hugely simplifying and

reductionist about these complex schools of thought.

6 'Glossary of terms', DAC website, www.oecd.org/document/ 32/0,3 343,en_2649_33721_42632800_1_1_1_1, 00.html#ODA, accessed 7 December 2010.

7 Reisen (2010) charts the extraordinary plurality and incoherence of the multilateral sector, noting that there are over two hundred multilateral organizations, including forty-seven UN agencies, funds and commissions; two IMF trust funds; five World Bank bodies; four European Union bodies, and so on (see also Kharas 2007; Hammad and Morton 2009). Rajan and Subramanian (2005) argue that multilateral aid is also subject to poor management, interference, replication and so on. As we shall see later in this book, there is a strong view that the current multilateral system is ominously creaky in the face of rapid and major shifts in wealth and power, and given the nature of global public problems in the new millennium (Leipziger 2011).

8 See Clemens and Moss (2005) and Glennie (2008) on the problematic history and nature of this target.

9 Dietz and Houtcamp (1995) point out that Soviet aid to African partners had been declining since the early/mid-1980s, while Western aid to some of these countries increased considerably in the same period. Although 1991 marked a sea-change in global geopolitics which certainly had significant impacts for the politics of foreign aid, changes were taking place prior to this.

10 For the DAC's own assessment, see the survey released in September 2011: www.aideffectiveness. org/busanhlf4/en/newsroom/519-aid-effectiveness-global-views-on-a-global-scorecard.html, accessed 24 February 2012.

2 Histories and lineages

1 As ever, a review of this nature tends to homogenize and simplify what were complex, diverse and dynamic relations between different countries over time, which were shaped by competing individuals, institutions and agendas. A detailed analysis of Russian–Nigerian relations from 1960 to 1991 (Matusevich 2003) ably demonstrates this. I am grateful to Patty Gray for drawing my attention to this book.

2 P. Halaxa and P. Lebeda (1998), 'Mnohostranná rozvojová pomoc České republiky', *Mezinárodní politika*: 7–9.

3 Bayly also discusses similar themes in relation to India, although in this publication she concentrates on Vietnam.

4 In a different category, Vietnam also provided unskilled and manual labour to regimes experiencing labour shortages. These workers joined Koreans, Cubans, Chinese and others in labour-needy places like Czechoslovakia and East Germany.

5 The Colombo Plan for Cooperative Economic Development in South and South-East Asia (now 'for Cooperative Economic and Social Development in Asia and the Pacific') was launched in 1951 following a Commonwealth Conference on Foreign Affairs conference in Sri Lanka in 1950. It was created in the context of rising US hegemony, the decline of formal British colonialism in Asia, and what was seen as a growing communist threat within Asia (Tarling 1986). As well as promoting the transfer of capital and skills from its developed-country to

less-developed-country members, it was also committed to South–South cooperation. However, as Tarling demonstrates, British enthusiasm for the Asian-led components of the Plan was driven by concerns that they should not appear to be dictating the agenda. In fact it was aimed primarily at blunting the appeal of communism by supporting economic growth and development. Securing India's cooperation was seen as vital.

6 ssc.undp.org/content/ssc.html, accessed 25 February 2012.

7 The majority of OPEC members are Arab countries in the Gulf region, and as donors they share many attributes in their agendas, institutions and cultures – although they are by no means homogeneous. They are the focus of this section, although this misses some of the similarities and differences with the non-Arab OPEC donors, Ecuador, Nigeria and Venezuela.

8 Although Shushan and Marcoux (2011) report that Qatar is in the process of establishing a sovereign agency known as the Qatar Development Fund. They also suggest that Iraq, which was a donor from 1974 to 1982, may return to aid activities.

9 www.trialog.or.at/start. asp?ID=96.

10 Many DAC donors have also been aid recipients – both Korea and Japan were significant aid recipients at different points in their histories, and a number of European countries were beneficiaries of the post-Second World War Marshall Plan. However, as Rowlands (2008) argues, in the case of the latter, this did not establish a sense of solidarity (real, imagined or contrived) with poorer countries. Rather, he suggests, they were reconstructing rather than developing, and thus 're-establishing their prior and self-deemed rightful place near the apex of the global hierarchy. Consequently, they retained either the fiction or reality of their role as imperial powers, with a superior status to poorer countries that were usually former colonies' (ibid.: 8).

11 For an excellent case study, see Oglesby (2011) on the multiple ways in which India's experiences as a recipient have shaped its approach to development cooperation as a 'donor'.

3 (Re-)emerging development partners

1 In April 2011 the DAC issued a formal statement on 'New Partnerships in Development Cooperation', in which it stated that reporting aid flows would have no bearing on a country's status as an aid recipient (OECD-DAC 2011a).

2 www.chinaafricarealstory.com/, accessed 10 February 2012.

3 One reason for caution about aid data is the distinction between aid/development cooperation pledged and the final amount disbursed. For instance, in Afghanistan, India had disbursed by 2008 only 22 per cent of the pledged amount for the period FY2002–FY2011, making it the second-worst performance among twenty-seven bilateral and multilateral donors examined; better only than that of Spain, which came in at 10 per cent (Waldman 2008, cited in Kondoh et al. 2010). However, as this example makes clear, this is both a DAC and a non-DAC issue.

4 In 2010 only five DAC countries had achieved this target (Denmark, Luxembourg, Norway, the Netherlands and Sweden). Whether they

will sustain this ration is questionable, and overall this does seem to be a somewhat unrealistic aspiration for the CEE states at present.

5 As ever, though, the detail is more complicated. For example, India, China and South Africa are UN Disaster Assessment and Coordination (UNDAC) member countries, which means that they financially support their participation in the UNDAC system through depositing funds with OCHA (in so-called 'mission accounts') to cover the deployment costs of their national UNDAC members on UNDAC missions. Brazil, on the other hand, is a UNDAC participating country, which means that it provides experts to be part of the UNDAC team but does not cover their costs of deployment. The cost of deployment is covered by voluntary contributions of donor countries; www.unocha.org/what-we-do/coordination-tools/undac/membership, accessed 23 February 2012. I am grateful to Pranay Sinha for bringing this example to my attention.

6 www.southsouth.info/forum/topics/it-is-a-good-practice-the, accessed 17 February 2012.

7 europafrica.net/2010/10/29/south-africa-plans-aid-agency-to-boost-african-development/, accessed 17 February 2012.

8 www.oecd.org/document/38/0,3746,en_2649_3236398_45675430_1_1_1_1,00.html, accessed 25 February 2012.

9 www.ibon.org/, accessed 28 February 2012.

10 www.realityofaid.org/roa-reports/index/secid/373/South-South-Development-Cooperation-A-challenge-to-the-aid-system, accessed 28 February 2012.

11 Details of this project and initial research findings can be found at www.geog.cam.ac.uk/research/projects/foreignaidperceptions/, accessed 17 February 2012.

12 See, for example, a story in the *Global Times* (28 November 2011) on a critical reaction to China's donation of buses to Macadonia: www.globaltimes.cn/NEWS/tabid/99/ID/686033/Government-must-look-before-it-leaps.aspx, accessed 23 February 2012.

13 Michael Hubbard and Pranay Sinha at Birmingham University (UK) have been working on a detailed technical analysis of the IATI, including whether and how it can enrol both DAC and non-DAC donors and development partners, and thus meaningfully capture 'traditional' ODA and South–South cooperation flows. Presentations, papers and videos can be accessed at www.birmingham.ac.uk/schools/government-society/departments/international-development/events/future-aid-data.aspx, accessed 17 February 2012.

14 www.thebrokeronline.eu/Blogs/Busan-High-Level-Forum/The-case-for-including-other-public-flows-for-development2, accessed 23 February 2012.

4 Modalities and practices

1 Dividing the various elements of development assistance up like this is of course arbitrary, and does not reflect the ways in which different countries may characterize the various elements themselves. For example, the Government of China (2011) lists eight aid instruments: complete projects, goods and materials, technical cooperation, human resource development cooperation, medical teams sent abroad, emergency humanitarian aid,

volunteer programmes in foreign countries, and debt relief. The UAE's 2009 Foreign Aid Report makes a distinction between three types of assistance: humanitarian, developmental and charity. The latter refers to assistance for cultural or religious purposes (Saidi and Wolf 2011).

2 www.chinaafricarealstory.com/2010_12_01_archive.html, accessed 17 February 2012.

3 As noted in Chapter 3, this may have contemporary resonances. Nissanke and Söderberg (2011) suggest that China and other development partners are starting to move towards more open competition and tendering. State support, including through the 'aid' element of development cooperation, has helped these firms to get a foothold by building experience and building up business relations and networks. In some cases they are ready to transition to a more competitive model. Approaches may change and differ, but in some respects the (re-) emerging development partners are now doing what the 'traditional' donors did in the past.

5 Discourse, imagery and performance

1 The introduction to gift theory and discussion of South–South development cooperation are based on a previously published paper (Mawdsley 2012). I am grateful to the editors and publishers of *Transactions of the Institute of British Geographers* for allowing me to reproduce it in part here.

2 That these anthropological ideas could be extended to contemporary states (and not just modern individuals and societies) was an argument developed quite explicitly by Mauss in his essay. Influenced by Durkheim's ideas on alienation in industrializing societies, and also by the catastrophic impacts of the First World War, Mauss looked to ways in which 'gift giving' between states could redirect antagonism and competition, subduing the Hobbesian state of 'primitive anarchy' between states.

3 Hattori critiques attempts by some liberal scholars to view foreign aid as an extension of the ideal of the welfare state. He argues that 'foreign aid is a voluntary practice of donor states, whereas welfare is a right of citizens' (2001: 636).

4 indiahighcom-mauritius.org/ MOS_nov3a.php, accessed 17 March 2012.

5 Interestingly, Jordan (2010) notes that Russia also attempts to assert a shared affinity and understanding with Africa, and position itself as a 'bridge' between North and South.

6 Moisés Naím was the Venezuelan minister for trade and industry in the early 1990s within a right-wing regime. He also served as director of Venezuela's Central Bank and as an executive director of the World Bank.

7 Available at lcweb2.loc.gov/frd/ cs /vetoc.html, accessed 17 February 2012.

6 Institutional overtures

1 This is of course complicated by whether or not these values should be understood as 'Western', and by the contested nature of these ideas and principles within and across the West and non-West. For example, some Sudanese feminists may embrace the liberating potential of Enlightenment-based secularist principles, while evangelical US senators may reject them.

2 Inevitably there are some major omissions in this list, notably the European Union, which is a very significant actor within global development governance. See Carbone (2007); Grimm et al. (2009).

3 siteresources.worldbank. org/INTLAC/Resources/FactSheet-BogotaConference.pdf, accessed 18 February 2012.

4 Individual members of the DAC have their own attitudes and approaches to the issue of the non-DAC development partners more broadly, and to individual (re-) emerging donors. Here we focus on the DAC as an institution, but recognize that it is the subject of considerable internal differences and pressures.

5 See www.oecd.org/dac/open-doors, accessed 18 February 2012.

6 www.oecd.org/dataoecd/45/0/ 44390151.pdf, accessed 18 February 2012.

7 www.oecd.org/document/7/0, 3746,en_2649_3236398_43364487_ 1_ 1_1_1,00.html, accessed 26 April 2012.

8 www.oecd.org/da-taoecd/16/63/45539861.pdf, accessed 18 February 2012.

9 Available at www.china. org.cn/business/g20/2009-04/02/ content_17545478.htm, accessed 18 February 2012.

10 Different individuals can make a great deal of difference. A particularly energetic, effective and robust recent Indian high commissioner to Ethiopia, Shri Gurjit Singh, actively deployed ITEC in promoting strategic and, he argued, mutually beneficial relations (Singh, personal communication, 2011).

7 From aid to development effectiveness

1 Laura Collins and Sungmi Kim, personal communication, 2012.

2 www.oecd.org/document/36/0, 3746,en_2649_34621_44173540_1_1_1_1 ,00.html, accessed 28 February 2012.

Bibliography

ABC (Agência Brasileira de Cooperação [Brazilian Cooperation Agency]) (2010) *Catálogo ABC de Cooperação Técnica do Brasil para a África* [ABC Catalogue for Brazil's Technical Cooperation with Africa], Brasilia: ABC.

Abdenur, A. (2007) 'The strategic triad: form and content in Brazil's triangular cooperation practices', International Affairs Working Paper 1007/6.

Abrahamsen, R. (2000) *Disciplining Democracy: Development Discourse and Good Governance in Africa*, London: Zed Books.

ACGI (Arab Coordination Groups Institutions) (2011) *The 2011 High-Level Partnership Dialogue. ACGI and the OECD-DAC*, www.oecd. org/dataoecd/23/5/48345739.pdf, accessed 22 February 2012.

ADB, OECD, UNECA and UNDP (2011) *African Economic Outlook 2011*, Paris/Nairobi: OECD/African Economic Research Consortium.

Adler, E. (2001) 'Constructivism and international relations', in W. Carlsnaes, T. Risse and B. A. Simmons (eds), *Handbook of International Relations*, London: Sage, pp. 95–118.

AECID (2010) 'Triangular cooperation in the context of aid effectiveness: experiences and views of European donors', Ministerio de Asuntos Exteriores y de Cooperación, Government of Spain.

Agarwal, M. (2010) 'G20 and development: reforms in the international economic system', in T. Fues and P. Wolff (eds), *G20 and Global Development: How can the new summit architecture promote pro-poor growth and sustainability?*, Bonn: DIE (German Development Institute).

Agensky, J. and J. Barker (2012) 'Indonesia and the liberal peace: recovering southern agency in global governance', in P. Amar (ed.), *Global South to the Rescue: Emerging Humanitarian Superpowers and Globalizing Rescue Industries*, London: Routledge.

Agrawal, S. (2007) *Emerging Donors in International Development Assistance – the India Case*, Canada: International Development Research Centre.

Alden, C. (2005a) 'South Africa's economic relations with Africa: hegemony and its discontents', *Journal of Modern African Studies*, 45: 367–92.

— (2005b) 'The new diplomacy of the South: South Africa, Brazil, India and trilateralism', *Third World Quarterly*, 26(7): 1077–95.

— (2007) *China in Africa*, London: Zed Books.

Alden, C. and G. le Pere (2004) 'South Africa's post-apartheid foreign policy: from reconciliation to ambiguity?', *Review of African Political Economy*, 100: 283–97.

Alden, C., D. Large and R. Soares de Oliveira (eds) (2008) *China Returns to Africa: A Superpower* and a Continent Embrace, London: Hurst.

Alden, C., S. Morphet and M. A. Vieira (2010) *The South in World Politics*, Basingstoke: Palgrave Macmillan.

Alesina, A. and D. Dollar (2000) 'Who gives foreign aid to whom and why?', *Journal of Economic Growth*, 5(1): 33–63.

Allyón, B. (2009) *South–South Cooperation (SSC) and Multilateral Governance of the Aid System: The implications for Spanish aid*, Madrid: Fundación para las Relaciones Internacionales y el Diálogo Exterior, www. fride.org/descarga/COM_CSS_ Gobernanza_Ayllon_ENG.pdf, accessed 23 February 2010.

Amar, P. (2012) 'Introduction: Global South to the rescue', in P. Amar (ed.), *Global South to the Rescue: Emerging Humanitarian Superpowers and Globalizing Rescue Industries*, London: Routledge.

Americas Forum for Freedom and Prosperity (2011) 'Venezuela's state-owned subsidiary Citgo relaunches program for America's poor', 13 December, www.americasforum.com/ content/venezuelas-state-owned-subsidiary-citgo-relaunches-program-americas-poor, accessed 10 February 2012.

Amin, S. (2009) 'Aid for development', in H. Abbas and Y. Niyiragira (eds), *Aid to Africa: Redeemer or Coloniser?*, Cape Town: Pambazuka Press, pp. 59–75.

Appadurai, A. (1986) *The Social Life of Things: Commodities in cultural perspective*, Cambridge: Cambridge University Press.

Arase, D. (2005) *Japan's Development Aid: Old Continuities and New Perspectives*, London: Routledge.

Armijo, L. E. (2007) 'The BRICs countries (Brazil, Russia, India, China) as an analytical category: mirage or insight', *Asian Perspectives*, 31(4): 7–42.

Arts, K. (2004) 'Changing interests in EU development cooperation: the impact of EU membership and advancing integration', in K. Arts and A. Dickson (eds), *EU Development Cooperation: From model to symbol?*, Manchester: Manchester University Press.

Ashoff, G. (2008) *The Development Cooperation Forum (DCF) in the Context of the International Aid Effectiveness Agenda*, Bonn: DIE (German Development Institute).

— (2010) 'Triangular cooperation: opportunities, risks and conditions for effectiveness', Special Report, *Development Outreach*, World Bank Institute, pp. 22–4, siteresources.worldbank.org/WBI/ Resources/213798-1286217829056/ ashoff.pdf, accessed 24 February 2011.

Åslund, A. (2010) 'Does Russia belong in the BRICs?', *Economists Forum*, 20 January, blogs.ft.com/ economistsforum/2010/01/ does-russia-belong-in-the-brics/#axzz1n6KVW6ho, accessed 22 February 2010.

Aycut, D. and A. Goldstein (2007) 'Developing country multinationals: South–South investment comes of age', in *Industrial Development for the 21st Century: Sustainable Development Perspectives*, United Nations, pp. 85–105.

Baaz, M. (2005) *The Paternalism of Partnership: A Postcolonial Reading of Identity in Development Aid*, London: Zed Books.

Bachman, J. (2012) 'Kenya and international security: enabling globalization, stabilising "stateness," and deploying "humanitarian counterterrorism"', in P. Amar (ed.), *Global South to the Rescue: Emerging Humanitarian Superpowers and Globalizing Rescue Industries*, London: Routledge.

Baginski, P. (2007) 'Polish foreign assistance in the EU context', Presentation at public hearing of European Parliament, Committee on Development, 30 January.

Bagoyoko, N. and M. Gilbert (2009) 'The linkage between security, development and governance: the European Union in Africa', *Journal of Development Studies*, 45(5): 789–814.

Baker, K. M. and R. L. Edmonds (2004) 'Transfer of Taiwanese ideas and technology to the Gambia, West Africa: a viable approach to rural development?', *Geographical Journal*, 170(3): 189–211.

Banks, G., W. A. Murray, J. Overton and R. Scheyvens (2011) 'Paddling on one side of the canoe? The changing nature of New Zealand's development assistance programme', NZADDS Working Paper, nzadds.org.nz/publications/, accessed 22 February 2012.

Barder, O. (2011) 'Global aid data governance for both DAC and non DAC donors – which institution is fit for purpose: OECD or UNDCF or any new one?', *A Future for Aid Data*, Workshop, University of Birmingham, October, www.birmingham.ac.uk/schools/government-society/departments/international-development/events/future-aid-data.aspx, accessed 22 February 2012.

Barnett, C. and L. Land (2007) 'Geographies of generosity: beyond the "moral turn"', *Geoforum*, 38: 1065–75.

Bayar, R. and F. Keyman (2012) 'Turkey: an emerging hub of globalization and internationalist humanitarian actor?, in P. Amar (ed.), *Global South to the Rescue: Emerging Humanitarian Superpowers and Globalizing Rescue Industries*, London: Routledge.

Bayly, S. (2007) *Asian Voices in a Postcolonial Age. Vietnam, India and Beyond*, Cambridge: Cambridge University Press.

— (2009) 'Vietnamese narratives of tradition, exchange and friendship in the worlds of the global socialist ecumene', in H. West and P. Raman (eds), *Enduring Socialism: Explorations of Revolution, Transformation and Restoration*, Oxford: Berghahn Books, pp. 125–47.

Beaudry-Somcynsky, M. and C. M. Cook (1999) *Japan's System of Official Development Assistance*, Ottawa: International Development Research Centre (IDRC).

Bellamy, A. J. (2005) 'Responsibility to protect or Trojan horse? The crisis in Darfur and humanitarian intervention after Iraq', *Ethics and International Affairs*, 19(2): 31–54.

— (2010) 'The responsibility to protect – five years on', *Ethics and International Affairs*, 24(2): 143–69.

Benthall, J. and J. Bellion-Jourdan (2009) *The Charitable Crescent: Politics of Aid in the Muslim World*, London: I. B. Tauris.

Beri, R. (2003) 'India's Africa policy in the post-Cold War era: an assessment', *Strategic Analysis*, 27(2), April–June.

— (2008) 'India's role in keeping peace in Africa', *Strategic Analysis*, 32(2): 197–221.

Better Aid (2011) *Statement on the Global Partnership for Effective*

Development Cooperation, 1 December.

Biesemans, S. (2007) 'New EU donors', Presentation at public hearing of European Parliament, Committee on Development, 30 January.

Bijoy, C. R. (2009) 'India – transiting to a global donor', in A. J. Tujan (ed.), *South–South Cooperation: A Challenge to the Aid System?*, Philippines: IBON Books, pp. 65–76.

Bilal, S. and F. Rampa (2011) 'Emerging economies in Africa and the development effectiveness debate', Discussion Paper 107, Maastricht: ECDPM.

Birdsall, N., H. Kharas, A. Mahgoug and R. Perakis (2010) *Quality of Official Development Assistance*, Washington, DC: Center for Global Development.

Bissell, R. E. (1980) 'Soviet interests in Africa', in W. Weinstein and T. H. Henriksen (eds), *Soviet and Chinese Aid to African Nations*, New York: Praeger.

Bjerg, O. (2005) 'To give or not to give: ethics after the tsunami', in Nordic Institute of Asian Studies (NIAS), *The Tsunami and Its Social and Political Implications*, pp. 16–17.

Black, R. and H. White (2003) *Targeting Development: Critical Perspectives on the Millennium Development Goals*, London: Routledge.

Bogotá Statement (2010) 'Towards effective and inclusive development partnerships', High Level Event on South–South Cooperation and Capacity Development, 25 March.

Boughton, J. and C. Bradford (2007) 'Global governance: new players, new rules', *Finance and Development*, 44(4).

Bourdieu, P. (1977) *Outline of a Theory of Practice*, trans. R. Nice, Cambridge: Cambridge University Press.

— (1990) *The Logic of Practice*, trans. R. Nice, Cambridge: Polity Press.

Braude, W., P. Thandrayan and E. Sidiropoulos (2008) 'Emerging donors in international development assistance: the South Africa case', in D. Rowlands (ed.), *Emerging Donors in International Development Assistance*, Canada: Partnership and Business Development Division, IDRC.

Bräutigam, D. (1998) *Chinese Aid and African Development: Exporting Green Revolution*, London: Macmillan Press.

— (2008) *China's African Aid: Transatlantic Challenges*, Washington, DC: German Marshall Fund of the United States, www.gmfus.org/doc/Brautigam0410aFINAL.pdf.

— (2009) *The Dragon's Gift: The Real Story of China in Africa*, Oxford: Oxford University Press.

— (2010) 'China, Africa and the international aid architecture', Africa Development Bank Group Working Paper 107, April.

— (2011) 'Aid "with Chinese characteristics": Chinese foreign aid and development finance meet the OECD-DAC aid regime', *Journal of International Development*, 23(5): 752–64.

Braveboy-Wagner, J. A. (2009) *Institutions of the Global South*, London: Routledge.

Broadman, H. G. (2007) *Africa's Silk Road: China and India's New Economic Frontier*, Washington, DC: World Bank.

Brown, S. (2007) 'From demiurge to midwife: changing donor roles in Kenya's democratization process', in G. R. Murunga and

S. W. Nasong'o (eds), *Kenya: The Struggle for Democracy*, London and Dakar: Zed Books and Council for the Development of Social Science Research in Africa, pp. 301–31.

— (2009) 'Donor responses to the 2008 Kenya crisis: finally getting it right?', *Journal of Contemporary African Studies*, 27(3): 389–406.

Bucar, M., M.-J. Marques, A. Mesic and E. Plibersek (2007) *Towards a Division of Labour in European Development Co-operation: Case Studies*, Bonn: DIE (German Development Institute).

Bull, H. (1977) *The Anarchical Society: A Study of Order in World Politics*, Oxford: Clarendon Press.

Bullion, A. (1997) 'India and UN peacekeeping operations', *International Peacekeeping*, 4(1): 98–114.

— (2001) 'India in Sierra Leone: a case of muscular peacekeeping', *International Peacekeeping*, 8(4): 77–91.

Burall, S. (2007) 'Multilateral donors: stakehold perceptions revealed', ODI Project Briefing, London: Overseas Development Institute.

Cabral, L. and J. Weinstock (2010) 'Brazil: an emerging aid player', ODI Briefing Paper 64, October.

Camilleri, J. (1980) *Chinese Foreign Policy: The Maoist era and its aftermath*, Oxford: Martin Robertson.

Carbone, M. (2004) 'Development policy', in N. Nugent (ed.), *EU Enlargement*, Basingstoke: Palgrave.

— (2007) *The European Union and International Development*, London: Routledge.

Carey, R. (2011) 'Aid governance and aid reporting: current issues in a historical perspective', *A Future for Aid Data*, Workshop, University of Birmingham, October, www.birmingham.ac.uk/schools/ government-society/departments/ international-development/ events/future-aid-data.aspx, accessed 22 February 2012.

Carmody, P. (2009) 'An Asian-driven economic recovery in Africa? The Zambian case', *World Development*, 37(7): 1197–207.

— (2011) *The New Scramble for Africa*, Cambridge: Polity Press.

Castellano, M. (2000) 'Japan's foreign aid program in the new millennium: rethinking "development"', Japan Economic Institute Report 6.

CGP (Center for Global Prosperity) (2010) 'The index of global philanthropy and remittances', Washington, DC: Hudson Institute, www.hudson. org/files/ pdf_upload/Index_ of_Global_Philanthropy_and_ Remittances_2010.pdf, accessed 20 December 2010.

Chahoud, T. (2008) 'Financing for Development series: Southern non-DAC actors in development cooperation', DIE Briefing Paper 13/2008.

Chan, G. (1997) 'Taiwan as an emerging foreign aid donor: developments, problems, and prospects', *Pacific Affairs*, 70(1): 37–56.

Chanana, D. (2009) 'India as an emerging donor', *Economic and Political Weekly*, 21 March, pp. 11–14.

Chandler, D. (2004) 'The responsibility to protect? Imposing the "Liberal Peace"', *International Peacekeeping*, 11(1): 59–81.

Chandy, L. and H. Kharas (2011) 'Why can't we all just get along? The practical limits of international development cooperation', *Journal of International Development*, 23(5).

Chang, H.-J. (2002) *Kicking Away the*

Ladder: Development Strategy in Historical Perspective, London: Anthem.

— (2010) 'Hamlet without the Prince of Denmark: how development has disappeared from today's "development" discourse"', in S. Khan and J. Christiansen (eds), *Towards New Developmentalism: Market as Means Rather than Master*, Abingdon: Routledge.

Chari, S. and K. Verdery (2009) 'Thinking between the posts: postcolonialism, postsocialism, and ethnography after the Cold War', *Comparative Studies in Society and History*, 51: 6–34.

Chatterjee, D. K. (2004) *The Ethics of Assistance: Morality and the Distant Needy*, Cambridge: Cambridge University Press.

Chaturvedi, S., T. Fues and E. Sidiropoulos (2012) *Development Cooperation and Emerging Powers: New Partners or Old Patterns?*, London: Zed Books.

Chenery, H., R. Jolly, M. S. Ahluwalia, C. L. Bell, C. L. and J. H. Duloy (1974) *Redistribution with Growth: Policies to Improve Income Distribution in Developing Countries in the Context of Economic Growth*, Oxford: Oxford University Press.

Cheru, F. and C. Obi (2010) *The Rise of China and India in Africa*, London and Uppsala: Zed Books and the Nordic Africa Institute.

Childress, S. (2011) 'Brazil may aid in eurozone crisis', Global Post, www.globalpost.com/dispatches/globalpost-blogs/que-pasa/brazil-may-aid-euro-zone-crisis, accessed 26 April 2011.

Chin, G. (2010) 'How to help rather than hinder: the G20 in global development', in T. Fues and P. Wolff (eds), *G20 and Global*

Development: How can the new summit architecture promote pro-poor growth and sustainability?, Bonn: DIE (German Development Institute).

Chisholm, L. and G. Steiner-Khamsi (eds) (2009) *South–South Cooperation in Education and Development*, New York and Cape Town: Teachers College Press and HRSC Press.

Chun, H.-M., N. E. Munyi and H.-J. Lee (2010) 'South Korea as an emerging donor: challenges and changes on its entering OECD/DAC', *Journal of International Development*, 22: 788–802.

Clemens, M. A. and T. J. Moss (2005) 'Ghost of 0.7%: origins and relevance of the international aid target', Working Paper no. 68, Center for Global Development, September.

Collier, P. (2008) *The Bottom Billion: Why are the Poorest Countries Failing and What Can be Done about It?*, Oxford: Oxford University Press.

Collier, P. and D. Dollar (1998) 'Aid allocation and poverty reduction', Policy Research Working Paper no. 2041, Washington, DC: World Bank.

Collins, S. D. (2007) 'The emerging pluralism of economic statecraft and its impact on American foreign policy', Paper presented at the 2007 Annual Meeting of the International Studies Association, Chicago, IL, 28 February–3 March.

Comaroff, J. and J. Comaroff (1993) 'Introduction', in J. Comaroff and J. Comaroff (eds), *Modernity and Its Malcontents. Colonial Power and Postcolonial Africa*, Chicago, IL: University of Chicago Press.

Constantine, J. (2011) 'Brazil as a development cooperation partner',

A Future for Aid Data, Workshop, University of Birmingham, October, www.birmingham.ac.uk/schools/government-society/departments/international-development/events/future-aid-data.aspx, accessed 22 February 2012.

Constantine, J. and A. Shankland (2011) 'Brazilian imaginaries of Africa and social technology transfers', Paper presented at 'Brazil in Africa: Africa in Brazil' conference, Centre for African Studies, Cambridge University, May.

Cooper, A. F. and A. Antkiewicz (eds) (2008) *Emerging Powers in Global Governance: Lessons from the Heiligendamm Process*, Waterloo: Wilfrid Laurier University Press.

Cooper, O. and C. Fogarty (1979) 'Soviet economic and military aid to the less developed countries, 1954–1978', in US Congress Joint Economic Committee (compilers), *Soviet Economy in a Time of Change*, Committee Print, 96th Congress, 1st session, Washington, DC: Government Printing Office.

Copestake, J. (2010) 'The global financial crisis of 2008–2009: an opportunity for development studies?', *Journal of International Development*, 22: 699–713.

Corbridge, S. (1993) 'Marxisms, modernities and moralities: development praxis and the claims of distant strangers', *Environment and Planning D: Society and Space*, 11: 449–72.

— (1998) 'Development ethics: distance, difference, plausibility', *Ethics, Place and Environment*, 1: 35–53.

Cornelissen, S. (2009) 'Awkward embraces: emerging and established powers and the shifting fortunes of Africa's international relations in the twenty-first century', *Politikon*, 36(1): 5–26.

Corrales, J. (2008) 'Venezuela's domestic politics and foreign policy: current trends', Testimony before the US House Committee on Foreign Affairs, 17 July.

Cotterrell, L. and A. Harmer (2005) 'Diversity in donorship: the changing landscape of official humanitarian aid – aid donorship in the Gulf States', HPG background paper, London: ODI, September, www.odi.org.uk/resources/hpg-publications/background-papers/2005/aid-donorship-gulf-states.pdf.

Craig, D. and D. Porter (2006) *Development beyond Neoliberalism? Governance, poverty reduction and political economy*, London: Routledge.

Crane, G. T. (1994) 'Collective identity, symbolic mobilization, and student protest in Nanjing, China, 1988–1989', *Comparative Politics*, 26(4): 395–413.

Crewe, E. and E. Harrison (1998) *Whose Development? An Ethnography of Aid*, London: Zed Books.

Da Silva, K. C. (2008) 'Aid as gift: an initial approach', *Mana*, 4.

Dang, H.-A., S. Knack and H. Rogers (2009) 'International aid and financial crises in donor countries', World Bank Policy Research Working Paper 5162.

Daniel, J., V. Naidoo and S. Naidu (2003) 'The South-Africans have arrived: post-apartheid corporate expansion into Africa', in J. Daniel, A. Habib and R. Southall (eds), *State of the Nation: South Africa 2003–4*, Cape Town: Human Sciences Research Council Press, pp. 368–90.

Darnton, A. (2007) 'Global poverty

and the public – desk research: driving public engagement in global poverty', London: DfID.

Davies, P. (2008) 'Aid effectiveness and non-DAC providers of development assistance', Background document to Round Table 9: 'The changing aid architecture: implications for aid effectiveness', Third High Level Forum on Aid Effectiveness (HLF-3), Accra, Ghana.

— (2010) 'South–South cooperation: moving towards a new aid dynamic', *Poverty in Focus*, International Policy Centre for Inclusive Growth Poverty Practice, Bureau for Development Policy, UNDP, pp. 11–13.

— (2011) 'The role of the private sector in the context of aid effectiveness', Final report, 2 February, www.oecd.org/data oecd/7/58/47088121.pdf, accessed 20 May 2011.

DCIS (Development Cooperation Information System) (2010) 'The triangular/trilateral cooperation within South–South cooperation: the South African experience', February, www. dcis.gov.za/PopUpDialog. aspx?DescriptionID=182&Type=1, accessed 18 November 2010.

De Freitas Barbosa, A. and R. Mendes (2010) 'Is there a Brazilian strategy for the G20?', in T. Fues and P. Wolff (eds), *G20 and Global Development: How can the new summit architecture promote pro-poor growth and sustainability?*, Bonn: DIE (German Development Institute).

De Haan, A. (2011) 'Will China change international development as we know it?', *Journal of International Development*, 23(5): 881–908.

Derrida, J. (1992) *Given Time*, vol. 1: *Counterfeit Money*, Chicago, IL: University of Chicago Press.

Deudney, D. and J. Ikenberry (1999) 'Nature and sources of liberal international order', *Review of International Studies*, 25: 179–96.

Dietz, T. and J. Houtcamp (1995) 'Foreign aid to Africa: a geographical analysis', *Tijdschrift voor Economische en Sociale Geografie*, 86(5): 278–95.

Dijkstra, G. and K. Komives (2011) 'The PRS approach and the Paris Agenda: experiences in Bolivia, Honduras and Nicaragua', *European Journal of Development Research*, 23(1): 191–207.

Diven, P. and J. Constantelos (2009) 'Explaining generosity: a comparison of US and European public opinion on foreign aid', *Journal of Transatlantic Studies*, 7(2): 118–32.

DN (2003) 'Aid: old morality and new realities', *Economic and Political Weekly*, 14 June.

Dosch, J. (2007) *The Changing Dynamics of Southeast Asian Politics*, Boulder, CO: Lynne Rienner.

Doty, R. L. (1996) *Imperial Encounters: The Politics of Representation in North–South Relations*, Minneapolis, MN: University of Minnesota Press.

Drazkiewicz, E. (2007) 'Challenging development: Polish experiences', Unpublished master's thesis, University of Cambridge.

— (2011) 'An emergent donor: the case of Polish developmental involvement in Africa', Unpublished PhD thesis, University of Cambridge.

Drodz, M. (2007) 'The new face of "Solidarity": a brief survey of Polish aid', Paper presented at International Mobility Conference

2007, akson.sgh.waw.pl/~trusek/im/papers/Drozd_wshop.pdf, accessed 15 March 2012.

Droeze, F. H. (2008) *Policy Coherence for Development*, www.dpwg-lgd.org/cms/upload/pdf/policy_coherence_for_development.pdf, accessed 26 April 2012.

Duffield, M. (2001) *Global Governance and the New Wars: The Merging of Development and Security*, London: Zed Books.

— (2007) *Development, Security and Unending War*, Cambridge: Polity Press.

Easterly, W. (2007) *The White Man's Burden: Why the West's Efforts to Aid the Rest Have Done So Much Ill and So Little Good*, Oxford: Oxford University Press.

Easterly, W. and T. Phutze (2008) 'Where does the money go? Best and worst practices in foreign aid', *Journal of Economic Perspectives*, 22(2): 29–52.

EC (European Commission) (2007) 'EU report on policy coherence for development', EU Coherence Programme, September.

ECDPM (2011) 'Offence is the best defence: the EU's past and future engagement in promoting effective development cooperation: ideas for Busan', Briefing note, European Centre for Development Policy Management, Maastricht: ECDPM.

ECDPM, Particip, ICEI (2007) 'Evaluation study on the EU institutions and member states' mechanisms for promoting policy coherence for development', May.

Economic Times (2011) 'India bailing out Europe', 3 August 2011, economictimes.indiatimes.com/news/economy/finance/india-to-give-2bn-to-fund-bailouts-in-

europe/articleshow/9463556.cms, accessed 8 August 2011.

ECOSOC (2008) 'Trends in South–South and triangular development cooperation', Background study for the Development Cooperation Forum, United Nations Economic and Social Council, New York.

Ellmers, B. (2011) 'Four months until Busan aid forum and a long way from more effective aid', European Network on Debt and Development, Brussels, 7 July, www. eurodad.org/whatsnew/articles.aspx?id=4584, accessed 26 April 2012.

Escobar, A. (1995) *Encountering Development: The Making and Unmaking of the Third World*, Princeton, NJ: Princeton University Press.

— (2004) 'Beyond the Third World: imperial globality, global coloniality and anti-globalisation social movements', *Third World Quarterly*, 25: 207–30.

Eurobarometer (2007) 'Europeans and development aid', Eurobarometer 280, ec.europa.eu/public_opinion/archives/ebs/ebs_280_en.pdf.

Eurodad (2011) 'Aid effectiveness: European Commission puts Europe in tough situation for Busan', eurodad.org/?p=4657.

Eyben, R. (2006a) *Relationships for Aid*, London: Earthscan.

— (2006b) 'The power of the gift and the new aid modalities', *IDS Bulletin*, 37(6), Brighton: Institute of Development Studies.

— (2008) 'Power, mutual accountability and responsibility in the practice of international aid: a relational approach', IDS Working Paper 305, Brighton: Institute of Development Studies.

— (2010) 'Hiding relations. The

irony of "effective aid"', *European Journal of Development Research*, 22(3): 382–97.

Fang, J. (2010) 'G20 and the development agenda', in T. Fues and P. Wolff (eds), *G20 and Global Development: How can the new summit architecture promote pro-poor growth and sustainability?*, Bonn: DIE (German Development Institute).

Ferguson, J. (1994) *The Anti-Politics Machine: 'Development,' Depoliticization, and Bureaucratic Power in Lesotho*, Minneapolis, MN: University of Minnesota Press.

— (1999) *Expectations of Modernity. Myths and Meanings of Urban Life on the Zambian Copperbelt*, Berkeley, CA: University of California Press.

Finnemore, M. (1996) *National Interests in International Society*, Ithaca, NY: Cornell University Press.

Finnemore, M. and K. Sikkink (1998) 'International norm dynamics and political change', *International Organization*, 52(4): 887–917.

Flint, M. and H. Goyder (2006) 'Funding the tsunami response', London: Tsunami Evaluation Coalition.

FOCAC (Forum on China–Africa Cooperation) (2006) *Beijing Summit and Third Ministerial Conference on China–Africa Cooperation*, english.focacsummit.org/.

— (2009) *Declaration of the Beijing Summit of the Forum on China–Africa Cooperation*, www.focac.org/eng/ltda/dscbzjhy/DOC32009/t606841.htm.

Fordelone, T. Y. (2009) 'Triangular cooperation and aid effectiveness', Paper prepared for Policy Dialogue on Development Cooperation, OECD-DAC, Mexico City, 28/29 September, www.oecd.org/dataoecd/63/37/43704891.pdf, accessed 20 October 2010.

Foster, V., W. Butterfield, C. Chen and N. Pushak (2008) 'Building bridges: China's growing role as infrastructure financier for sub-Saharan Africa', Trends and Policy Options no. 5, Washington, DC: World Bank/PPIAF.

Foy, C. and H. Helmich (1996) *Public Support for International Development*, Development Centre of the Organisation for Economic Co-operation and Development.

Friedman, J. (2009) 'Soviet policy in the developing world and the Chinese challenge in the 1960s', *Cold War History*, 10(2): 247–72.

Frynas, J. G. and M. Paulo (2007) 'A new scramble for African oil? Historical, political, and business perspectives', *African Affairs*, 106(423): 229–51.

Fues, T. (2010) 'Competing aid regimes: will the UN be able to challenge the dominant role of the OECD-DAC in international development cooperation', Manuscript, Bonn: DIE (German Development Institute).

— (2011) 'Beyond the DAC: the rising donors and the UN Development Cooperation Forum', Unpublished paper.

— (2012) 'The development agenda of the G20', *G20 Update*, 10, Heinrich Böll Stiftung, February.

Fues, T. and P. Wolff (eds) (2010) *G20 and Global Development: How can the new summit architecture promote pro-poor growth and sustainability?*, Bonn: DIE (German Development Institute).

Fues, T., S. Chaturvedi and E. Sidiropoulos (2012) 'Conclusion: towards a global consensus on development cooperation',

in S. Chaturvedi, T. Fues and
E. Sidiropoulos (eds), *Develop-
ment Cooperation and Emerging
Powers: New Partners or Old
Patterns?*, London: Zed Books,
pp. 243–62.

Fukuyama, F. (1992) *The End of History and the Last Man*, New York:
Free Press.

G20 (2009) *Communiqué of the G20
Summit in London*, www.china.
org.cn/business/g20/2009-04/02/
content_17545478.htm.

G20 Development Working Group
(2011) *2011 Report of Development
Working Group*, Cannes: G20.

G77 (Group of 77) (2003) *Marrakech
Declaration on South–South Cooperation*, www.g77.org/marrakech/
Marrakech-Declaration.htm,
accessed 26 April 2012.

— (2005) 'Development Cooperation Forum launched at
ECOSOC meeting', *Journal of
the Group of 77*, www.g77.org/
nc/journal/makejournal.php?
id=0707#item070702, accessed
4 September 2010.

Gallagher, J. (2009) 'Healing the
scar: idealising Britain in
Africa, 1997–2007', *African Affairs*,
108(432): 435–51.

Ghaus, K. (2010) 'G20 and development: a view from Pakistan', in
T. Fues and P. Wolff (eds), *G20
and Global Development: How
can the new summit architecture
promote pro-poor growth and sustainability?*, Bonn: DIE (German
Development Institute).

Gilman, N. (2003) *Mandarins of the
Future: Modernization Theory in
Cold War America*, Baltimore, MD:
Johns Hopkins University Press.

Gilmartin, M. and L. Berg (2007)
'Commentary: locating postcolonialism', *Area*, 39: 120–24.

Glennie, J. (2008) *The Trouble with
Aid: Why Less Could Mean More
for Africa*, London: Zed Books.

— (2011a) 'The role of aid to middle-
income countries: a contribution
to evolving EU development
policy', ODI Working Paper 331,
London: Overseas Development
Institute, June.

— (2011b) 'What's driving the rise
of southern aid agencies?',
Guardian, 20 January, www.guard-
ian.co.uk/global-development/
poverty-matters/2011/jan/20/
south-africa-aid-agency-
motivation, accessed 8 February
2011.

— (2011c) 'Who should lead the
aid effectiveness debate in the
future?', Speech at the first ODI
Busan Debate, House of Com-
mons, London.

— (2012) 'The West has no right to
criticize the China–Africa relationship', *Guardian*, 8 February,
www.guardian.co.uk/global-de-
velopment/poverty-matters/2012/
feb/08/west-no-right-to-criticise-
china, accessed 22 February 2012.

Glennie, J. and A. Rogerson (2011)
'Global reach is the prize
at Busan', ODI Opinion 154,
London: ODI, September.

Godelier, M. (1999) *The Enigma of the
Gift*, Chicago, IL: University of
Chicago Press.

Goldman Sachs (2003) 'Dreaming
with BRICs: the path to 2050',
Global Economics Paper no. 99,
www2.goldmansachs.com/ideas/
brics/book/ 99-dreaming.pdf,
accessed 21 August 2009.

Goldstein, A., N. Pinaud, H. Reisen
and X. Chen (2006) *The Rise of
China and India: What's in it for
Africa?*, Paris: OECD Development Centre.

Gould, J. (ed.) (2005) *The New Conditionality: The Politics of Poverty*

Reduction Strategies, London: Zed Books.

Government of China (2007) Remarks by Ambassador Li Baodong at the launching ceremony of the Development Cooperation Forum, www.china-un.ch/eng/qtzz/wtojjwt/t339665.htm, accessed 27 February 2012.

— (2010) Keynote speech by Mr Yi Xiaozhun, Vice-Minister of Commerce, People's Republic of China, at 2010 High-Level Segment Development Cooperation Forum, www.china-un.org/eng/hyyfy/t712924.htm, accessed 24 February 2012.

— (2011) *White Paper on China's Foreign Assistance*.

Government of Pakistan (2010) Statement by Sardar Muhammad Latif Khan Khosa at the 2010 DCF, www.un.org/en/ecosoc/julyhls/pdf10/pakistan.pdf.

Gray, P. (2011) 'Looking "The Gift" in the mouth: Russia as donor', *Anthropology Today*, 27(2): 5–8.

Griffin, K. (1991) 'Foreign aid after the Cold War', *Development and Change*, 22: 645–85.

Griffith-Jones, S., D. Griffith-Jones and D. Hertova (2008) 'Enhancing the role of regional development banks; the time is now', G24 Discussion Paper Series no. 50, United Nations Conference on Trade and Development.

Grimm, S. and A. Harmer (2005) 'Diversity in donorship: the changing landscape of official humanitarian aid: aid donorship in central Europe', HPG Background Paper, September.

Grimm, S., J. Humphrey, E. Lundsgaarde and S. John de Souza (2009) 'European development cooperation to 2020: challenges by new actors in international development', EDC Working Paper no. 4, Bonn: DIE (German Development Institute), www.edc2020.eu/fileadmin/Textdateien/EDC2020_WP4_Webversion.pdf, accessed 24 February 2010.

Gulrajani, N. (2011) 'Transcending the great foreign aid debate: managerialism, radicalism and the search for aid effectiveness', *Third World Quarterly*, 32(2): 199–216.

Hackenesch, C. (2009) 'China and the EU's engagement in Africa: setting the stage for cooperation, competition or conflict?', Discussion Paper 16, Bonn: DIE (German Development Institute).

Hammad, L. and B. Morton (2009) 'Non-DAC donors and reform of the international aid architecture', Issues Brief, Development Cooperation Series, Ottawa: North–South Institute.

Hancilova, B. (2000) 'Czech humanitarian assistance 1993–1998', *Journal of Humanitarian Assistance*, 9 April.

Handousa, H. (1991) 'The impact of foreign aid on Egypt's economic development, 1952–1986', in U. Lele and I. Nabi (eds), *Transitions in Development: The Role of Aid and Commercial Flows*, San Francisco, CA: International Center for Economic Growth, pp. 195–224.

Hansen, H. and F. Tarp (2000) 'Aid effectiveness disputed', in F. Tarp (ed.), *Foreign Aid and Development: Lessons learnt and directions for the future*, London: Routledge, pp. 103–28.

Harmer, A. and L. Cotterrell (2005) 'Diversity in donorship: the changing landscape of official humanitarian aid', HPG Research

Report 20, London: Overseas Development Institute.

Harrigan, J. (2007) 'The doubling of aid to sub-Saharan Africa: promises and problems', *Journal of Contemporary African Studies*, 25(3): 369–89.

Harris, D. and D. Azzi (2006) 'ALBA – Venezuela's answer to "free trade": the Bolivarian alternative for the Americas', Occasional Paper 3, São Paulo and Bangkok: Focus on the Global South, October.

Harriss, J., J. Hunter and C. Lewis (eds) (1995) *The New Institutional Economics and Third World Development*, London: Routledge.

Hattori, T. (2001) 'Reconceptualising foreign aid', *Review of International Political Economy*, 8(4): 633–60.

— (2003) 'The moral politics of foreign aid', *Review of International Studies*, 29: 229–47.

He, W. (2006) 'Educational exchange and cooperation between China and Africa', Paper in 3rd Round-table Discussion on 'Comparative culture and education in African and Asian Societies', African Studies Group, University of Hong Kong.

Heiligendamm Process (2009) *Concluding Report of the Heiligendamm Process*, www.oecd.org/dataoecd/4/53/43288908.pdf, accessed 26 April 2012.

Henry, M. (2012) 'Peacexploitation? Interrogating labor hierarchies and global sisterhood amongst Indian and Uruguayan female peacekeepers', in P. Amar (ed.), *Global South to the Rescue: Emerging Humanitarian Superpowers and Globalizing Rescue Industries*, London: Routledge.

Hickey, S. and G. Mohan (2008) 'Poverty reduction strategies, participation and the politics of accountability', *Review of International Political Economy*, 15(2): 234–58.

Hill, A. (2012) 'Globalising security culture and knowledge in practice: Nigeria's hybrid model', in P. Amar (ed.), *Global South to the Rescue: Emerging Humanitarian Superpowers and Globalizing Rescue Industries*, London: Routledge.

Hindley, D. (1963) 'Aid to Indonesia and its political implications', *Pacific Affairs*, 36(2): 107–19.

Hobart, M. (1993) *An Anthropological Critique of Development. The Growth of Ignorance*, London: Routledge.

Horky, O. (2006) 'Development policy in new EU member states: re-emerging donors on the way from compulsory altruism to global responsibility', 4th CEEISA Convention: 'Reflecting on a wider Europe and beyond: norms, rights and interests', Tartu (Estonsko), CEEISA, 25–27 June, www.ceeisaconf.ut.ee/orb.aw/class=file/action=preview/id=166463/horky.pdf.

— (2011) 'Depoliticization, instrumentalization and legitimacy of Czech development cooperation: a case of imposed altruism?', *Éthique et économique* [Ethics and Economics], 8(1), papyrus.bib.umontreal.ca/jspui/bitstream/1866/4585/1/Horky.pdf, accessed 24 February 2012.

Hosono, A., S. Honda, M. Sato and M. Ono (2011) 'Inside the black box of capacity development', in H. Kharas, K. Makino and W. Jung (eds), *Catalysing Development: A New Vision for Aid*, Washington, DC: Brookings Institution.

Hout, W. (2004) 'Political regimes

and development assistance: the political economy of aid selectivity', *Critical Asian Studies*, 36(4): 591–613.

Howell, J. and J. Lind (2009) 'Changing donor policy and practice in civil society in the post-9/11 aid context', *Third World Quarterly*, 30(7): 1279–96.

— (2010) 'Securing the world and challenging civil society: before and after the "War on Terror"', *Development and Change*, 41(2): 279–91.

Hubbard, M. and P. Sinha (2011) 'Beyond Busan: the case for including other public flows for development', *A Future for Aid Data*, Workshop, University of Birmingham, October, www. birmingham.ac.uk/schools/ government-society/departments/ international-development/ events/future-aid-data.aspx, accessed 22 February 2012.

Hudson, A. and L. Jonsson (2009) 'Beyond aid for sustainable development', Project Briefing 22, Overseas Development Institute, May.

Hulme, D. and S. Fukuda-Parr (2009) 'International norm dynamics and the "end of poverty": understanding the Millennium Development Goals', Brooks World Poverty Institute Working Paper 96.

Hunter, S. (1984) *OPEC and the Third World: The Politics of Oil*, Bloomington, IN: Indiana University Press.

Hurrell, A. (2006) 'Hegemony, liberalism and global order: what space for would-be great powers', *International Affairs*, 82: 1–19.

— (2007) *On Global Order: Power, Values and the Constitution of International Society*, Oxford: Oxford University Press.

Hyden, G. (2008) 'After the Paris Declaration: taking on the issue of power', *Development Policy Review*, 26(3): 259–74.

Ikenberry, J. (2008) 'The rise of China and the future of the West', *Foreign Affairs*, 87(1): 23–37.

Institute of Development Studies (2005) 'The impact of Asian Drivers on the developing world', Globally networked research programme coordinated by the IDS at the University of Sussex, www. ids.ac.uk/files/IDSAsianDrivers ProgrammeFeb05.pdf.

— (2006) 'Asian Drivers: opportunities and threats', *IDS Bulletin*, 37(1), January.

Jaffrelot, C. (ed.) (2009) *Emerging States: The Wellspring of a New World Order*, New York: Columbia University Press

James, W. and N. J. Allen (eds) (1998) *Marcel Mauss: A centenary tribute*, Oxford: Berghahn Books.

Jerve, A. M. (2007) 'Asian models for aid: is there a non-western approach to development assistance?', CMI Report, Chr. Michelsen Institute, Bergen.

John de Sousa, S.-L. (2010) 'Brazil as an emerging actor in international development cooperation: a good partner for European donors?', DIE Briefing Paper 5/2010.

Jolly, R. (2010) 'Future directions for the G20: towards legitimacy and universality', in T. Fues and P. Wolff (eds), *G20 and Global Development: How can the new summit architecture promote pro-poor growth and sustainability?*, Bonn: DIE (German Development Institute).

Jordan, P. A. (2010) 'A bridge between the global North and Africa? Putin's Russia and G8 development commitments', *African Studies Quarterly*, 11(4): 83–115.

Kaag, M. (2008) 'Transnational Islamic NGOs in Chad: Islamic solidarity in the age of neoliberalism', *Africa Today*, 54(3): 3–18.

Kagame, P. (2009) 'Why Africa welcomes the Chinese', *Guardian*, 2 November.

Kamau, P. and D. McCormick (2011) 'The impact of India–Kenya trade relations on the Kenya garment industry', in E. Mawdsley and G. McCann (eds), *India in Africa: Changing Geographies of Power*, Cape Town: Pambazuka Press, pp. 70–87.

Kang, S. J., H. Lee and B. Park (2011) 'Does Korea follow Japan in foreign aid: relationships between aid and foreign investment', *Japan and the World Economy*, 23(1): 19–27.

Kaplinsky, R. (2005) *Globalization, Poverty and Inequality*, Cambridge: Polity Press.

Kaplinsky, R. and M. Farooki (2009) 'Africa's development cooperation with new and emerging development partners: options for Africa's development', Report prepared for the Office of the Special Advisor on Africa (OSAA), Department of Economic and Social Affairs (DESA), United Nations, New York.

Kaplinsky, R. and D. Messner (2008) 'Introduction: the impact of Asian Drivers on the developing world', *World Development*, 36(2): 197–209.

Kaplinsky, R. and M. Morris (2009) 'The Asian Drivers and SSA: is there a future for export-oriented African industrialisation?', *World Economy*, 32(11).

Kapoor, I. (2008) *The Postcolonial Politics of Development*, London: Routledge.

Katzenstein, P. (1996) *Cultural Norms and National Security*, Ithaca, NY: Cornell University Press.

KCG (2003) *Donor Harmonisation: Joint Statement by Development Partners at the Kenya Consultative Group Meeting*, November, siteresources.worldbank.org/KENYAEXTN/Resources/donor-harmonization.pdf, accessed 26 April 2012.

Keohane, R. O. (1989) *International Institutions and State Power: Essays in International Relations Theory*, Boulder, CO: Westview Press.

Ketkar, S. and D. Ratha (eds) (2009) *Innovative Financing for Development*, Washington, DC: World Bank.

Kharas, H. (2007) 'The new reality of aid', Brookings Blum Roundtable, www.brookings.edu/research/papers/2007/08/aid-kharas, accessed 20 June 2012.

Kharas, H. and L. Chandy (2011) 'Measuring for success at the Busan High Level Forum on Aid Effectiveness', Global Views Policy Paper 2011-6, Washington, DC: Brookings Institution.

Kharas, H., K. Makino and W. Jung (eds) (2011) *Catalysing Development: A New Vision for Aid*, Washington, DC: Brookings Institution.

Kiala, C. (2010) 'The impact of China–Africa aid relations – the case of Angola', Policy Brief no. 1, Nairobi: African Economic Research Consortium.

Killen, B. and A. Rogerson (2010) 'Global governance for international development: who's in charge?', OECD Development Brief 2.

Killick, T. with R. Gunatilaka and

A. Marr (1999) *Aid and the Political Economy of Policy*, London: Routledge.

Kim, S. (2010) 'Korea: "something old" and "something borrowed"', *Norrag News: Network for Policy Research Review and Advice on Education and Training*, 44, September.

— (2011) 'Bridging troubled worlds? An analysis of the ethical case for South Korean aid', *Journal of International Development*, 23(6): 802–22.

Kim, S. and S. Lightfoot (2011) 'Does "DAC-ability" really matter? The emergence of non-DAC donors: introduction to policy arena', *Journal of International Development*, 23(5): 711–21.

Kindornay, S. and H. Besada (2011) 'Multilateral development cooperation: current trends and future prospects', *Canadian Development Report 2011*, Ottawa: North–South Institute.

King, K. (ed.) (2010) 'A brave new world of "emerging", "non-DAC" donors and their differences from "traditional" donors', *Norrag News: Network for Policy Research Review and Advice on Education and Training*, 44, September.

— (ed.) (2011) 'The geopolitics of overseas scholarships and awards. Old and new providers, East and West, North and South', *Norrag News*, 45.

Klingebiel, S. (2011) 'Transparency and accountability as one of the critical perspectives on the legitimacy of future development cooperation', *A Future for Aid Data*, Workshop, University of Birmingham, October, www.birmingham.ac.uk/schools/government-society/departments/international-development/events/future-aid-data.aspx, accessed 22 February 2012.

Kloke-Lesch, A. and C. Gleichmann (2010) 'Global development beyond the North–South paradigm', in T. Fues and P. Wolff (eds), *G20 and Global Development: How can the new summit architecture promote pro-poor growth and sustainability?*, Bonn: DIE (German Development Institute).

Knack, S. and A. Rahman (2007) 'Donor fragmentation and bureaucratic quality in aid recipients', *Journal of Development Economics*, 83: 176–97.

Kondoh, H., T. Kobayashi, H. Shiga and J. Sato (2010) 'Impact of non-DAC donors in Asia: a recipient's perspective: diversity and transformation of aid patterns in asia's "emerging donors"', JICA Research Institute no. 21.

Korf, B. (2007) 'Antimonies of generosity: moral geographies and post-tsunami aid in Southeast Asia', *Geoforum*, 38: 366–78.

Korf, B., S. Habullah, P. Hollenbach and B. Klem (2010) 'The gift of disaster: the commodification of good intentions in post-tsunami Sri Lanka', *Disasters*, 34: 60–77.

Kornegay, F. and C. Landsberg (2009) 'Engaging emerging powers: Africa's search for a "common position"', *Politikon*, 36(1): 171–91.

Kosky, J. L. (1997) 'The disqualification of intentionality: the gift in Derrida, Levinas, and Michael Henry', *Philosophy Today*, 41(Supplement): 186–97.

Kothari, U. (2005) *A Radical History of Development Studies: Individuals, Institutions and Ideologies*, London: Zed Books.

— (2007) 'Geographies and histories of development', *Journal für Entwicklungspolitik* [Austrian Journal of Development Research], 23(2): 28–44.

Kragelund, P. (2008) 'The return of the non-DAC donors to Africa: new prospects for African development', *Development Policy Review*, 26(5): 555–84.

— (2010) 'The potential role of non-traditional donors' aid in Africa', Issue Paper no. 11, International Centre for Trade and Sustainable Development.

— (2011) 'Back to basics? The rejuvenation of non-traditional donors' development cooperation with Africa', *Development and Change*, 42(2): 585–607.

Kraxberger, B. M. (2005) 'The United States and Africa: shifting geopolitics in an "Age of Terror"', *Africa Today*, 52(1): 47–68.

Kumar, A. (2010) 'G20 and global governance: a new "new deal" for the global poor!', in T. Fues and P. Wolff (eds), *G20 and Global Development: How can the new summit architecture promote pro-poor growth and sustainability?*, Bonn: DIE (German Development Institute).

Kuuisk, R. (2006) 'Estonia's development cooperation: power, prestige and practice of a new donor', in A. Kasekamp (ed.), *Estonian Foreign Policy Yearbook*, Tallinn: Eesti Välispoliitika Instituut.

Kuziemko, I. and E. Werker (2006) 'How much is a seat on the Security Council worth? Foreign aid and bribery at the United Nations', *Journal of Political Economy*, 114(5): 905–30.

Lai, K. P. Y. (2006) '"Imagineering" Asian emerging markets: financial knowledge networks in the fund management industry', *Geoforum*, 37(4): 627–42.

Laidlaw, J. (2000) 'A free gift makes no friends', *Journal of the Royal Anthropological Institute*, 6: 617–34.

Lancaster, C. (2007) *Foreign Aid: Diplomacy, development, domestic politics*, Chicago, IL: University of Chicago Press.

Langan, M. and J. Scott (2011) 'The false promise of aid for trade', Brooks World Poverty Institute Working Paper no. 160.

Large, D. (2008) 'China and the contradictions of "non-interference" in Sudan', *Review of African Political Economy*, 115: 93–106.

Larkin, B. D. (1971) *China and Africa, 1949–1970: The foreign policy of the People's Republic of China*, University of California Press.

Lawson, C. (1987) 'Soviet economic aid: volume, function and importance', *Development Policy Review*, 5: 257–76.

Lawson, C. W. (1980) 'Socialist relations with the Third World: the case study of the New International Economic Order', *Economics of Planning*, 16: 148–60.

— (1983) 'National independence and reciprocal advantages: the political economy of Romanian South relations', *Soviet Studies*, 35: 362–75.

— (1988) 'Soviet economic aid to Africa', *African Affairs*, 87(349): 501–18.

Lawson, V. (2007) 'Geographies of care and responsibility', *Annals of the Association of American Geographers*, 97: 1–11.

Le Pere, G. (2010) 'Africa and poor countries must be central to the G20's Seoul development agenda', in T. Fues and P. Wolff (eds), *G20 and Global Development: How can the new summit architecture promote pro-poor growth and sustainability?*, Bonn: DIE (German Development Institute).

Lee, P. K., G. Chan and L.-H. Chan (2010) 'China in Darfur: humanitarian rule-maker or rule-taker?', *Review of International Studies*, 1(22).

Lee, R. and D. M. Smith (eds) (2004) *Geographies and Moralities: International perspectives on development justice and place*, Oxford: Blackwell.

Leftwich, A. (1993) 'Governance, democracy and development in the Third World', *Third World Quarterly*, 14(3): 605–24.

Leheny, D. and K. Warren (2009) *Japanese Aid and the Construction of Global Development: Inescapable Solutions*, London: Routledge.

Leipziger, P. (2011) *Multilateralism, the Shifting Global Economic Order, and Development Policy*, Canadian Development Report 2011, Ottawa: North–South Institute.

Lensink, R. and H. White (1999) 'Is there an aid Laffer Curve?', CREDIT Working Paper 99/6, Centre for Research in Economic Development and International Trade, University of Nottingham.

Leung, A. (2010) 'A new China–Africa: financial, investment and business partnership', Presentation to the African Banking and Financial Institutions Seminar, Accra, Ghana, April.

Lévi-Strauss, C. (1987) *Introduction to the Work of Marcel Mauss*, London: Routledge.

Li, T. M. (2007) *The Will to Improve. Governmentality, Development and the Practice of Politics*, London: Duke University Press.

Lightfoot, S. (2008) 'Enlargement and the challenge of EU development', *Perspectives on European Politics and Society*, 9(2): 128–42.

— (2010) 'The Europeanisation of international development

policies: the case of central and eastern European states', *Europe–Asia Studies*, 62: 329–50.

Lin, J. Y. and J. B. Nugent (1995) 'Institutions and economic development', in H. Chenery and T. N. Srinivasan (eds), *Handbook of Development Economics*, vol. 3, Elsevier, pp. 2301–70.

Lindelow, M., I. Kushnarova and K. Kaiser (2006) 'Measuring corruption in the health sector: what can we learn from public expenditure tracking and service delivery services in developing countries', in *Global Corruption Report 2006*, Transparency International, pp. 29–36.

Lockhart, C. (2004) 'From aid effectiveness to development effectiveness: strategy and policy coherence in fragile states', Background paper prepared for the Senior Level Forum on Development Effectiveness in Fragile States, Overseas Development Institute, www.odi.org.uk/resources/docs/4829.pdf.

Lumsdaine, D. et al. (2007) 'Changing values and the recent rise in Korean development assistance', *Pacific Review*, 20(2): 221–55.

Lumsdaine, D. H. (1993) *Moral Vision in International Politics*, Princeton, NJ: Princeton University Press.

Lutz, C. A. and J. L. Collins (1993) *Reading 'National Geographic'*, Chicago, IL: University of Chicago Press.

Mahadeo, M. and J. McKinney (2007) 'Media representations of Africa: still the same old story?', *Policy and Practice: A Development Education Review*, 4: *Voices from the Global South*, www.developmenteducationreview.com/issue4-focus2.

Mahon, R. and S. McBride (2009)

'Standardizing and disseminating knowledge: the role of the OECD in global governance', *European Political Science Review*, 1(1): 83–101.

Mamdani, M. (2010) *Saviors and Survivors: Darfur, Politics and the War on Terror*, New York: Random House.

— (2011) 'Responsibility to protect or right to punish?', in P. Cunliffe (ed.), *Critical Perspectives on the Responsibility to Protect: Interrogating Theory and Practice*, London: Routledge.

Manning, R. (2006) 'Will "emerging" donors change the face of international cooperation?', *Development Policy Review*, 24(4): 371–83.

— (2008) 'The DAC as a central actor in development policy issues: experiences over the past four years', DIE Discussion Paper 7/2008.

Marten, R. and J. M. Witte (2008) 'Transforming development? The role of philanthropic foundations in international development cooperation', Global Public Policy Research Paper no. 10, Berlin: Global Public Policy Institute, www.gppi.net/fileadmin/gppi/GPPiRP10_Transforming_Development_20080526final.pdf, accessed 27 February 2009.

Massey, D. (2004) 'Geographies of responsibility', *Geografiska Annaler, Series B*, 86: 5–18.

Matusevich, M. (2003) *No Easy Row for a Russian Hoe: Ideology and pragmatism in Nigerian–Soviet relations, 1960–1991*, Trenton, NJ: Africa World Press

Mauss, M. (1990) *The Gift*, trans. W. D. Hall, London: Routledge.

Mawdsley, E. (2008) 'Fu Manchu versus Dr Livingstone in the Dark Continent? Representing China, Africa and the West in British broadsheet newspapers', *Political Geography*, 27(5): 509–29.

— (2010) 'The non-DAC donors and the changing landscape of foreign aid: the (in)significance of India's development cooperation with Kenya', *Journal of Eastern African Studies*, 4(2): 361–79.

— (2012) 'The changing geographies of foreign aid and development cooperation: contributions from Gift Theory', *Transactions of the Institute of British Geographers*, 37(2): 256–72.

Mawdsley, E. and G. McCann (2010) 'The elephant in the corner? Reviewing India–Africa relations in the new millennium', *Geography Compass*, 4(2): 81–93.

— (eds) (2011) *India and Africa: Changing Geographies of Power and Development*, Cape Town: Pambazuka Press.

Mawdsley, E. et al. (2011a) 'The Conservatives, the Coalition and international development', *Area*, 43(4): 506–7.

— (2011b) 'Public perceptions of development cooperation in China, India, Poland, Russia and South Africa', Project details at www.geog.cam.ac.uk/research/projects/foreignaidperceptions/, accessed 26 April 2012.

McCann, G. (2011) 'Diaspora, political economy and India's postcolonial relations with Kenya', in E. Mawdsley and G. McCann (eds), *India in Africa: Changing Geographies of Power*, Cape Town: Pambazuka Press.

McClintock, A. (1984) '"Unspeakable secrets": the ideology of landscape in Conrad's "Heart of Darkness"', *Journal of the Midwest Modern Language Association*, 17(1): 38–53.

McCormick, D. (2008) 'China and India as Africa's new donors: the impact of aid on development', *Review of African Political Economy*, 35(115): 73–92.

McCulloch, N. and A. Sumner (2009) 'Will the global financial crisis change the development paradigm?', www.eadi.org/file admin/MDG_2015_Publications/ Does_the_crisis_change_the_ dev_paradigm.pdf.

McEwan, C. (2009) *Postcolonialism and Development*, London: Routledge.

McEwan, C. and E. Mawdsley (2012) 'New global development partnerships: trilateral development cooperation and the changing geographies of foreign aid', *Development and Change* (forthcoming).

McGee, R. and J. Gaventa (2011) 'Shifting power? assessing the impact of transparency and accountability initiatives', IDS Working Paper 383, Brighton: Institute of Development Studies.

Meernik, J., E. L. Krueger and S. C. Poe (1998) 'Testing models of U.S. foreign policy: foreign aid during and after the Cold War', *Journal of Politics*, 60(1): 63–85.

Mehta, P. S. and N. Nanda (2005) 'Trilateral development cooperation: an emerging trend', CUTS-CITEE Briefing Paper, www.cuts-international.org/pdf/ BP1-2005.pdf, accessed 16 September 2010.

Meier, C. and C. Murthy (2011) 'India's growing involvement in humanitarian assistance', Global Public Policy Institute.

Mihaly, E. B. (1965) *Foreign Aid and Politics in Nepal: A Case Study*, Oxford: Oxford University Press.

Ministry of Foreign Affairs (2003) 'Strategia polskiej współpracy na rzecz rozwoju', www.polskapomoc.gov.pl/files/dokumenty_publikacje/Strategia_2003.doc.

Ministry of Foreign Affairs of the PRC (2006) *China's African Policy*, www.fmprc.gov.cn/eng/zxxx/ t230615.htm, accessed 9 December 2009.

Mitchell, A. (2011) 'Emerging powers and the international development agenda', Transcript of a speech delivered at Chatham House, 15 February, www. chathamhouse.org/publications/ papers/view/109585, accessed 21 August 2011.

Mohan, G. (2012) 'The rising powers and accountable development', Unpublished paper.

Mohan, G. and M. Power (2008) 'New African choices? The politics of Chinese engagement in Africa and the changing architecture of international development', *Review of African Political Economy*, 35(1): 23–42.

— (2009) 'Africa, China and the "new" economic geography of development', *Singapore Journal of Tropical Geography*, 30: 24–8.

Mohan, G. and M. Tan-Mullins (2009) 'Chinese migrants in Africa as new agents of development? An analytical framework', *European Journal of Development Research*, 21: 588–605.

Mohan, G., E. Brown and B. Milward (2000) *Structural Adjustment, Practices, Theory and Impacts*, London: Routledge.

Mold, A. (2009) *Policy Ownership and Aid Conditionality in the Light of the Financial Crisis: A Critical Review*, Development Centre Studies, Paris: OECD.

Monson, J. (2009) *Africa's Freedom Railway: How a Chinese Develop-*

ment Project Changed Lives and Livelihoods in Tanzania, Bloomington, IN: Indiana University Press.

Monye, E. A. and E. Orakwue (2010) 'Easy to declare, difficult to implement: the disconnect between the aspirations of the Paris Declaration and donor practices in Nigeria', *Development Policy Review*, 26(6): 749–70.

Morgenthau, H. (1962) 'A political theory of foreign aid', *American Political Science Review*, June, pp. 301–9.

Morrison, D. (1998) *Aid and Ebb Tide: A History of CIDA and Canadian Development Assistance*, Waterloo: Wilfrid Laurier Press.

Mosse, D. (2004) 'Is good policy unimplementable? Reflections on the ethnography of aid policy and practice', *Development and Change*, 35: 639–71.

— (2005) *Cultivating Development*, London: Pluto Press.

— (2011) *Adventures in Aidland: The anthropology of professionals in international development*, vol. 6: *Studies in Public and Applied Anthropology*, New York: Berghahn Books.

Mosse, D. and D. Lewis (eds) (2006) *Development Brokers and Translators. The Ethnography of Aid and Agencies*, Bloomfield, CT: Kumarian Press.

Moyo, D. (2009) *Dead Aid: Why aid is not working and how there is a better way for Africa*, New York: Farrar, Straus and Giroux.

Muhr, T. G. E. (2011) *Venezuela and the ALBA: Counter-Hegemony, Geographies of Integration and Development, and Higher Education for All*, VDM.

— (2012) 'Bolivarian globalization?: the New Left's struggle in Latin America and the Caribbean to negotiate a revolutionary approach to humanitarian militarism and international intervention', in P. Amar (ed.), *Global South to the Rescue: Emerging Humanitarian Superpowers and Globalizing Rescue Industries*, London: Routledge.

Murray, W. E. and J. D. Overton (2011) 'Neoliberalism is dead, long live neoliberalism? Neostructuralism and the international aid regime of the 2000s', *Progress in Development Studies*, 11(4): 307–19.

Myers, G. A. (2001) 'Introductory human geography textbook representations of Africa', *Professional Geographer*, 53(4): 522–32.

Naidu, S. (2011) 'Representation, legitimacy and accountability: emerging donors and multilaterals in Africa', *Canadian Development Report 2011*, Ottawa: North–South Institute.

Naím, M. (2007) 'Rogue aid: what's wrong with the foreign aid programs of China, Venezuela and Saudi Arabia? They are enormously generous. And they are toxic', *Foreign Policy*, 159: 96.

Narayanaswamy, L. (2010) 'Gender, power and the knowledge-for-development agenda', Doctoral thesis, Durham University, etheses.dur.ac.uk/530/.

Narlikar, A. (2010) *New Powers: How to become one and how to manage them*, London/New York: Hurst/Columbia University Press.

— (2012) *Deadlocks in Multilateral Negotiations: Causes and Solutions*, Cambridge: Cambridge University Press.

Nel, P. (2010) 'Redistribution *and* recognition: what emerging regional powers want', *Review of International Studies*, 36: 951–74.

Nel, P. and M. Stephen (2010) 'The

foreign economic policies of regional powers in the developing world', in D. Flemes (ed.), *Regional Leadership in the Global System: Ideas, Interests and Strategies of Regional Powers*, Farnham: Ashgate, pp. 71–92.

Nelson, J. (2011) 'The private sector and aid effectiveness: towards new models of engagement', in H. Kharas, K. Makino and W. Jung (eds), *Catalysing Development: A New Vision for Aid*, Washington, DC: Brookings Institution, pp. 83–111.

Neumayer, E. (2003a) 'What factors determine the allocation of aid by Arab countries and multilateral agencies?', *Journal of Development Studies*, 39(4): 134–47.

— (2003b) *The Pattern of Aid Giving: The Impact of Good Governance on Development Assistance*, London: Routledge.

— (2004) 'Arab-related bilateral and multilateral sources of development finance: issues, trends, and the way forward', *World Economy*, 27(2): 281–300.

Nevaer, L. E. V. (2007) 'Mexico–Venezuela clash over oil as foreign aid', *New America Media*, 29 January, news.newamerica media.org/news/view_article. html?article_id=722f51257c1e7 43b89fa1d459711 c481, accessed 10 February 2012.

Nissanke, M. and M. Söderberg (2011) 'The changing landscape of aid relations in Africa – can China's engagement make a difference to African development', UI papers 2011/02, Stockholm: Swedish Institute of International Affairs.

Nonneman, G. (1988) *Development, Administration and Aid in the Middle East*, London: Routledge.

Nordtveit, B. (2011) 'An emerging donor in education and development: a case study of China in Cameroon', *International Journal of Educational Development*, 31: 99–108.

North, D. (1990) *Institutions, Institutional Change and Economic Performance*, Cambridge: Cambridge University Press.

Noxolo, P. (2011) 'One world, big society: a discursive analysis of the Conservative Green Paper for international development', *Geographical Journal*, 178(1): 31–41.

Nussbaum, M. (2011) *Creating Capabilities: The Human Development Approach*, Cambridge, MA: Belknap Press.

Nye, J. (2011) *The Future of Power*, Washington, DC: Public Affairs.

O' Gorman, E. (2011) *Conflict and Development*, London: Zed Books.

O'Keefe, D. (2006) 'Venezuelan, Cuban foreign policy promotes solidarity', *Seven Oaks: A Magazine of Politics, Culture and Resistance*, 14 September.

O'Neill, H. (2007) 'Ireland's foreign aid in 2006', *Irish Studies in International Affairs*, 18.

O'Neill, J. (1999) 'What gives (with Derrida)?', *European Journal of Social Theory*, 2: 131–45.

— (2012) 'The rise of the BRICs', Presentation at 'Rising Powers in the International System: Harnessing Opportunities, Managing Challenges' conference, CRASSH/POLIS/Centre for Rising Powers, University of Cambridge, 25 February.

Obiorah, N. (2007) 'Who's afraid of China in Africa? Towards an African civil society perspective on China–Africa relations', in F. Manji and S. Marks (eds), *African Perspectives on China in Africa*,

Cape Town: Pambazuka Press, pp. 35–56.

Odén, B. and L. Wohlgemuth (2011) 'Where is the Paris Agenda heading? Changing relations in Tanzania, Zambia and Mozambique', Briefing Note 21, European Centre for Development Policy Management, Maastricht: ECDPM.

ODI (1980) 'OPEC aid', Overseas Development Institute Briefing Paper no. 4.

OECD (2005) *Policy Coherence for Development, Promoting Institutional Good Practice*, Paris: OECD.

OECD-DAC (1996) *Shaping the 21st Century: The Contribution of Development Co-operation*, Paris: OECD.

— (2003) *Japan: DAC Peer Review. Main Findings and Recommendations*, Paris: OECD.

— (2006) *DAC in Dates: The History of OECD's Development Assistance Committee*, www.oecd.org/dataoecd/3/38/1896808.pdf, accessed 15 March 2012.

— (2008) *The Paris Declaration on Aid Effectiveness and the Accra Agenda for Action*, www.oecd.org/dataoecd/11/41/34428351.pdf, accessed 15 March 2012.

— (2011a) 'Welcoming new partnerships in international development co-operation', OECD Development Assistance Committee statement, Paris: OECD.

— (2011b) *Implementing the 2001 DAC Recommendation on Untying Aid: 2010–2011 Review*, Paris: OECD.

— (2012a) *Working Party on Aid Effectiveness: Working arrangements for the Global Partnership for Effective Development Co-operation – identifying key characteristics*, Meeting of the Post-Busan Interim Group, 13/14 February, Paris.

— (2012b) *Working Party on Aid Effectiveness: Arrangements for consultation and decision making in shaping the Global Partnership for Effective Development Co-operation and its associated monitoring framework*, Meeting of the Post-Busan Interim Group, 13/14 February, Paris.

Oglesby, R. (2011) 'India's evolution from aid recipient to humanitarian aid donor', Unpublished master's thesis, University of Cambridge.

Olsen, G. (2005) 'The EU's development policy: shifting priorities in a rapidly changing world', in P. Hoebink and O. Stokke (eds), *Perspectives on European Development Co-operation*, London: Routledge.

Onuf, N. (1989) *World of Our Making*, Columbia, SC: University of South Carolina Press.

Orbie, J. (2003) 'EU development policy integration and the Monterrey Process: a leading and benevolent identity?', *European Foreign Affairs Review*, 8: 395–415.

Orbie, J. and H. Versluys (2008) 'The European Union's international development policy: leading and benevolent?', in J. Orbie (ed.), *Europe's Global Role*, Farnham: Ashgate.

Orford, A. (2003) *Reading Humanitarian Intervention: Human Rights and the Use of Force in International Law*, Cambridge: Cambridge University Press.

— (2011) *International Authority and the Responsibility to Protect*, Cambridge: Cambridge University Press.

Ori, K. O. (2010) 'Haiti: Congo joins Senegal in rare poor-help-poor diplomacy', en.afrik.com/article16800.html, accessed 24 March 2010.

Orr, R. M. (1990) *The Emergence of Japan's Foreign Aid Power*, New York: Columbia University Press.

Osteen, M. (2002) *The Question of the Gift: Essays across disciplines*, London: Routledge.

Park, K. (2011) 'New development partners and a global development partnership', in H. Kharas, K. Makino and W. Jung (eds), *Catalysing Development: A New Vision for Aid*, Washington, DC: Brookings Institution, pp. 38–60.

Parry, J. (1986) 'The gift, the Indian gift, and the "Indian gift"', *Man*, 21: 453–73.

Patey, L. (2011) 'Fragile fortunes: India's oil venture into war-torn Sudan', in E. Mawdsley and G. McCann (eds), *India in Africa: Changing Geographies of Power*, Cape Town: Pambazuka Press, pp. 153–64.

Paulo, S. and H. Reisen (2010) 'Eastern donors and western soft law: towards a DAC donor peer review of China and India?', *Development Policy Review*, 28(5): 535–52.

Payne, A. (2008) 'The G8 in a changing global economic order', *International Affairs*, 84(3): 519–33.

PCPP (Partner Countries' Position Paper) (2011) 'Partner countries' vision and priority issues for HLF4', 12 June.

Pearson, N. O. (2006) 'Chavez spreads wealth to aid UN cause', www.freerepublic.com/focus/f-news/1719935/posts.

Peet, R. and E. Hartwick (2009) *Theories of Development: Contentions, Arguments, Alternatives*, 2nd edn, New York: Guildford Press.

People's Republic of China (2011) *China's Foreign Aid: White Paper*, Information Bureau of the State Council of the PRC, April, www.scio.gov.cn/zxbd/wz/201104/t896900.htm, accessed 2 June 2011.

Piçarra, M. (2011) 'Revisiting Mozambique's sovereignty: China's impact', Unpublished master's thesis, University of Bristol.

Picciotto, R. (2005) 'Policy coherence and development evaluation, concepts, issues and possible approaches', in OECD, *Fostering Development in a Global Economy, a Whole of Government Perspective*.

Picciotto, R., C. Alao, E. Ikpe, M. Kimani and R. Slade (2004) 'Striking a new balance: donor policy coherence and development cooperation in difficult partnerships', Global Policy Project, 30 December.

Pogge, T. (2010) *Politics as Usual: What Lies behind the Pro-Poor Rhetoric*, Cambridge: Polity Press.

Potter, D. M. (2008) *Modes of Asian Development Assistance*, Nagoya: Nanzan University.

Power, M. and G. Mohan (2010) 'Towards a critical geopolitics of China's engagement with African development', *Geopolitics*, 15(3): 462–95.

Power, M., G. Mohan and M. Tan-Mullins (2012) *Powering Development: China's energy diplomacy and Africa's future*, London: Palgrave Macmillan.

Prashad, V. (2008) *The Darker Nations: A people's history of the Third World*, New York: The New Press.

Price, G. (2005) 'Diversity in donorship: the changing landscape of official humanitarian aid: India's official aid programme', Overseas Development Institute HPG Background Paper.

Publish What You Fund (2011) 'Why aid transparency matters, and the global movement for aid transparency', Briefing Paper 1.

Puri, H. (2010) 'Rise of the global South and its impact on South–South cooperation', Special Report, Development Outreach, Washington, DC: World Bank.

Quibria, M. G. (2004) 'Development effectiveness: what does recent research tell us?', Working Paper 1, Asian Development Bank, October.

Raffer, K. (1998) 'Looking a gift horse in the mouth: analysing donors' aid statistics', *Zagreb International Review of Economics and Business*, 1(2): 1–21.

Raja Mohan, C. (2004) *Crossing the Rubicon: The Shaping of India's New Foreign Policy*, London: Palgrave Macmillan.

Rajan, R. and A. Subramanian (2005) 'Aid and growth: what does the cross-country evidence really show?, IMF Working Paper 05(127), Washington, DC.

Reardon, J. (2011) 'U.S. poor to benefit from 6th year of subsidized Venezuelan heating oil', VenezuelaAnalysis.com, 28 January, venezuelanalysis.com/news/5965, accessed 10 February 2012.

Rehbichler, S. (2006) 'The unfinished eastward enlargement', *World Economy and Development*, April/May, www.word-economy-and-development.org, accessed 30 May 2006.

Reisen, H. (2010) 'The multilateral donor non-system: towards accountability and efficient role assignment', *Economics: The Open-Access, Open-Assessment E-Journal*, vol. 4.

Reisen, H. and S. Ndoye (2008) 'Prudent versus imprudent lending in Africa: from debt relief to emerging lenders', OECD Development Centre Working Paper no. 268, Paris: OECD, www.oecd.org/dataoecd/62/12/40152567.pdf/.

Renard, R. (2005) 'The cracks in the new aid paradigm', Paper presented at the EADI conference, Bonn, September.

Rhee, H. (2010) *South–South Cooperation*, KOICA.

— (2011) 'Promoting South–South cooperation through knowledge exchange', in H. Kharas, K. Makino and W. Jung (eds), *Catalysing Development: A New Vision for Aid*, Washington, DC: Brookings Institution.

Richelle, K. (2002) 'EU enlargement and European development policy for a changing world', EADI 10th Global Conference, Ljubljana, Slovenia, 19 September.

Richey, L. A. and S. Ponte (2011) *Brand Aid: Shopping Well to Save the World*, Minneapolis, MN: Minnesota University Press.

Riddell, R. (2007) *Does Foreign Aid Really Work?*, Oxford: Oxford University Press.

Rist, G. (2003) *The History of Development: From Western Origins to Global Faith*, Expanded edn, London: Zed Books.

Rix, A. (1993) *Japan's Foreign Aid Challenge*, London: Routledge.

Roberts, S. (2011) 'Foreign assistance for development: USAID and the world of development contractors', Presentation at AAG national meetings, Seattle.

Roeder, P. G. (1985) 'The ties that bind: aid, trade and political compliance in Soviet–Third World relations', *International Studies Quarterly*, 29(2): 191–216.

Rogerson, A. (2005) 'Aid harmonisation and alignment: bridging the gaps between reality and the

Paris reform agenda', *Development Policy Review*, 23(5): 531–52.

— (2011a) 'Key Busan challenges and contributions to the emerging development effectiveness agenda', ODI Background Note, November.

— (2011b) 'What if development aid were truly "catalytic"?', ODI Background Note, November.

Rogerson, A. and S. Steensen (2009) 'Aid orphans: whose responsibility?', *Development Brief*, 1, July, Paris: OECD, www.oecd.org/dataoecd/14/34/43853485.pdf.

Rogerson, A., A. Hewitt and D. Waldenberg (2004) 'The international aid system 2005–2010: forces for and against change', ODI Working Paper 235, London: Overseas Development Institute.

Roodman, D. (2007) 'The 2007 Commitment to Development Index: components and results', CGD Brief, Center for Global Development, Washington, DC, October.

Rosenthal, G. (2005) 'The Economic and Social Council of the United Nations', Occasional Paper no. 15, New York: Friedrich-Ebert-Stiftung.

Rowlands, D. (2008) 'Emerging donors in international development assistance: a synthesis report', PBDD Report, January.

Saavedra, M. (2009) 'Representations of Africa in a Hong Kong soap opera: the limits of enlightened humanitarianism in the last breakthrough', *China Quarterly*, 199: 760–76.

Sachs, J. (2005) *The End of Poverty: How we can make it happen in our lifetime*, London: Penguin.

Sagasti, F., K. Bezanson and F. Prada (2005) *The Future of Development Financing: Challenges and Strategic Choices*, New York: Palgrave Macmillan.

Sahlins, M. (1972) *Stone Age Economics*, Chicago, IL: Aldine.

Said, E. W. (1978) *Orientalism*, New York: Vintage.

Saidi, M. and C. Wolf (2011) 'Recalibrating development cooperation: how can African countries benefit from emerging partners?', OECD Development Centre Working Paper no. 302.

Sato, J. (2007) 'Aid policies of Thailand, Singapore, and Malaysia: emerging donors in Southeast Asia', *Journal of JBIC Institute*, 35: 40–71.

Sato, J., H. Shiga, T. Kobayashi and H. Kondoh (2010) 'How do "emerging" donors differ from "traditional" donors? An institutional analysis of foreign aid in Cambodia', JICA Research Institute Working Paper 2, March.

— (2011) '"Emerging donors" from a recipient perspective: an institutional analysis of foreign aid in Cambodia', *World Development*, 39(12): 2091–104.

Sautman, B. (1994) 'Anti-black racism in post-Mao China', *China Quarterly*, 138(434).

Schaefer, B. and A. Kim (2010) 'U.S. foreign aid recipients show little support for America when voting at the United Nations', Backgrounder no. 2395, 6 April, Washington, DC: Heritage Foundation.

Scheyvens, H. (2005) 'Reform of Japan's official development assistance: a complete overhaul or merely a fresh coat of paint?', *Progress in Development Studies*, 5(2): 89–98.

Schläger, C. (2007) 'New powers for global change? Challenges for international development cooperation – the case of Brazil',

Briefing Papers, March, Berlin: Friedrich-Ebert-Stiftung.

Schmitz, H. (2007) 'The rise of the East: what does it mean for development studies', *IDS Bulletin*, 38(2): 51–8.

Schoeman, M. (2003) 'South Africa as an emerging middle power', in J. Daniel, A. Habib and R. Southall, *State of the Nation: South Africa 2003–4*, Cape Town: Human Sciences Research Council Press, pp. 349–67.

Schulz, N.-S. (2008) 'From Accra to 2011: perspectives for the global governance of aid', FRIDE Comment, Madrid: Fundación para las Relaciones Internacionales y el Diálogo Exterior, www.fride.org/descarga/COM_Accra 2011_ENG_sep08.pdf, accessed 26 April 2012.

— (2009) 'On track towards the global governance of aid (in turbulent times)', FRIDE Comment, Madrid: Fundación para las Relaciones Internacionales y el Diálogo Exterior, www.ituc-csi.org/IMG/pdf/Global_governance_of_aid_90.pdf, accessed 26 April 2012.

— (2010a) 'The third wave of development players', FRIDE Policy Brief no. 60, November.

— (2010b) 'South–South cooperation in the context of aid effectiveness: telling the story of partners in 110 cases of South–South and triangular cooperation', Task Team on South–South Cooperation, March, api.ning.com/files/SwykFuav-XMFudJpnX2l*2EX0Ed PUD07BvWjU5H*VcEOKEiZ2m KyfaqG2z98s14x5RzkIe6DUO1x2u CFxpxov91huRYUf7yo/TTSSC Casestoriessummaryreportdraft 20100317.pdf, accessed 1 November 2010.

Scott, J., M. vom Hau and D. Hulme (2010) 'Beyond the BRICS: identifying the "emerging middle powers" and understanding their role in global poverty reduction', BWPI Working Paper 137, December.

Sen, A. (2001) *Development as Freedom*, Oxford: Oxford University Press.

— (2011) 'Quality of life: India vs. China', *New York Review of Books*, 12 May.

Severino, J.-M. and O. Ray (2009) 'The end of ODA: death and rebirth of a global public policy', Working Paper no. 167, Washington, DC: Center for Global Development.

— (2010) 'The end of ODA (II): the birth of hypercollective action', Working Paper 218, Washington, DC: Center for Global Development.

Shah, A. (2006) 'Media, propaganda and Venezuela', Global Issues, www.globalissues.org/article/403/media-propaganda-and-venezuela, accessed 26 April 2012.

— (2011) 'Foreign aid for development assistance', www.globalissues.org/article/35/foreign-aid-development-assistance.

Shrivastava, M. (2009) 'India and Africa: from political alliance to economic partnership', *Politikon*, 36(1): 117–43.

Shushan, D. and C. Marcoux (2011) 'The rise (and decline?) of Arab aid: generosity and allocation in the oil era', *World Development*, 39(11): 1969–80.

Sidaway, J. (2012) 'Geographies of development: new maps, new visions?', *Professional Geographer*, 64(2): 1–14.

Sidaway, J. D. and M. Pryke (2000) 'The strange geographies of "emerging markets"', *Transactions of the Institute of British Geographers*, NS 25(2): 187–201.

Silk, J. (2004) 'Caring at a distance: gift theory, aid chains and social movements', *Social and Cultural Geography*, 5: 229–50.

Singh, S. K. (2007) 'India and West Africa: a burgeoning relationship', Briefing Paper, Chatham House Africa Programme, April.

Singh, V. K. (2010) 'Rising above political boundaries may hold the key to G20 success', in T. Fues and P. Wolff (eds), *G20 and Global Development: How can the new summit architecture promote pro-poor growth and sustainability?*, Bonn: DIE (German Development Institute).

Sinha, P. (2010) 'Indian development cooperation with Africa', in F. Cheru and C. Obi (eds), *The Rise of China and India in Africa*, London and Uppsala: Zed Books and the Nordic Africa Institute.

Sinha, P. and M. Hubbard (2011) 'Convergence and divergence among established players and new global players: where is the common ground?', *A Future for Aid Data*, Workshop, University of Birmingham, October, www.birmingham.ac.uk/schools/government-society/departments/international-development/events/future-aid-data.aspx, accessed 22 February 2012.

Six, C. (2009) 'The rise of postcolonial states as donors: a challenge to the development paradigm?', *Third World Quarterly*, 30(6): 1103–21.

Slater, D. (2004) *Geopolitics and the Post-Colonial: Rethinking North–South Relations*, Oxford: Blackwell.

Smart, A. (1993) 'Gifts, bribes and guanxi: a reconsideration of Bourdieu's social capital', *Cultural Anthropology*, 8: 385–408.

Smith, D. (2005) 'Roaring China shows how to help the poor', *The Times*, 20 February.

Smith, D. M. (2000) *Moral Geographies: Ethics in a world of difference*, Edinburgh: Edinburgh University Press.

Smith, K. (2011) 'Non-DAC donors and humanitarian aid: shifting structures, changing trends', Global Humanitarian Assistance Briefing Paper.

Smith, K., T. Fordelone and F. Zimmerman (2010) 'Beyond the DAC: the welcome role of other providers of development cooperation' DCD Issues Brief, May, Paris: OECD-DAC.

Smith, M. (2010) 'Terrorism thinking: "9/11 changed everything"', in M. Smith, *Securing Africa*, Aldershot: Ashgate, pp. 1–28.

Smith, M. and H. Yanacopulos (2004) 'The public faces of development', *Journal of International Development*, 16: 741–9.

Snow, P. (1988) *The Star Raft: China's Encounter with Africa*, Ithaca, NY: Cornell University Press.

Soderberg, M. (2002) 'Changes in Japanese foreign aid policies', European Institute of Japanese Studies Working Paper 157.

Sogge, D. (2002) *Give and Take: What's the matter with foreign aid?*, London: Zed Books.

Sorensen, J. S. (ed.) (2010) *Challenging the Aid Paradigm: Western Currents and Asian Alternatives*, Basingstoke: Palgrave Macmillan.

South Centre (2008) *Developing Country Perspectives on the Role of the Development Cooperation Forum: Building Strategic Approaches to Enhancing Multilateral Develop-*

ment Cooperation, Analytical Note SC/GGDP/AN/GEG/10, Geneva: South Centre.

Ssewakiryanga, R. (2011) 'From aid effectiveness to development effectiveness', 29 November, www. devex.com/en/news/from-aid-effectiveness-to development/ 76786, accessed 29 February 2012.

Stiglitz, J. (2002) Globalization and Its Discontents, New York: W. W. Norton & Co.

Stirrat, J. (2006) 'Competitive humanitarianism: relief and the tsunami in Sri Lanka', Anthropology Today, 22: 11–16.

Stirrat, R. L. and H. Henkel (1997) 'The development gift: the problem of reciprocity in the NGO world', Annals of the American Academy of Political and Social Science, 554: 66–80.

Stokke, O. (ed.) (1989) Western Middle Powers and Global Poverty: The Determinants of the Aid Policies of Canada, Denmark, The Netherlands, Norway and Sweden. Uppsala: Scandinavian Institute of African Studies.

Strauss, J. (2009) 'The past in the present: historical and rhetorical lineages in China's relations with Africa', in J. Strauss and M. Saavedra (eds), China and Africa: Emerging patterns in globalization and development, China Quarterly Special Issues 9, Cambridge: Cambridge University Press, pp. 777–95.

Stuenkel, O. (2011) 'India and Brazil's foreign aid and their role in the future development architecture', A Future for Aid Data, Workshop, University of Birmingham, October, www. birmingham.ac.uk/schools/ government-society/departments/ international- development/

events/future-aid-data.aspx, accessed 22 February 2012.

Sumner, A. (2010) 'Global poverty and the new bottom billion: three-quarters of the world's poor live in middle-income countries', IDS Working Paper 349, Brighton: Institute of Development Studies.

Sumner, A. and C. Melamed (2010) 'The MDGs and beyond', IDS Bulletin, 41(1), Brighton: Institute of Development Studies.

Suzuki, S. (2011) 'Why does China participate in intrusive peacekeeping? Understanding paternalistic Chinese discourses on development and intervention', International Peacekeeping, 18(3): 271–85.

Taela, K. (2011) 'Gender equality at home and abroad: Brazil's development cooperation with Mozambique in the field of HIV and AIDS', Unpublished MA dissertation, Institute of Development Studies, University of Sussex.

Tan-Mullins, M., G. Mohan and M. Power (2010) 'Redefining "aid" in the China–Africa context', Development and Change, 41(5): 857–81.

Tandon, Y. (2008) Ending Aid Dependence, Cape Town: Fahamu Books.

— (2009) Development and Globalisation: Daring to think differently, Cape Town: Pambazuka Press.

Tansky, L. (1966) 'Soviet foreign aid to the less developed countries', in New Directions in the Soviet Economy, compiled by US Congress Joint Economic Committee 949-974, Committee Print, 89th Congress, 2nd session, Washington, DC: Government Printing Office.

Tarling, N. (1986) 'The United Kingdom and the origins of

the Colombo Plan', *Journal of Commonwealth and Comparative Politics*, 24(1): 3–34.

Taylor, I. (1998) 'China's foreign policy towards Africa in the 1990s', *Journal of Modern African Studies*, 36(3): 443–60.

— (2000) 'Ambiguous commitment: the People's Republic of China and the anti-apartheid struggle in South Africa', *Journal of Contemporary African Studies*, 18(1): 91–106.

— (2002) 'Taiwan's foreign policy and Africa: the limitations of dollar diplomacy', *Journal of Contemporary China*, 11(30): 125–40.

— (2006) *China and Africa: Engagement and compromise*, London: Routledge.

— (2009) 'Growing multipolarity, coalitions and global governance: the India–Brazil–South Africa Dialogue Forum', in D. Lesage and P. Vercauteren (eds), *Contemporary Global Governance: Multipolarity vs New Discourses on Global Governance*, Brussels: P.I.E. Peter Lang, pp. 63–80.

— (2010) *China's New Role in Africa*, Boulder, CO: Lynne Rienner.

Tierney, M. (2011) 'Experience with including non DAC donors' aid information in AidData database', *A Future for Aid Data*, Workshop, University of Birmingham, October, www.birmingham.ac.uk/schools/government-society/departments/international-development/events/future-aid-data.aspx, accessed 22 February 2012.

Titmuss, R. M. (1992) *The Gift Relationship: From human blood to social policy*, London: Allen and Unwin.

Tsopanakis, G. (2011) 'Japan International Cooperation Agency: a brand "new" international development organisation or a traditional bureaucratic actor?', Working Paper no. 5, Manchester: Centre for Organisations in Development.

TT-SSC (2011a) 'Towards effective South–South and triangular cooperation: Good Practice Paper', October.

— (2011b) 'Triangular cooperation: towards horizontal partnerships, but how?', Bali Workshop Report, 27 February–1 March.

Tull, D. (2006) 'China's engagement in Africa: scope, significance and consequences', *Journal of Modern African Studies*, 4(3): 459–79.

— (2008) 'Political consequences of China's return to Africa', in C. Alden, D. Large, R. Soares de Oliveira (eds), *China Returns to Africa – a Rising Power and a Continent Embrace*, London: Hurst & Co., pp. 111–28.

UN (United Nations) (2008) *First Report of the Development Cooperation Forum*, ECOSOC, United Nations.

UNCTAD (United Nations Conference on Trade and Development) (2010) *South–South Cooperation: Africa and the New Forms of Development Partnership*, Geneva, www.unctad.org/templates/WebFlyer.asp?intItemID=5491&lang=1, accessed 26 April 2012.

UNDP (2001) 'Development effectiveness review of evaluative evidence', www.undp.org/evaluation/documents/der2001.pdf.

— (2009) 'Enhancing South–South and triangular cooperation. Study of the current situation and existing good practices in policy, institutions, and operation of South–South and triangular cooperation', New York: UNDP.

Unsworth, S. (2009) 'What's politics got to do with it?: why donors find it so hard to come to terms with politics, and why this matters', *Journal of International Development*, 21(6): 883–94.

Usher, G. (2009) 'India in Afghanistan', *London Review of Books*, 9 April.

Valkenier, E. K. (1979) 'The USSR, the Third World, and the global economy', *Problems of Communism*, 28(4): 17–33.

Van den Boogaerde, P. (1991) 'Financial assistance from Arab countries and Arab regional institutions', International Monetary Fund.

Van Reisen, M. (2007) 'The enlarged EU and the developing world', in A. Mold (ed.), *EU Development Policy in a Changing World*, Amsterdam University Press, pp. 29–65.

Vandemoortele, L. (2011) 'The MDG story: intention denied', *Development and Change*, 42(1): 1–21.

Vaz, A. C. and C. A. Inoue (2007) 'Emerging donors in international development assistance: the Brazil Case', in D. Rowlands, *Emerging Donors in International Development Assistance*, Canada: Partnership and Business Development Division, IDRC.

Vieira, M. (2011) 'Will China, India and Brazil make "South–South" cooperation a reality?', *A Future for Aid Data*, Workshop, University of Birmingham, October, www.birmingham.ac.uk/schools/government-society/departments/international-development/events/future-aid-data.aspx, accessed 22 February 2012.

Villanger, E. (2007) 'Arab foreign aid: disbursement patterns, aid policies and motives', CMI Report 2/2007, Oslo: Christian Michelsen Institute.

Vines, A. (2008/09) 'India's strategy in Africa: looking beyond the India–Africa Forum', *South African Yearbook of International Affairs 2008/9*.

Vines, A. and I. Campos (2008) *Angola and China: A pragmatic partnership?*, Washington, DC: Center for Strategic and International Studies, www.csis.org/media/csis/pubs/080306_angolachina.pdf/, accessed 2 August 2009.

Vines, A., L. Wong, M. Weimer and I. Campos (2009) *Thirst for African Oil: Asian National Oil Companies in Nigeria and Angola*, London: Chatham House.

Vittek, M. and S. Lightfoot (2010) 'The Europeanization of Slovak development cooperation?', *Contemporary European Studies*, 1: 21–37.

Vittorini, S. and D. Harris (2011a) 'India goes over to the other side: Indo-West African relations in the 21st century', in E. Mawdsley and G. McCann (eds), *India in Africa: Changing Geographies of Power*, Cape Town: Pambazuka Press.

— (2011b) 'African governmental responses to Indian ventures on the continent: a changing arena of African politics?', in *New Topographies of Power? Africa Negotiating an Emerging Multipolar World*, Leiden: Brill.

Wade, R. (1996) 'Japan, the World Bank, and the art of paradigm maintenance: the East Asian miracle in political perspective', *New Left Review*, 217: 3–36.

— (2010) 'After the crisis: industrial policy and the developmental state in low-income countries', *Global Policy*, 1(2).

Warden, S. (2007) *Joining the Fight against Global Poverty: A Menu for Corporate Engagement*, Washington, DC: Center for Global Development.

Watts, J. (2005) 'No questions, no lies in China's quest for oil: inside Asia', *Guardian Weekly*, 3 June.

Wedel, J. R. (2001) *Collision and Collusion: The Strange Case of Western Aid to Eastern Europe 1989–1998*, New York: St Martin's Press.

Weisbrot, M. (2006) 'Latin America shifts left: it's the economy', Center for Economic and Policy Research, 21 January, www.cepr.net/index.php/Op-Eds-Columns/Op-Eds-Columns/latin-america-shifts-left-its-the-economy, accessed 15 March 2012.

Wendt, A. (1999) *Social Theory of International Politics*, Cambridge: Cambridge University Press.

Wendt, A. E. and R. Duvall (1989) 'Institutions and international order', in E. O. Czempieland and J. N. Rosenau (eds), *Global Changes and Theoretical Challenges*, Lexington, MA: Lexington Books, pp. 51–74.

White, H. (2001) 'Will the new aid agenda help promote poverty reduction?', *Journal of International Development*, 13(7): 1057–70.

Wilkinson, R. and K. Pickett (2009) *The Spirit Level: Why Equality is Better for Everyone*, Harmondsworth: Penguin.

Wissenbach, U. (2010) 'A new Seoul consensus on development: the G20 needs to reconcile effective ODA with emerging country economic cooperation', in T. Fues and P. Wolff (eds), *G20 and Global Development: How can the new summit architecture promote pro-poor growth and sustainability?*, Bonn: DIE (German Development Institute).

Wood, B., J. Betts, F. Etta, J. Gayfer, D. Kabell, N. Ngwira, F. Sagasti and M. Samaranayake (2011) 'The evaluation of the Paris Declaration', Final Report, Copenhagen: Danish Institute for International Studies, May.

Wood, R. E. (1986) *From Marshall Plan to Debt Crisis: Foreign Aid and Development Choices in the World Economy*, Berkeley, CA: University of California Press.

Woods, N. (2008) 'Whose aid? Whose influence? China, emerging donors and the silent revolution in development assistance', *International Affairs*, 84(6): 1205–21.

— (2010) 'Global governance after the financial crisis: a new multilateralism or the last gasp of the Great Powers?', *Global Policy*, 1(1): 51–63.

— (2011) 'Rethinking aid coordination', in H. Kharas, K. Makino and W. Jung (eds), *Catalysing Development: A New Vision for Aid*, Washington, DC: Brookings Institution, pp. 112–26.

Woods, T. (2003) 'Giving and receiving: Nuruddin Farah's gifts, or, the postcolonial logic of Third World aid', *Journal of Commonwealth Literature*, 38: 91–112.

World Bank (1997) *World Development Report: The State in a Changing World*, Washington, DC: World Bank.

— (1998) *Knowledge for Development: World Development Report 1998/99*, Washington, DC: World Bank.

— (2008) *Aid Architecture: An Overview of the Main Trends in Official Development Assistance Flows*, Washington, DC: World Bank.

— (2010) *Arab Development Assistance: Four Decades of Cooperation*, Washington, DC: World Bank.

— (2011a) *Global Development*

Horizons 2011. Multipolarity: The new global economy, Washington, DC: World Bank.

— (2011b) *World Development Report: Conflict, Security and Development*, Washington, DC: World Bank.

Worthington, S. A. and T. Pipa (2010) 'International NGOs and foundations: essential partners in creating an effective architecture', in *Making Development Aid More Effective. The 2010 Brookings Blum Roundtable Policy Briefs*, Brookings Institution, www. brookings.edu/~/ media/Files/rc/ papers/2010/09_development_ aid/09_development_aid.pdf.

WP-EFF (2011) *Busan Partnership for Effective Development Cooperation. Outcome Document of the Fourth High Level Forum on Aid Effectiveness*, Busan, Republic of Korea, 2 November–1 December.

Wrighton, N. (2010) 'Participation, power and practice in development: a case study of theoretical doctrines and international agency practice in Tuvalu', Unpublished master's thesis, University of Victoria, Wellington.

Xu, J. (2011) 'The political economy of development cooperation: China's unintentional influence on the aid effectiveness debate', Paper presented at 'Unpacking foreign aid effectiveness: examining donor dynamics', London School of Economics, 21 June.

Yahuda, M. B. (1978) *China's Role in World Affairs*, London: Croom Helm.

— (1983) *Towards the End of Isolationism: China's foreign policy after Mao*, London: Macmillan.

Yanacopolos, H. (2011) 'The emerging powers and the changing landscape of foreign aid and development cooperation: public perceptions of development cooperation in South Africa', www. geog.cam.ac.uk/research/projects/ foreignaidperceptions/, accessed 15 March 2012.

Young, R. C. (2003) *Postcolonialism: A Very Short Introduction*, Oxford: Oxford University Press.

Yu, G. (1975) *China's Africa Policy: A Study of Tanzania*, New York: Praeger.

Zhang, H. (2010) 'G20 and global governance: challenges and impacts', in T. Fues and P. Wolff (eds), *G20 and Global Development: How can the new summit architecture promote pro-poor growth and sustainability?*, Bonn: DIE (German Development Institute).

Zimmermann, F. and K. Smith (2011) 'More actors, more money, more ideas for international development co-operation', *Journal of International Development*, 23(5): 722–38.

Index

with aid orthodoxy, 180; reporting of aid volumes, 108; reporting of ODA disbursements, 80; symbolic politics of, 145; use of term, 5–7
non-governmental organizations (NGOs), 31
non-state actors, 4
non-traditional donors, use of term, 5, 7
North-South relations, 3, 64, 199, 202; binary construct, 3, 9, 130, 194; model, 124
Norway, aid to Cameroon, 162

odious regimes, collaboration with, 115–16
official development assistance (ODA), 29–33; as lending, 33; as policy tool, 87; calculations overvalue commodities, 33; definition of, 109
oil: affordable, provided by Venezuela and Mexico, 170; prices, rise of, 15, 63, 65
ONGC Videsh company, 99
Organisation for Economic Co-operation and Development (OECD), 46, 217; Convention on Combating of Bribery of Foreign Public Officials, 143; Development Assistance Committee (DAC), 5–7, 16, 31, 151, 174, 183, 185–7 (as mainstream paradigm, 211; at heart of global aid system, 45; charity model of, 78–85; classification of donors, 150; Creditors Reporting System (CRS), 79; impacted by non-DAC development actors, 8; Outreach Strategy, 186; role in Development Cooperation Forum, 191; Western make-up of, 175; Working Party on Aid Effectiveness (WP-EFF) *see* Working Party on Aid Effectiveness); Development Cooperation Directorate, 85, 108; recommendations on tied aid, 137, 138

Organization of the Petroleum Exporting Countries (OPEC), 48, 168; creation of, 65–7
OPEC Fund for International Development, 66, 87, 95, 113, 168
Orientalism, 147
other official flows (OOF), 30, 81, 82, 109, 121, 144
ownership of programmes, 40, 128, 210

Pacific countries, China's relations with, 178
Pakistan, 71, 72, 204; floods in, 89; view of Development Cooperation Forum, 192
Palestinian Authority, corruption in, 142
Pan-African e-Network, 125
Paris Agenda, 16, 17, 28, 42, 44, 94, 128, 151, 202, 207, 210, 214; an evolving process, 44; Brazil's view of, 178; in Bolivia, 42; in Honduras, 42; in Mozambique, 43; in Nicaragua, 42; in Tanzania, 43; in Zambia, 43
Paris Declaration, 39, 65, 177, 180, 186–7, 188; summary of, 40
Partai Komunis Indonesia (PKI), 51
partnership, use of term, 7, 43, 151
People in Need Foundation (Czech Republic), 89
Poland, 1, 5, 7, 16, 19, 68, 99–100; advisory role on democratic transition, 129; as classic borderland, 164–5; candidacy for EU membership, 164; development assistance of, 163–7; food aid of, 118; Millennium Development Goals project, 69; return to donor activities, 146
policy coherence for development, 46
Polish Humanitarian Action, 89
poor and middle income countries, lack of voice, 183
population growth, 214
Portugal, 7

hegemony of, rejected, 168; image of, damaged, 117; India's relations with, 71, 204; poverty in, 20; tied aid of, 137; Turkey's relationship with, 176
Uzbekistan, human rights abuses in, 116

Venezuela, 1, 16, 48, 124, 170; assistance to US cities, 115; cancels Haitian debt, 10; development cooperation of, 146, 167–71; foreign aid policies of, 11; humanitarian aid of, 103; loan to Argentina, 169; seeks seat on UN Security Council, 169; switches from World Bank, 87
Vietnam, 48, 49, 58–61, 104, 125; representation of, 162–3
volunteering, 126

Walesa, Lech, 129
war on terror, 35, 77
Washington Consensus, 35
West: critique of, 167; relations with China, 181
West Bank, aid to, 89
Western, use of term, 7

Western dominance of aid agendas, 1, 2, 23, 26, 44, 90, 149, 212, 218
Western models of development cooperation, 6
Western values, 173; aspiration to, 165
Working Party on Aid Effectiveness, 183, 187–9, 211, 216–17
World Bank, 16, 19, 35, 37, 44, 74, 79, 98, 99, 113, 118, 131, 168, 169, 174, 176, 183–5, 189, 194, 197, 198, 204; funding for African agriculture, cut, 131; reaction to reform, 184–5; *World Development Report*, 124–5; voting rights in, 12
World Bank Institute trust fund, 185
World Food Programme (WFP), 88, 91, 92–3, 118, 197
world systems theory, 26–7
World Trade Organization (WTO), 19, 74

Yugoslavia, 62

Zambia, 55
Zhou En-lai, tour of Africa, 154
Zimbabwe, 116, 181